THE MARRIAGE BUYOUT

The Marriage Buyout

The Troubled Trajectory of U.S. Alimony Law

Cynthia Lee Starnes

NEW YORK UNIVERSITY PRESS

New York and London

NEW YORK UNIVERSITY PRESS
New York and London
www.nyupress.org

References to Internet websites (URLs) were accurate at the time of writing.
Neither the author nor New York University Press is responsible for URLs that
may have expired or changed since the manuscript was prepared.

Library of Congress Cataloging-in-Publication Data

Starnes, Cynthia, author.
The marriage buyout : the troubled trajectory of U.S. alimony law / Cynthia Lee Starnes.
pages cm. — (Families, law, and society series)
Includes bibliographical references and index.
ISBN 978-0-8147-0824-8 (hardback)
1. Alimony—United States. 2. Alimony—Economic aspects—United States. 3. Alimony—
Social aspects—United States. I. Title.
KF537.S73 2014
346.7301'663—dc23
                              2013049126

New York University Press books are printed on acid-free paper,
and their binding materials are chosen for strength and durability.
We strive to use environmentally responsible suppliers and materials
to the greatest extent possible in publishing our books.

Manufactured in the United States of America
10 9 8 7 6 5 4 3 2 1

Also available as an ebook

To Michael, to Brad and Zach, and to Jim
my family all

CONTENTS

ACKNOWLEDGMENTS

Thanks to the many people who helped me through this project: To my late friend and colleague Craig Callen, who exemplified and inspired independent thought and precision. To my colleagues Kevin Saunders and David Thronson, whose comments on portions of earlier drafts guided and inspired me. To Associate Dean Chuck Ten Brink and the tireless librarians he leads at Michigan State University College of Law, including Hildur Hanna, Jane Meland, Kathy Prince, Robin Doutre, Janet Hedin, Brent Domann, and Brooke Moynihan, and especially to Allison Eicher and Barbara Bean, whose professional dedication and expert focus made me feel as if I were their only client. To Dean Joan Howarth and attorney John F. Schaefer, whose support was genuine and generous. To doctoral candidate Matt Piszczek, who insisted on statistical and linguistic rigor, always with a happy spirit. To my many talented student research assistants, including Scott Milligan, Alice Newlin, and Sarah Primrose. To Nancy Dowd, a smart and supportive editor who critiques without wounding. And to my dear husband, Michael Gorman, who pulled me through many a tough moment.

This book draws on and sometimes reproduces portions of my prior writings, including the following: "Lovers, Parents, and Partners: Disentangling Spousal and Co-Parenting Commitments," *Arizona Law Review* 54 (2012): 197; "Alimony Theory," *Family Law Quarterly* 45 (2011): 271; "Mothers, Myths and the Law of Divorce: One More Feminist Case for Partnership," *William and Mary Journal of Women and the Law* 13 (2006): 203; "One More Time: Alimony, Intuition, and the Remarriage-Termination Rule," *Indiana Law Journal* 81 (Summer 2006): 971; "Mothers as Suckers: Pity, Partnership, and Divorce Discourse," *Iowa Law Review* 90 (2005): 1513; "Victims, Breeders, Joy and Math: First Thoughts on Compensatory Spousal Payments under The Principles," *Duke Journal of Gender Law and Policy* 8 (2001): 137; "Reflections on Betty Crocker, Soccer Mom, and Divorce: A Message from Detergent Manufacturers," *Wisconsin Law Review* (1997): 285; "Applications of a Contemporary Partnership Model for Divorce," *Brigham Young University Journal of Public Law* 8 (1993): 107; and "Divorce and the Displaced Homemaker: A Discourse on Playing with Dolls, Partnership Buyouts and Dissociation under No-Fault," *University of Chicago Law Review* 60 (1993): 67.

Introduction

Marriage is a vital social institution. The exclusive commitment of two individuals to each other nurtures love and mutual support; it brings stability to our society. For those who choose to marry, and for their children, marriage provides an abundance of legal, financial, and social benefits. In return it imposes weighty legal, financial, and social obligations.
—*Goodridge v. Dep't of Public Health*, 798 N.E.2d 941, 948 (Mass. 2003) (holding Massachusetts's ban on same-sex marriage unconstitutional)

Promises that matter have consequences. Even children know this. Consider the case of little Brad, who hid behind his brother's bedroom door after helping himself to an unauthorized share of his brother's Halloween candy.

"Did you eat Zach's candy?" I asked.

"No," said Brad through chocolate lips.

"Are you sure?" I asked.

"Well, I ate some," he said.

"Promise me you won't eat any more," I said, stashing the plastic pumpkin head of sweets on a high closet shelf.

"I promise," said Brad.

Brad's promise bought him a reprieve from a time-out. But he knew that if he broke his promise, if he climbed on a chair, retrieved the pumpkin head, and helped himself to another serving of his brother's candy, there would be a price to pay: the reprieve would be revoked and the dreaded time-out imposed. Brad's promise mattered.

Promises come in many forms, and we all expect that the serious ones will have consequences if they are broken. I promise to sing in your opera, to paint your house, to repair your Cessna or your vacuum cleaner; I promise to sell you hamburger that isn't spoiled or a bathtub that doesn't leak—all these promises have consequences that make it safe for a promisee to rely on them.

So what of marriage promises? Do they matter? Family law's answer to this question is surprising and troubling: marriage promises matter very much in judicial rhetoric, but otherwise hardly at all. Contemporary courts, especially those addressing same-sex marriage, may wax eloquent on the significance of the marriage commitment, but when marriage promises are broken, they are largely ignored, relegated to the status of a pitch by a used-car salesperson—assurances on which only the foolish rely.

For me, this is Casey's story. Casey (not her real name) could have been male or female, black or white, gay or straight. As it happened, she was a petite, white, heterosexual woman, probably in her early fifties, with short brown hair and a quiet way about her. I met Casey at the small law firm where I worked as a paralegal many years ago. One day when I reported for work, Casey was there, sitting behind a tiny desk that had been squeezed into a hallway leading to the firm's trio of offices. No one was aware of any plan to hire a receptionist. Looking back, I imagine one of the attorneys spontaneously created the position just for Casey.

As I later learned, Casey had been a full-time homemaker, married to a professor at a major university in a nearby state. The couple's children were grown and gone when one day the professor came home with some startling news: he had fallen in love with another woman and wanted out of the marriage. The couple divorced and Casey ran away, ending up in our city, where she rented a room and took a minimum-wage job as our receptionist. Casey reported that she got next to nothing from the marriage—scant property, no alimony, and of course no child support.

One day Casey didn't show up for work. We phoned her home but got no response and figured she had walked out on us. Who could blame her? Hers wasn't much of a job—low wages, lots of tedium, little respect. As it was, Casey had made a darker choice: She had traveled back to her hometown, to her old house, to her old garage, where she sat in a car and took her life.

Of course, I don't know the whole story of Casey's marriage. Maybe she was a scoundrel, a reprobate disguised as a vulnerable, middle-aged mother. Maybe. But I wondered then and I wonder now why she should be reduced to a near-poverty existence after so many years as a home-maker and wife of a well-positioned husband. It didn't seem right then and it doesn't seem right now.

What makes Casey's fate seem so wrong? Surely, it is sad to see decent folks fall on hard times. But I believe the discomfort occasioned by Casey's story goes deeper—to an unsettling awareness that the law turned her into a sucker for relying on the marriage promise. As we will see in the following chapters, primary caregivers like Casey typically experience lost opportunities and declining human capital as a result of their marital role, while their spouses often experience human capital gains as a result of career or job investments. If these gains and losses are not shared at divorce, the result is that one partner enjoys most of the long-term benefits of family teamwork while the other bears most of the costs. This outcome devalues the contributions of caregivers in raising the next generation, encourages an individualistic rather than a communal vision of marriage, and makes reliance on the marriage promise a dangerous, foolhardy proposition.

Casey is no dinosaur; she cannot be dismissed as part of a dying breed of Betty Crockers and soccer moms. Casey is my colleague's wife, my gay neighbor, my beautiful thirty-something niece—all the many varieties of marital partners who take on the lion's share of family labor, a role that describes many contemporary homes. The point is not that the law should encourage primary caregiving—a posture that would trouble many of us for many reasons—but rather that the law should not denigrate and penalize this choice, surprising unwary caregivers with the news that they were foolish to invest in their families, foolish to think their marriage promises mattered.

So how exactly should the law respond to the financial peril of divorc-ing caregivers? Family law gives divorce courts three (and only three) financial tools: child support, property distribution, and alimony. While child support orders are commonly entered at the time of divorce, their focus is not the spouses' responsibility to each other, but rather their responsibility to common children. The distribution of marital prop-erty is a more appropriate tool for imposing divorce consequences, but its usefulness is limited by the fact that while most divorcing couples have the ability to produce future income, they have few existing assets. Alimony is thus often the *only* available tool for addressing the financial consequences of a divorce. To be sure, alimony is not always a practical tool. When spouses have barely enough income to keep one of them out of poverty, an alimony award is useless. But in very many middle- and upper-class marriages, alimony is an important tool for ensuring that the long-term costs of marital roles do not fall exclusively on family caregivers. Yet alimony as currently conceptualized is not up to this task.

Commentators have long bemoaned the sorry state of alimony law—the broad judicial discretion that makes alimony orders unpredictable and inconsistent, the lack of any coherent theory to justify alimony, and the general disdain for alimony, which ensures that few awards are made. The word "alimony" itself has a nasty connotation, inspiring visions of spoiled and greedy women sipping martinis poolside while their hapless ex-husbands struggle to make ends meet.

Indeed, such visions have long played a role in popular fiction. Take the 1933 movie *Alimony Madness,* in which a cruel ex-wife takes a man's last twenty dollars to pay the vet bill for a Pekinese dog.[1] This heartless alimony grab is the final straw that drives the man's new wife temporarily mad; she kills the ex-wife, but (in a happy ending) is acquitted by an understanding jury. Alimony misadventures are told with similar relish in *Alimony—Preying on Innocent Dupes*, the 1949 movie that tells the "Daring inside story of the alimony racket";[2] *Guilty Conscience*, a 1985 television movie about an attorney (Anthony Hopkins) who fantasizes about killing his wife (Blythe Danner) to avoid paying her alimony;[3] and the book *Remember the Alimony*, a 2007 murder mystery about a beauty queen who has an affair with her husband's attorney.[4]

These alimony tales are entertaining—notorious and delicious, with a touch of schadenfreude. But today's stories in the blogosphere have a very different tone—one that is impassioned, angry, and indignant. Check out the website Alimony Nightmares,[5] where you will see reports of alimony payors who are living in motor homes and working odd jobs to make ends meet, payors who are thrown in jail because they cannot pay their alimony, and who are committing suicide because they "have lost all hope." Similar reports and sentiments appear at the websites New Jersey Alimony Reform, where you will see tales of alimony abuse "more frightening than any Hollywood horror film,"[6] and Alimony Slaves in America, where the blog name says it all.[7] The Alimony Nightmares website doesn't mention Casey. Nor do reports of alimony horrors tend to mention that, despite popular perceptions to the contrary, alimony is uncommon, usually short-term, and often limited to the rehabilitation of a needy spouse.

Alimony is complex—more complex than Alimony Nightmares or popular fiction or Casey's story can fully convey. Alimony is a mirror of American culture, a reflection of changing views of women, of marriage, and of personal commitment. Its history is a richly layered account of the tension between individual and collective responsibility for dependency, of aspirational reform surprised by the intractability of gender-driven roles and the cruel judgment of well-intentioned dreamers. Alimony is a tale of notoriety and hype, of risk and high stakes, of the danger of myth and the powerful symbolism of money. It is at once a grand narrative of the evolution of law, and a personal story of an intimate relationship—a story of betrayal, desperation, and bravado, of investment, regret, and freedom to start over, a story of self-sacrifice aging into lost opportunity and financial responsibility hardening into involuntary servitude. And it is a tale without a grand finale, a still-evolving story of what is sometimes cast as the lone holdout in family law's dramatic progression from coverture to partnership marriage.

Alimony is at a crossroads. Even as today's alimony reform groups publicize reports of abuse designed to inspire anti-alimony fervor and statutory limits on alimony awards, the American Law Institute identifies a contemporary rationale for alimony and advances a reform template designed to promote predictable awards. In the end, alimony's fate will depend on whether it is understood, yet the general disdain for alimony has made it a much-neglected topic of study.

This book aims to further our understanding of alimony by examining the history and current state of alimony law, theory, and practice, and then to advance a reconceptualization of alimony as a marriage buyout. Buyouts draw on a loose analogy to partnership—a compelling metaphor for contemporary marriage, with its principles of mutual contribution, reciprocal responsibility, shared fate, and default rules that assume equality of status. Buyouts do not depend on who files for divorce or who commits marital fault; nor do they aim to penalize a spouse who wants out or compel specific performance of the marriage promise. What buyouts do, however, is significant: they replace alimony with a financial award consistent with norms of contemporary marriage; they provide a presumptive quantification formula that injects predictability and certainty into the law; and they go far in ensuring that primary caregivers are not thrown under the bus when their marriages end. The book's final chapter looks beyond alimony, describing a co-parenting partnership between committed couples who add children to their family, and a conceptual basis for a new form of income sharing between divorced parents of minor children.

PART I

Alimony Reflections

Once upon a time,
there was a woman who discovered
she had turned into the wrong person.
—Anne Tyler, *Back When We Were Grownups* (New York:
Knopf, 2001), 3

Stacy and Tracy were lovers. They graduated from college, found full-time teaching jobs at a local high school, and in a small ceremony attended by happy friends and family, committed to each other as life partners. The world looked bright. A year passed, the couple gave birth to a daughter, and like many young couples, Tracy and Stacy assumed they would equally share their daughter's care. This they did during the first summer of her life. But in the fall, when Stacy and Tracy returned to full-time teaching, life proved more complicated than they supposed it would be. Household tasks multiplied with their daughter's birth, and while the couple initially shared these chores, it was Tracy who took time off from work when the child's sneezes and coughs, rashes, and ear infections precluded day care. A year passed and more. The couple bore a son, Stacy acquired a master's degree and a nice salary increase, and Tracy quit her teaching job, planning to return when their son entered kindergarten. Four years later, Tracy did return to teaching, but took a part-time position. Life went on. Tracy continued to assume the majority of child care and household responsibilities, though no one much noticed. Stacy took an administrative position with the school district, the family enjoyed a rising standard of living, the children graduated high school, and then something incredible, something unforeseen by either party more than twenty years ago, happened. Stacy fell in love with a young colleague and determined to leave Tracy.

Stacy's decision puts Tracy in a hell of a spot. Like many contemporary couples, Stacy and Tracy have no significant assets. They are underwater on their home mortgage, and consume most of their income as it comes in. Given her age and the bleak employment market, Tracy despairs of finding a full-time teaching job or ever recovering her many years of lost seniority. Tracy, it seems, has become someone she never imagined she would be. Has she turned into the wrong person—the family sucker who stupidly invested in family labor rather than a career, and so must bear the consequences of her own folly? Or must Stacy share the costs of the family's division of labor? What is the "right" answer, the answer that best comports with principles of social justice, with feminism and egalitarianism, with norms of public responsibility, with respect for individualism, private ordering, and the integrity of a promise? The law's answer to these questions will be life-altering for Tracy and for Stacy, and will send an important message to other committed couples—to a broad audience of same-sex and opposite-sex partners, to couples who are married or cohabiting; childful or childless; older or younger; richer or poorer; of majority or minority race and ethnicity; highly or barely educated; traditional, egalitarian, or postmodern; to couples who keep their promises and to those who break them, sooner or later. At bottom, the answer to the question of Tracy's and Stacy's responsibility to each other depends on the meaning of intimate commitment, for that is where their story began.

In the United States, marriage is still the most common signal of intimate commitment. While not every committed couple is married, and not every married couple is committed, marriage is a cultural symbol of commitment to a life partner that is readily visible to outsiders and so serves as a useful starting point for an inquiry into the consequences of intimate promises. If Stacy and Tracy formalized their commitment through marriage, the question of Tracy's economic fate becomes, at least in the conventional script, an inquiry into the legitimacy of alimony.

But Stacy and Tracy are not real; as far as I know, I made them up. If alimony is an issue worth thinking about, if alimony matters, it is because the story of Stacy and Tracy generally describes a mass of real people.

1

Who Cares about Alimony?

In most households, someone is cleaning the toilet. Hardly anyone likes this job. And then there is the vacuuming, the laundering, the grocery shopping, the cooking, the bill paying, the dusting, the bed making. If the family includes children, these tasks multiply and new ones are added: the feeding, the bathing, the managing of child care on sick days and snow days and regular school days that don't match job hours, the homework supervising, the transporting to soccer and dance and medical appointments, the bedtime storytelling. Not all unpleasant tasks to be sure, but responsibilities that demand time and energy, often driving primary caregivers into part-time employment, employment gaps, and paid work that is flexible enough to accommodate family work. Meanwhile, the caregiver's labor frees her spouse to participate in the paid economy as an "ideal worker" unshackled by primary home responsibilities.[1] Teamwork thus allows the couple to enjoy together a home with children and a family wage.

It's a common story and a convenient one—at least so long as the partners' commitment endures. But if affection fades, divorce may unmask the reality that teamwork has disparately impacted the spouses' earning capacity. Over time, investments in family labor tend to reduce earning capacity for a primary caregiver, while investments in paid labor tend to increase earning capacity for a primary breadwinner. A clean break at divorce thus means the primary caregiver will bear most of the long-term costs of family roles while the primary wage-earner will enjoy most of the benefits in the form of enhanced earning capacity. When marital property is scant, as it usually is, alimony is the only judicial tool for addressing this inequity. This is the nutshell version of why alimony matters.

To be sure, alimony will not always be an exclusive or appropriate answer to a caregiver's lost earning capacity. If a divorcing couple has significant assets, a sizable property award can considerably ease a caregiver's financial straits, though some high-asset spouses have fought for and won large alimony awards in addition to property.[2] If, on the other hand, a potential payor has little income, an alimony award large enough to do much good might thrust that spouse into poverty, an outcome few would support. But both the very high-asset cases and the very low-income cases lie at the extremes of the spectrum. For the great pool of middle-class couples who divorce with little property but with a steady income stream, alimony is the only available tool for addressing disparate earning capacity related to marital roles. For these many couples, like Stacy and Tracy, alimony matters very much indeed.

The case for alimony begins with a look at the work of primary caregivers in most contemporary families.

A. Kinder, Küche, Kirche

The American home is not an equal opportunity employer.[3] While alimony is gender-neutral, and should be,[4] family roles have long made women the primary alimony candidates and alimony recipients. Between 2001 and 2006, only 3.6 percent of all alimony awards went to men;[5] in 2011, this figure was 8 percent.[6] The history of alimony is thus part of a larger story of gender roles within the family, a story with roots in the ideology of separate spheres, the notion that women are better suited for the private sphere of home and hearth and men for the public sphere of the marketplace. As Justice Bradley explained in 1872, a married woman has no right to practice law since "the civil law, as well as nature herself, has always recognized a wide difference in the respective spheres and destinies of man and woman. . . . [T]he domestic sphere . . . properly belongs to the domain and functions of womanhood."[7]

Such candid expressions of separate-spheres ideology sound peculiar to most modern ears. Yet the ideology persists in more subtle forms, casting women as natural nurturers—warm, selfless, sensitive, relationship-focused, better purveyors of family care—and men as tough, competitive, and ambitious, natural breadwinners for whom nurturing is awkward and even unmanly.[8] Most significantly, separate-spheres ideology underscores a gender script that continues to describe the division of labor in most contemporary marriages. Married women, even if they are full-time wage-earners, continue to assume primary caregiving responsibilities in the home.

This gender script becomes more vivid when we return to a time when it was more openly expressed. In the 1950s, for example, the view that women belonged in the home was trumpeted in startlingly frank fashion. A woman's "central function," observed one sociologist of the day, "remains that of creating a life style for herself and for the home in which she is life creator and life sustainer."[9] As the anthropologist Margaret Mead explained, a female has two choices: either she proclaims herself "a woman, and therefore less an achieving individual, or an achieving individual and therefore less a woman."[10]

The popular press of the day proclaimed the homemaker a

> wondrous creature [who] marries younger than ever, bears more babies and looks and acts far more feminine than the "emancipated" girl of the 1920's or even '30's. Steelworker's wife and Junior Leaguer alike do their own housework. . . . Today, if she makes an old-fashioned choice and lovingly tends a garden and a bumper crop of children, she rates louder hosannas than ever before.[11]

Such housewives were applauded as "feminine, women with truly feminine attitudes, admired by men for their miraculous, God-given, sensationally unique ability to wear skirts, with all the implications of that fact."[12]

The marketplace duplicated this view of the proper role of women, exhibiting an "almost universal opposition to employment of middle-class married women."[13] Most married women did not work outside their homes, and those who did worked "as a way of filling a hope chest or buying a new home freezer [while] gracefully conced[ing] the top jobs to men."[14] Such women took jobs not "out of a desire to compete with men but rather to help the family—a traditional role."[15] Not surprisingly, the majority of wage-earning women were segregated in low-paying jobs. In 1950, female wages were 53 percent of male wages.[16]

As Stephanie Coontz points out, however, not all married women of the 1950s were happy *Ozzie and Harriet* housewives.[17] The reality of housewives' experience was more complex; in many cases, it was homemaking that frustrated women. But women who by force of spirit resisted the cultural norm and pursued a career rather than a home freezer were cast by the media as "neurotic, unfeminine, unhappy women."[18] As one popular magazine explained, "Few women would want to thumb their noses at husbands, children and community and go off on their own. Those who do may be talented individuals, but they rarely are successful women."[19] As a *New York Times* editorial opined, while some housewives "admit to being deeply frustrated at times by the lack of privacy, the physical burden, the routine of family life, the confinement of it, . . . none would give up her home and family if she had the choice to make again."[20]

Women today clearly enjoy more choices than their 1950s counterparts. But separate-spheres ideology has proven curiously tenacious. Consider Anne-Marie Slaughter's 2012 article in the *Atlantic*, "Why Women Still Can't Have It All." After a two-year stint in Washington, D.C., with the State Department, Slaughter decided to go home to her two teenage sons, her husband, and her tenured position at Princeton. Recognizing that she was stepping "onto treacherous ground, mined with stereotypes," Slaughter explained her decision:

> Men are still socialized to believe that their primary family obligation
> is to be the breadwinner; women, to believe that their primary family
> obligation is to be the caregiver. . . . But it may be more than that: . . . a
> maternal imperative felt so deeply that the "choice" is reflexive.[21]

And then there was Lisa Belkin's 2003 *New York Times* article, "The Opt-Out Revolution." Interviewing a book club of female Princeton grads, Belkin recounted the views of two stay-at-home moms.[22] "This is what I was meant to do," said one mom. "I mean this is what I was meant to do at this time. I know that's very un-p.c., but I like life's rhythms when I'm nurturing a child." Said another stay-at-home mom, "I think some of us are swinging to a place where we enjoy, and can admit we enjoy, the stereotypical role of female/mother/caregiver. . . . I think we were born with those feelings."

Consider too the words of Katy McLaughlin in her 2012 article in the *Wall Street Journal*, "New Dreams, When the Old Ones Don't Fit."[23] The mother of two sons, McLaughlin confessed,

> When I was a young feminist, I would have been appalled by the notion of erasing my own passions and subsuming them into a husband and kids. . . . [But] the day our eldest was born, I lost the ambitious spirit that once propelled me on artistic exploits around the globe. My world became our home, our future and every hair on our child's head.

Separate-spheres ideology is powerful indeed. And its draw is not limited to professional women, who can presumably hire someone else to clean their toilets. For reasons that may seem mysterious, family labor—both housework and child care—is still largely a female role even though most married women today also work outside their homes. In Arlie Hochschild's famous words, married women typically work two shifts—one in the marketplace and another in the home, where they perform the lion's share of family labor.[24] Although Hochschild's supporting data were from the 1980s, her observations still describe a majority of contemporary families. In 2012, the Bureau of Labor Statistics reported that on an average day in 2011, 18.9 percent of men did housework—such as cleaning, doing laundry, or scrubbing toilets—compared with 47.8 percent of women.[25] That same year, 40.1 percent of men engaged in food preparation or cleanup, compared with 66 percent of women. In another study of married mothers and fathers, Bianchi, Robinson, and Milkie found that married mothers spent 19.4 hours a week in primary housework activities in 2000, compared with 9.7 hours in primary housework for married fathers.[26]

In an interesting study from the Panel Study of Income Dynamics (PSID) conducted at the University of Michigan, researchers found that having a husband actually creates more housework for women—seven extra hours each week—while having a wife saves men about an hour of housework each week.[27] The study used 2005 time-diary data and defined "housework" to include "core" tasks such as cooking, cleaning, and doing other basic work around the house, but not gardening, home repairs, or washing the car. The PSID researchers found that in 2005, women averaged about seventeen hours of housework weekly compared with thirteen hours for men. For married couples with more than three children, women averaged about twenty-eight hours of housework each week in 2005, while men averaged about ten hours. As the director of the PSID study observed, in general "[i]t's a well-known pattern. There's still a significant reallocation of labor that occurs at marriage; men tend to work more outside the home, while women take on more of the household labor. . . . And the situation gets worse for women when they have children."

Although the gap seems to be narrowing, women also typically undertake a larger share of child care than men. Bianchi, Robinson, and Milkie found that in 2000, mothers performed almost twice as much routine child care as fathers, taking on the majority of tasks such as feeding and dressing children, arranging medical care, and providing travel associated with child care.[28] Fathers, however, participated more equally in interactive enrichment activities such as teaching children, talking or reading to them, and engaging in indoor or outdoor playtime.[29] Married mothers spent 12.9 hours each week in *all* child care activities during 2000 (9.5 hours in routine activities and 3.3 hours in interactive activities), while married fathers spent 6.5 hours (4.1 hours in routine activities and 2.4 hours in interactive activities).[30] These figures represent an increase over 1965 figures, when married mothers spent 10.6 hours weekly in *all* child care activities (9.1 hours in routine activities and 1.5 hours in interactive activities) while married fathers spent 2.6 hours (1.3 hours in routine activities and 1.2 hours in interactive activities). The increase in child care time partly reflects increased multitasking, as parents combine child care with their own leisure activities.[31]

While the gender gap in family labor may be narrowing, for the moment women continue to assume the majority of that work. The American Law Institute summed up the current state of things:

Despite the dramatic changes in the workforce participation of married women over the last several decades, marital roles have persisted. . . . Whether or not women actually leave full-time employment after the birth of their children, studies consistently show that they usually perform far more than half of the married couple's domestic chores.[32]

So what gives? There are only so many hours in a day. If contemporary women are working for pay while taking on the lion's share of housework and devoting increasing time to child care, where do they find the time to do it all? Studies suggest that one source of extra time is reduced housework. The PSID researchers found that while women continue to take on the majority of housework, they are spending fewer hours on it. As previously noted, women averaged about seventeen hours of housework weekly in 2005.[33] In 1976, this figure was twenty-six hours—nine hours more than in 2005. Even as women are spending fewer hours on housework, men are spending more. The PSID researchers reported that in 1976 men spent six hours per week on housework, as compared with thirteen hours in 2005.[34]

The decreasing amount of housework appears even more dramatic when 1965 figures are used. In their study of married mothers and fathers, Bianchi, Robinson, and Milkie found that married mothers spent 34.5 hours weekly in primary housework in 1965, as compared with 19.4 hours in 2000. The married fathers in their study spent 4.4 hours weekly on primary housework in 1965, as compared with 9.7 hours in 2000.[35] The researchers surmised that to accommodate paid labor, mothers give up housework, sleep, discretionary time, and time with spouse, family, and friends.

The point is not that men are sloughing off. Indeed, studies show that the average *total workloads* of married mothers and fathers are almost equal—sixty-five hours for mothers and sixty-four hours for fathers.[36] Fathers, however, spend almost twice as many hours in paid work as mothers, while mothers spend twice as many hours in domestic work as fathers.[37]

While the division of labor in most contemporary families follows a gender script, primary caregiving is not limited to that script. In his study of fifty-two lesbian and gay families, Carrington found that one partner specialized in domestic labor in roughly three-fourths (thirty-eight) of the families.[38] As with many heterosexual couples, this specialization is not always a happy choice. As one gay man in Carrington's study explained, "Sterling never cleaned the toilets, he still doesn't clean toilets; he intends to clean the toilets, but right about the time when he gets to it, I have already cleaned the toilets."

Most work has its ups and downs, though cleaning toilets surely ranks low on the enjoyment hierarchy. Still, in the short term, while the family operates as a team, both partners may benefit from a primary breadwinner/primary caregiver arrangement. But for the caregiver this division of labor is risky. If the couple's commitment to each other ends, dissolution may expose the harsh reality that primary caregiving and the market disinvestment that often accompanies it have reduced the caregiver's earning capacity.

B. Market Disinvestment

Women who cook and launder and tutor and grocery shop and chauffeur and tell bedtime stories have less time and energy for other things. Not surprisingly, primary caregivers' home labor often limits their participation in the paid economy. This disinvestment may take several forms. A caregiver may work full-time in the home, forgoing paid work entirely for long or short periods, especially when children are young; or she may combine family work with paid work that is flexible, part-time, part-year, or that otherwise accommodates family responsibilities. Over time, a single caregiver may experiment with each of these disinvestment strategies.

1. Full-Time Caregivers and Gappers

Although it is no longer a grandly trumpeted norm or even a widely publicized fact, full-time homemaking has not disappeared. In 2012, the Bureau of Labor Statistics reported that when a child *under age one* was in the household, 56.9 percent of married mothers participated in the labor force in 2011 (56.3 percent in 2010).[39] When a child *under age three* was in the household, married mothers' participation rate was 59.4 percent in 2011 (59.3 percent in 2010). Of married mothers with children *under age six* in the household, 59.1 percent were employed in 2011 (58.9 percent in 2010). When the youngest child in the household was *age six to seventeen*, 70.5 percent of married mothers were employed in 2011 (70.7 percent in 2010).

In interpreting these data, BLS definitions are crucial. Significantly, the BLS defines labor force participation to include those who are working and *also those who are looking for work*. Under this definition, a married mother who cannot find but continues to search for flexible family-friendly work is counted as a labor force participant. The BLS definition of "employed" is also important, as it includes those who "did any work at all as paid employees"[40] and thus includes minimal part-time and seasonal workers. Perhaps most important is the BLS definition of "unemployed," which counts persons who did not work during the reference period despite "specific efforts to find employment." Under this definition a mother who drops out of the labor force to care for family is not *un*employed because she is not looking for paid work. "Not employed" thus differs significantly from "unemployed" under BLS terminology.

To estimate the number of married mothers who are *not employed* outside the home, we thus consider the flip side of the numbers on labor force participation and employment rather than the numbers of the "unemployed." In 2011, 43.1 percent of married mothers with a child *under age one* were not working for pay or looking for such work (43.7 percent in 2010).[41] Also in 2011, 40.6 percent of married mothers with a child *under age three* were not working for pay or looking for such work (40.7 percent in 2010). Of married mothers with children *under age six*, 40.9 percent were not working for pay or looking for such work in 2011 (41.1 percent in 2010). When the youngest child in the home was *age six to seventeen*, 29.5 percent of married mothers were not working for pay or looking for such work in 2011 (29.3 percent in 2010). Hardly insignificant numbers. Also interesting is the BLS comparison of labor force participation rates of married mothers and fathers. When the youngest child in the home was *under age eighteen*, 94 percent of married fathers were in the labor force in 2011, as compared with 68.7 percent of married mothers.[42] Taking the flip side of this latter figure, over 31 percent of married mothers with minor children did not work outside their homes, as compared with 6 percent of married fathers. Stay-at-home mothers are evidently still around.

As these data suggest, for some women, full-time homemaking is a temporary phenomenon, as they take gaps in employment, especially when children are young, and return to full-time or part-time work when children are older. Numerous studies have shown that women are more likely than men to spend time away from the paid labor force.[43] In her study of "highly qualified women," Sylvia Ann Hewlett found that 60 percent of these women had "nonlinear careers,"[44] taking off-ramps (stepping out of the workforce) and scenic routes (stepping back from—rather than stepping out of—the workforce) in an attempt to balance work and family responsibilities. Thirty-seven percent of these professional women voluntarily left their employment for some period, on average 2.2 years.[45] As a reason for their time-out, 45 percent of these women cited child care challenges, while 24 percent cited elder-care crises.[46] For women in the business sector aged forty-one to fifty-five (the sandwich generation), one in three women surveyed reported leaving paid employment to care for a family member other than a child.[47] African American women who care for elderly and extended family members are especially hard-hit by these responsibilities, spending 12.4 hours per week in that work, as compared with 9.5 hours for white women.[48] As Hewlett concludes, "if you are not derailed by a two-year-old at age thirty, you may be derailed by an eighty-year old at age fifty!"[49]

As Joan Williams observes, it is not clear that women who leave paid labor have opted out so much as they have been pushed out by a labor market that does not accommodate family priorities.[50] The unavailability of part-time work, inflexible hours, policies that don't look kindly on unplanned absences to care for a sick child, and stereotypes that disadvantage mothers may be driving caregivers out of the workplace. Moreover, the high cost of day care may make low-paid work irrational. In every state, the average cost of day care for a child under age one exceeds the average cost of college tuition at a state university.[51]

Pressure to drop out of paid employment increases when a husband's long work hours turn a married caregiver into a quasi-solo parent. One study found that having a husband who works more than sixty hours a week increases a wife's odds of quitting her job by 112 percent; having a husband who works more than fifty hours a week increases these odds by 44 percent.[52] As Shirley Tilghman, molecular biologist and Princeton president, observed, when ambitious men and women have children, "someone has to become less ambitious."[53]

Of course not all couples consist of two ambitious professionals. Full-time caregiving, however, crosses socioeconomic lines, with the highest rates appearing at lower income levels. A 2007 survey by the Pew Research Center revealed that stay-at-home mothers are slightly younger than mothers who work for pay, are less educated, and have lower household incomes.[54] Twenty-one percent of stay-at-home mothers are college graduates, as compared with 34 percent of mothers who work for pay. Another study found that between 2006 and 2008, 60 percent of low-income married mothers, 23 percent of middle-income married mothers, and 20 percent of professional-managerial-class married mothers did not work outside their homes.[55] One explanation for the higher rate of stay-at-home mothers in low-income groups may be the unavailability of family-friendly, flexible jobs in low-wage categories. Punching a clock is tough when a child is home sick.

Race may also affect the incidence of full-time homemaking. Pew researchers found that in 2007, 27 percent of stay-at-home mothers were Hispanic, 54 percent were white, and 9 percent were black.[56] In an interesting study of levels of depression in mothers returning to paid work, African American women experienced the least depression and immigrant Latina women the most.[57] A study by Riche Jeneen Daniel Barnes found that married black women are 1.5 times more likely to work full-time outside the home than married white women.[58] Barnes speculates that the explanation for this disparity may lie partly in the fact that black women are taught to avoid economic dependence on a man. Barnes reported that when they do become stay-at-home mothers, the black women in her study were motivated by a desire to protect their marriages rather than to tend to children. These data go far in explaining why about 90 percent of alimony recipients are white.[59]

While most of the caregiving data focus on heterosexual couples, we have seen that same-sex couples may also adopt a primary breadwinner/primary caregiver division of labor. In some of these families, the caregiver works full-time in the home. A 2004 analysis of randomly selected Census Bureau returns for same-sex couples with children revealed that 26 percent of gay male couples and 22 percent of lesbian couples included a stay-at-home parent.[60] In follow-up interviews, gay stay-at-home parents repeatedly explained that "staying at home constitutes the just and noble course of parenthood"—a sentiment curiously familiar to any student of the 1950s.

2. Neo-Traditional Caregivers

Most primary caregivers are not full-time homemakers, but rather neo-traditional caregivers who combine market labor with primary caregiving, working one shift at home and another in the paid economy. These caregivers often make compromises not required of their partners, limiting employment hours in order to accommodate family responsibilities. The Department of Labor reported that in 2010, women were almost twice as likely as men to work part-time (fewer than thirty-five hours per week).[61] In 2010, 26.6 percent of women worked part-time, as compared with 13.4 percent of men. The 2007 numbers are similar: in that year, about 25 percent of all employed women worked part-time.[62] The vast majority of part-time workers cite "noneconomic reasons," such as child care demands, other family obligations, and school work, as the reason for their work arrangement.[63] In 2003, 25 percent of all employed women worked part-time, as compared with 11 percent of employed men.[64]

In Hewlett's study of highly qualified women, 36 percent said they had worked part-time to balance work and personal life, 25 percent said they had reduced their hours in a full-time job, and 16 percent said they had declined a promotion.[65] Thirty-eight percent of these women said they had chosen employment with fewer responsibilities and lower pay in order to meet family responsibilities.

A study of popular attitudes by the Pew Institute in 2009 suggests that Americans may approve of such accommodations for family. Pew researchers reported that 40 percent of those surveyed in 2009 believed that the ideal situation for a young child is a mother who works part-time, and 42 percent thought that a stay-at-home mother was best for the child.[66] When asked what arrangement they believed was best for the mother of a young child, 44 percent said that part-time work was best for her; 38 percent thought it best if the mother didn't work outside the home at all.

The incidence of part-time employment among women doesn't tell the whole story of caregivers' market disinvestment, since part-time work is commonly defined as anything less than thirty-five hours per week. More enlightening are reports comparing the actual number of hours employed men and women spend in paid work. In a report on *working men and women* in 2011, the BLS found that on days when they worked, men spent forty-seven more minutes on the job than women.[67] This disparity partly reflects women's greater likelihood of working part-time, but even among full-time workers, men worked longer hours each day—8.3 hours as compared to 7.8 hours for women.

In a study of *employed mothers and fathers*, Bianchi, Robinson, and Milkie found that in 2000 fathers averaged more hours in paid labor than mothers and that mothers' hours in paid labor varied with the age of children. Employed mothers with a child under age one spent 31.3 hours in paid labor, while those with children over age six spent 36 hours.[68] By contrast, fathers' market participation appeared not to vary with the number or age of children. A 1996 study comparing the hours of paid labor by *married parents* found that fathers averaged far more hours on the job than mothers—2,132 hours as compared with 1,197 hours.[69]

The number of hours employed mothers spend in paid employment appears to vary with their education. In a 2003 study, Gornick and Meyers found that mothers without a high school diploma averaged twenty-one hours in paid labor each week, while mothers with a college degree averaged twenty-seven hours.[70] Bianchi, Robinson, and Milkie found that in 2000, married mothers with a postgraduate education averaged 33.5 hours of employment per week, compared with 41.5 hours for comparably educated single mothers and 47.2 hours for married fathers.[71] Interestingly, the more hours a father works, the more time the mother spends in child care and the less time she reads; the more hours a mother works, the more time the father sleeps or watches television.[72]

The point is not that primary caregiving and the market disinvestment that often accompanies it are good or bad, but only that they are real. It would be a mistake, however, to cast primary caregiving as a valueless endeavor, an unfortunate remnant of separate-spheres ideology. Caregiving is part of the teamwork that describes many contemporary families, and for these families it may have significant practical and emotional value. Indeed, primary caregiving may be viewed as a parental imperative. Consider Bellafonte's interviews of gay couples in which the stay-at-home parent repeatedly explained that "staying at home constitutes the just and noble course of parenthood."[73] Consider too the candid words of Anne Slaughter, who felt a deep "maternal imperative" to be with her children, and the stay-at-home mothers in Lisa Belkin's interviews who enjoyed the caregiving experience. Whether performed by a gay, lesbian, or straight parent, full-time caregiving has value, providing a supportive, connected, nondistracting environment that nurtures family members, including the caregiver. The problem, however, is that caregiving is not free.

C. The Motherhood Penalty

As we have seen, most primary caregivers are women, and primary caregiving women often disinvest in paid labor, especially when children are in the household. This disinvestment and the status of motherhood itself tend to reduce earnings in a phenomenon common enough to have a name—the motherhood penalty.

In his much-cited 1988 book *Women's Quest for Economic Equality*, the economist Victor Fuchs reported that the primary cause of the earnings gap between men and women is family responsibility that compromises women's workplace investments. Controlling for education, Fuchs found that the hourly wages of women aged thirty to thirty-nine declined proportionately with the number of children in the family. For women, concluded Fuchs, "the greatest barrier to economic equality is children."[74]

Other studies confirm a continuing motherhood penalty in the form of reduced earnings and earning capacity for women with children. In her blockbuster 2001 book *The Price of Motherhood*, Ann Crittenden characterizes a mother's lost earnings as a "mommy tax," which can exceed one million dollars for college-educated women.[75] For working-class women, says Crittenden, mothers' responsibility for children "is the most important factor in disposing women to poverty."[76] In her 1998 survey of the literature, Jane Waldfogel concluded that "researchers typically find a family penalty of 10 to 15 percent for women with children as compared to women without children."[77] In a 2003 study searching for educational predictors of the size of the motherhood penalty, Anderson, Binder, and Krause found that medium-skilled mothers experience more persistent and severe income losses than either low-skilled or high-skilled mothers.[78]

In a recently released study of earnings inequality among white women, researchers at the University of Massachusetts–Amherst found that "a significant motherhood penalty persists at all earnings levels."[79] Most hard-hit are the lowest-paid women: earnings losses ranged from 15 percent per child among low-wage workers to approximately 2.5 percent per child for the average highly paid worker. Although their study focused on white women, these researchers speculate that "the more bottom-heavy distribution of earnings among black women, combined with larger motherhood penalties among lower-paid white women, suggest strong negative effects of children on earnings among black women."

Primary caregivers who work part-time may not only receive less pay, but also fewer fringe benefits such as health insurance or retirement plans. This tradition of no-benefit part-time work dates to the post–World War II era, in which employers responded to the shortage of single women by creating part-time jobs for married women, who employers assumed would be covered by their husbands' benefit plans.[80]

Other studies have focused specifically on gappers, women who periodically drop out of the paid labor force. Women who drop out of the paid labor force for significant periods are likely to have lower lifetime earnings than women with uninterrupted labor force attachment, simply because of forgone wages during employment gaps. Most of the studies of wage depreciation in workers with career interruptions find a statistically significant depreciation effect, ranging from around 0.6 percent to over 5 percent annually.[81] Sigle-Rushton and Waldfogel, for example, compared the lifetime earnings of medium-educated mothers and childless women. They found that women with one child earned 89 percent of childless women's earnings and that women with two children earned 81 percent of childless women's earnings.[82]

In her study of highly qualified women, Hewlett found that even an average career gap of 2.2 years imposes a severe financial penalty—an 18 percent loss in earning power.[83] Women who took a gap of three or more years lost 37 percent of their earning capacity. As Hewlett notes, these data on the costs of gapping are consistent with other data showing that when women enter the workforce their earnings are comparable to those of men, but that over time a gender gap appears. At age twenty-five to twenty-nine, women earn 87 percent of men's wages, but at age forty to forty-four, women earn just 71 percent of men's wages. Hewlett also discovered that few gappers realize how difficult reentering the paid labor force will be. While 93 percent of the gappers studied wanted to return to paid jobs, only 74 percent were actually able to do so. Moreover, only 40 percent returned to full-time, mainstream employment, while 24 percent took part-time employment, and 9 percent became self-employed.[84]

The primary family responsibilities that lead married mothers to limit paid employment go far in explaining the motherhood penalty. Caregivers who prioritize family labor over work for an employer tend not be viewed as "ideal workers."[85] Caregivers' compromised investments in the job market often mean less pay, less advancement, and over time reduced earning capacity as opportunities disappear. The costs of caregiving, however, may not be apparent during marriage, as a mother shares the family wage with a higher-income spouse. In the 1950s, when norms of full-time caregiving pressured married women to stay home, their role was less risky than it is today. Implicit in the cultural message of the day was the predicate that a caregiver's home and family would be there for her. Divorce was rare, and restrictions on a husband's access to divorce insulated the homemaker against the depreciation in marketable human capital that ordinarily accompanies homemaking. No-fault divorce, however, removes this insulation.

D. Terry and Jack

Time for a true story. Here is the tale of Terry, who married a handsome marine named Jack and stuck with him as he made his way through Georgetown Law School. Terry and Jack moved to the lower Hudson Valley and bore five children. Jack became a judge and Terry became a stay-at-home mom. In 1977, Terry wrote an op-ed column for the *New York Times* about the challenges and joys of full-time caregiving in an age of liberated women. As Terry explained,

> I come from a long line of women more Edith Bunker than Betty Freidan, who never knew they were unfulfilled. I can't testify that they were happy, but they were cheerful. . . . They took pride in a clean, comfortable home and satisfaction in serving a good meal because no one had explained that the only work worth doing is that for which you get paid.

They enjoyed raising their children because no one ever told them that children belonged in church basements and their mother belonged somewhere else.[86]

Terry appeared on the *Today Show* and told her story to Charlie Rose, to Dinah Shore, and to Oprah. She appeared at lecterns around the country and in 1980 published *Ever since Adam and Eve*, in which she passionately defended her decision to forgo a career and assume the role of stay-at-home mom, extolling the virtues of "making a home," raising children, preparing family meals, and supporting a hardworking husband.

Forty years passed. Then something unimaginable happened, something unforeseen by Terry (and probably by Jack) forty years ago. On their fortieth wedding anniversary, Jack served Terry with divorce papers.[87] Terry was stunned, bitter, confused, and embarrassed to find herself, at this stage in her life, "marooned" and "discarded" by "the love of her life." "'Divorce,'" she wrote, "doesn't begin to describe the pain of this process. 'Canceled' is more like it. It began with my credit cards, then my health insurance and checkbook, until, finally, like a used postage stamp, I felt canceled too." She sold her engagement ring to pay a roofer, and was shocked when her first non-joint tax return informed her that she had become eligible for food stamps. Meanwhile, Jack vacationed in Cancún with his girlfriend. A divorce court awarded Terry four years of alimony in an amount "less than she was used to getting for household expenses" and suggested she undertake job training when she turned sixty-seven. Embittered and regretful of her caregiving role, Terry charged that "[d]ivorce has become a license for men to behave badly."

How could this happen? How could a stay-at-home mom of forty years with five children and six grandchildren be thrown to the wolves by a divorce court that awards her four years of alimony and advises her to reinvent herself at age sixty-seven? Something is terribly wrong here.

In Terry's case, the story ends rather well. In 2009 she published a second book, *Disregard First Book,* a cautionary tale for modern women about the financial perils of caregiving. While Terry's recovery is good news for her, it is hardly reassuring to other primary caregivers, given the slim chances of anyone becoming a famous writer. Indeed, Terry's tale should strike a chord of fear in any caregiver who is paying attention. For caregivers, for their families and friends and communities—indeed, for any observer concerned with the fairness and integrity of the legal system—Terry's story demands an explanation. Or does it?

It is easy to empathize with Terry, to insist that she should have received more than four years of alimony after forty years as a stay-at-home mom of five, to question the vision of equity that would lead a court to set her husband free to vacation in Cancún while Terry qualified for welfare. But these responses suppose that alimony is a legitimate answer to Terry's plight and to the plight of the many other full-time and primary caregivers who will one day divorce. Critics have charged, however, that alimony is an anachronism that has no place in an age of supposedly egalitarian marriage. Alimony, some charge, should be abandoned rather than reformed.

E. Alimony Objections: If It's Broke, Throw It Out

[S]o widespread is the idea that alimony is just another racket that it is not uncommon to hear people say that it should be done away with entirely.
—Catherine Groves Peele, "Social and Psychological Effects of the Availability and the Granting of Alimony on the Spouses," *Law and Contemporary Problems* 6 (1939): 291

If men and women are equally endowed, equally opportuned, and equally responsible for their individual fate, why, critics ask, should men be expected to support their ex-wives? This fundamental question drives several common objections to alimony, including arguments that alimony inappropriately perpetuates women's dependence on men, that it wrongly assumes private responsibility for what should be collective responsibility, and that it overcompensates primary caregivers who have already enjoyed a primary wage-earner's income during marriage. The answer to these objections ultimately depends on whether there is a convincing rationale for alimony consistent with contemporary visions of marriage as a partnership of equals, a subject we will consider in chapters 7 and 8. This section previews common objections to alimony since these objections should be part of any broad rethinking of the law of alimony.

1. Perpetuating and Privileging Female Dependence

As we have seen, the law of alimony is gender-neutral. Yet the overwhelming majority of alimony claimants and alimony recipients are female. The explanation of course lies in married women's continuing role as the primary family caregiver, a role that often makes divorce more costly for women than men. Critics have charged, however, that alimony perpetuates women's dependence on men, entrenching gender roles in ways contrary to women's best interests. As Herma Hill Kay explained long ago, the law should not encourage women to make "economically disabling" choices that perpetuate "their traditional financial dependence upon men and contribut[e] to their inequality with men at divorce."[88] "Female dependency," said Kay, "should no longer be the necessary result of motherhood."[89]

The premise that alimony encourages female dependence, however, is not beyond dispute. First, it is not clear that primary caregiving is so much a carefully weighed choice as it is a response to necessity, to the inadequacy of the U.S. day care system for both children and the elderly, to cultural expectations, to a game of "chicken" within the family, or simply to the daily tasks of maintaining a family that gradually default to one spouse who, over time, and almost as a surprise, realizes she has become a primary caregiver. To the extent that the role of primary caregiver is not the result of a conscious, free choice, the law's treatment of caregivers will neither induce nor dissuade married women from assuming this role.

Second, even when a primary caregiver makes a voluntary choice to assume this role, it is not clear that the law of divorce will have much effect on her decision. For many caregivers and others, the law of divorce is unknown or misunderstood. Alimony is already rare, although many people, including married women, seem not to realize this. One study of expectations found that although 80 percent of women assumed they would receive alimony if they divorced, in fact only about 8 percent of women were being awarded alimony.[90] The premise that the law will affect intimate decisions depends fundamentally on an assumption that decision makers have an accurate understanding of the law, an assumption that may be overly optimistic. Even if a caregiver's understanding of the law were more accurate—that is, even if alimony were eliminated and the caregiver were aware of this fact—it is not clear that her personal decision about how much time to spend caring for her family would be much affected. Until troubles arise in a marriage, couples tend not to think about the economics of divorce. Indeed, at the time of marriage the starry-eyed factor leads most couples to unrealistically discount the likelihood of divorce.

Finally, if alimony were abandoned, the consequence would often be to *punish* a divorcing spouse who had failed or refused to accede to the law's message that primary caregiving is a disapproved role. Such a response is inconsistent with the law's long-standing deference to private decision making within the family, with freedom of choice in intimate matters, and with respect for pluralism. In the end, concern for women's best interests would likely backfire, penalizing women who don't seem to understand or agree about what is best for them.

In a related argument, critics have objected that alimony privileges heterosexual, affluent white women. Twila Perry, for example, has argued that alimony both encourages women's dependence on men and contributes to a racial hierarchy among women.[91] Perry explains that the search for an alimony rationale rests on a racial stereotype—a vision of marriage as the union of an economically powerful husband and a dependent wife—that excludes most African American marriages. As Regina Austin observes, the experience of black women is often very different from that of white women. "[I]n some segments of the heterosexual black population, saving and asset accumulation are gender roles assigned to women," and "men [are] the chief cause of black women's asset poverty."[92] Laura Kessler adds that the problem of the primary caregiver with reduced earning capacity is "less relevant to women of limited economic means and women of color, who are less likely to ever be married and who, if married, are unlikely to be married to a man with the kind of job that would make a generous alimony award a promising path to economic independence."[93] Moreover, says Kessler, "reviving the remedy of support in the divorce context offers essentially nothing to same-sex couples denied the right of marriage or civil unions."

Similarly, Martha Fineman warns that income-sharing proposals privilege traditional, heterosexual women and do not meet women's needs at large.[94] Vicki Schultz agrees, adding that "joint property feminists tie homemakers' pay to their spouses' income—a methodology that introduces severe class bias."[95] Of great concern to Schultz is the possibility that "[t]he wife of a high-level executive who gets one-half his earnings for caring for the house and kids is paid much more than the wife of a janitor, for example, even though both wives may be doing essentially the same work." Moreover, says Schultz, feminists should not be encouraging women to invest in patriarchal relationships.[96]

To be sure, alimony should not be reserved for heterosexual, affluent white women. But it isn't. Alimony is neutral as to gender, race, and ethnicity, and as states continue to extend marriage rights to same-sex couples, it will increasingly be neutral as to sexual orientation. As we have seen, the limited available data suggest that same-sex couples often adopt a primary caregiver/primary wage-earner division of labor, which will presumably create a new pool of same-sex alimony claimants. It is true, as we have seen, that alimony is primarily a middle-class remedy, but this is a consequence of pragmatism rather than exclusion. Low-income couples have little income to share; high-income couples often have assets significant enough to reduce the need for alimony. The point is that alimony cannot address all the wrongs in our world or offer a one-size-fits-all remedy for every divorcing spouse. Still, alimony remains an important tool in ensuring equity in many divorces. To deny courts this tool because it is not appropriate or workable in every divorce would make the perfect the enemy of the good.

2. Collective Responsibility

Still other critics charge that alimony represents a private response to what should be a collective responsibility—that the costs of caring for children should be assumed by society at large rather than by any one individual. Some feminist commentators, most notably Martha Fineman, have urged public support of the work of caregivers.[97] Because caregiving has public value, reasons Fineman, it creates a "social debt—a debt that binds each and every member of society, not only individual family members or receivers of care."[98]

It is not clear, however, that public and private law solutions to the problem of a divorcing caregiver must be either/or propositions. Because caregiving often benefits both an individual spouse and society at large, both private and public measures seem appropriate. On the one hand, if a well-positioned spouse is not required to share income with the primary caregiver who has conferred direct benefits on him, that spouse will receive a windfall at the expense of society at large. On the other hand, when private resources are unavailable, either because a spouse's income is low or because the caregiver is alone or part of a couple, perhaps a same-sex couple, not subject to divorce law, public law solutions are necessary and appropriate.

Of course, a private-law income-sharing tool (like alimony) should not reinforce patriarchal marriage. The appropriateness of alimony as an answer to the costs of primary caregiving thus depends on identification of a rationale for alimony disentangled from the long-discarded notion of men as lifetime protectors of women. In chapter 8 we will identify such a rationale based on a vision of contemporary marriage as a partnership of equals.

3. The Overcompensation Argument

Though not so clearly articulated as the previous objections, a recurring sentiment is that alimony might overcompensate a primary caregiver who has already enjoyed the good life, namely, years of sharing the income of a primary wage-earner. A variation on this theme is that a primary caregiver has enjoyed more time with children, reaping psychic joy that the wage-earner has forgone in order to bring home the bacon. Each of these concerns suggests that a caregiver has "already had her cake" and shouldn't expect a second helping of dessert. A related concern is based on the premise that a caregiver has assumed the risk of her own declining human capital, perhaps after a personal cost-benefit calculation, and so shouldn't expect a former spouse to share the costs of her decision.

Each of these concerns is linked by a common thread—a vision of marriage as an association of two individuals who continue to operate in separate capacities, loosely linked by marriage, but at bottom separate persons who function separately, reap costs and benefits separately, and make contributions that should be counted and weighed and compared at divorce. If this weighing reveals that a caregiver has reaped more benefits than she has conferred, then she can hardly complain and deserves nothing from her ex-spouse. In this individualistic model, marriage looks much like cohabitation. Each party remains free, uncommitted, and individually responsible for whatever life choices he or she has made and whatever fate he or she experiences. If the couple intended more, they would have committed to each other. Wait. That's what married couples do, isn't it?

But it is perhaps too easy to respond that leaving a primary caregiver to bear all the costs of her marital role is unfair. The truth is that the answer to overcompensation concerns depends on whether we draw on an individualistic or communal model of marriage, on our view of the meaning of intimate commitment. If we view marriage as a partnership in which partners promise to share the costs and benefits of their life together, we will come to one conclusion. But if we view marriage as an at-will association of two individuals who each assume the costs and benefits of their independent lives, we will come to another conclusion. These competing visions of marriage lie at the core of the search for a rationale for alimony, and we will return to them in chapters 7 and 8.

With these objections to alimony in mind, we turn next to the intriguing story of alimony's history and the elusive search for its rationale.

2

Alimony's Heritage

The Helpless, the Blameless, and the Clean-Break Losers

A woman is not a breeding cow to be nurtured during her
years of fecundity, then conveniently and economically con-
verted to cheap steaks when past her prime. . . . This has
nothing to do with feminism, sexism, male chauvinism, or
any other trendy social ideology. It is ordinary common
sense, basic decency and simple justice.
—*In re Marriage of Brantner*, 136 Cal. Rptr. 635, 637 (1977)

The law's treatment of divorcing caregivers is a disturbing tale of divorce
serving as "a handy vehicle for the summary disposal of old and used
wives";[1] of divorce judges vested with broad discretion setting long-term
caregivers free to "enjoy" new lives with little income, little property,
and little hope of ever escaping the human capital costs of their family
role; of feminists' early insistence that gender equality leaves no place
for alimony. But this is supposedly the penultimate story, the horror
before family law's enlightened appreciation of the value of family care
and the economic vulnerability of divorcing caregivers. Maybe. But try
explaining that to Terry Hekker, the stay-at-home mom of five children
whose husband divorced her after forty years of marriage. As we saw
in the last chapter, Terry received four years of alimony, a suggestion
from the divorce judge that she undertake job retraining at age sixty-
seven, and a notice from the IRS that she qualified for food stamps. In
a 2011 interview, Terry, then seventy-nine, was still hoping that divorce

This chapter incorporates portions of an earlier article published as "Divorce and the Displaced Homemaker: A Discourse on Playing with Dolls, Partnership Buyouts and Dissociation under No-Fault," *University of Chicago Law Review* 60 (1993): 67.

laws would change, still worrying about young women who don't prepare themselves for financial independence, and still wishing that the National Organization for Women "would put its considerable clout behind the issue."[2]

A recitation of anecdotal inequities, however, will not tell the full story of divorcing caregivers. Their fate is part of a larger story of the history of alimony, a history that is inextricably linked with evolving views of the status of women, the meaning of marriage, the right to divorce, and the rationale for alimony. And so we take up the curious and at times disturbing tale of alimony's heritage.

A. Support for the Helpless and the Blameless: From Coverture to Fault

Once upon a time, caregivers were protected "favorites" of family law—at least that was the storyline. Prior to the English reforms of 1857, a man who married undertook a lifetime obligation to support his wife. Although he could obtain a legal separation (divorce *a mensa et thoro*), rarely could he obtain an absolute divorce—that is, a full severance of marital ties (divorce *a vinculo*). Whether or not spouses lived together, the husband's duty of support continued throughout the wife's life. Alimony was the mechanism, designed by the English ecclesiastical courts, for enforcing the husband's lifetime obligation to sustain his wife. Indeed, the word "alimony" derives from the Latin *alimonia*, which means "sustenance."

Underpinning the husband's support obligation was an assumption that married women should not and often could not support themselves. Employment opportunities for women were limited, and a married woman's property was subject to her husband's control. Indeed, according to the common-law concept of coverture, a married woman's identity merged into that of her husband, who bore a moral and legal obligation to provide for her. As Blackstone explained, "the very being or legal existence of the woman is suspended during the marriage, or at least is incorporated and consolidated into that of the husband, . . . under whose wing, protection, and cover, she performs every thing."[3] In Blackstone's view, this was not a bad deal for women, since "even the disabilities, which the wife lies under, are for the most part intended for her protection and benefit. So great a favourite is the female sex of the laws of England."[4] To be sure, this "favored" status demanded a steep price from married women, who were tethered to men and denied the respect and freedom most American women enjoy today. But at least these early English women were less easily thrown under the bus than their contemporary American counterparts.

The appearance of absolute divorce and the supposed end of coverture meant the end of caregivers' lifetime support ticket and also the end of a clear rationale for alimony. If marital ties are fully severed, how can a husband's duty of support survive? Although its original rationale is long gone, alimony mysteriously endures. A partial explanation may lie in Reva Siegel's observation that the law of coverture, so starkly described by Blackstone in 1765, continued to influence judicial thinking well into the twentieth century.[5] Courts may have also been inspired by the pragmatic concern that if a dependent wife were cut off from her source of support, she would become a public charge.

In colonial times, and even after independence, divorce law in the United States varied widely across the states, with southern states generally more inclined toward the English aversion to absolute divorce than their northern counterparts. By the late nineteenth century, every state had moved to a fault-based divorce regime, which authorized absolute divorce, but only for an innocent spouse who could prove that the other spouse had engaged in serious marital misconduct. Such misconduct typically included adultery, cruelty, or abandonment. Without proof of such wrongdoing, divorce was unavailable, no matter that the spouses disliked or even hated each other.

By the end of World War II, a shifting emphasis on individual happiness rather than family stability had sparked questions about the legitimacy of fault-based divorce laws, which were increasingly viewed as pesky anachronisms. Not surprisingly, spousal collusion was widespread. If both spouses wanted out of the marriage, they could game the system by together fabricating grounds for divorce. This collusion was no secret: the courts, the clerks, the lawyers, the parties—virtually everyone—was aware of its reality, but distaste for restrictive divorce laws led most to look the other way. For a time, collusion effectively transformed many fault-based laws into mutual-consent divorce regimes.

While fault-based restrictions on divorce and the collusion they inspired were not the finest moment in the history of American family law, this scheme did offer some protection to caregivers—at least to caregivers who had not committed marital fault and whose spouses were eager to escape the marriage. Such "innocent" caregivers could bargain for financial concessions, offering to collude in manufacturing grounds for divorce in return for a bigger share of marital property or generous alimony settlement. Of course, not every caregiver was innocent. Nor was every caregiver less eager to leave the marriage than her spouse or willing to lie to a court about the existence of grounds for divorce in order to improve her economic positioning. At most, fault-based divorce threw a few bargaining chips to some innocent caregivers.

At least in theory, fault-based divorce regimes also protected some innocent caregivers by providing a rationale for alimony. In an analogy to contract, a spouse who engages in marital misconduct might be said to have breached the marriage contract and thus be liable for alimony as damages. Under this reasoning, a husband who committed adultery, for example, would be required to pay alimony to an injured caregiver. Of course, such a fault-based rationale for alimony would protect only caregivers who are innocent and whose mates are guilty; that is, no innocent spouse would ever pay alimony and no guilty spouse would ever receive alimony. North Carolina law comes close to this scheme, providing that courts shall order a "supporting spouse" guilty of "illicit sexual behavior" to pay alimony, and shall not order alimony on behalf of a "dependent spouse" guilty of such conduct.[6] The statute further authorizes the court to deny alimony in its discretion when both spouses are guilty of "illicit sexual behavior." But such a limitation has never fully described the law of alimony and thus offers only an imperfect rationale.

Moreover, fault is a precarious friend of caregivers, who are presumably just as capable of committing marital offenses as their mates. Many states have at one time or another barred alimony awards to guilty claimants. South Carolina, for example, prohibits a court from awarding alimony to a spouse who commits adultery.[7] In a worst-case scenario, such a bar might ensure the economic undoing of a long-term caregiver who has a one-night stand with the tennis pro, an outcome we will consider in chapter 4.

Whatever their usefulness, fault-based rationales for alimony and fault-based grounds for divorce were compromised by the compelling philosophy of no-fault divorce.

B. Egalitarian Dreams and the "Liberation" of Caregivers

By 1969, dissatisfaction with state restrictions on divorce had led California to enact a statute allowing divorce without a showing of fault. The act went into effect under the signature of then Governor Ronald Reagan. Shortly thereafter, in 1970, the National Conference of Commissioners on Uniform State Laws boldly approved a Uniform Marriage and Divorce Act (UMDA), which authorized divorce upon a showing that a marriage was "irretrievably broken" without regard to marital fault.[8] The states quickly followed suit. By 1985, every state had amended or replaced its divorce statute to allow divorce without a showing of fault.[9]

Shunning views of divorce as a remedy for an innocent spouse, no-fault reforms viewed divorce not as the consequence of one spouse's fault, but rather as the product of complex spousal dynamics beyond the understanding and the appropriate inquiry of a court of law. Under this view, no one spouse's conduct could or should be singled out as the cause of divorce. No-fault laws thus made divorce available largely without reference to spousal conduct and typically, though unofficially, upon the request of only one spouse. The no-fault movement, however, did not eliminate fault from divorce proceedings. While fault is no longer the *exclusive* path to divorce, many states simply added a no-fault ground to their existing fault-based laws, offering parties alternative grounds for divorce—fault or no-fault. Even among states that disallow fault as a ground for divorce, marital fault may affect the economic consequences of divorce. While the concept of marital fault thus did not disappear with the appearance of no-fault divorce, the wildly popular no-fault philosophy significantly undercut fault-based rationales for alimony.

Central to the no-fault movement was a vision of divorce as an opportunity for a fresh start and a clean break. Since no one was to blame for the marital breakup, no one should suffer unnecessarily. At least in principle, no-fault divorce thus aims to provide each spouse with an opportunity to begin life anew, as free as possible from any lingering marital entanglements—emotional or financial. With this goal came final abandonment, at least in principle, of any shreds of the old English view of a husband's lifetime legal and moral responsibility for his wife.

At the heart of the no-fault reforms is the partnership notion that marriage is an association of individuals who may dissolve their relationship at will, compel the liquidation and distribution of their property, and upon winding up their affairs, leave the relationship with no further obligations to one another. This scheme initially held great appeal both for proponents of easy access to divorce and for women's rights advocates whose equality rhetoric disavowed the need for male financial support. Unexpectedly, however, no-fault reforms unmasked the reality that many caregivers were "just a man away from poverty."[10]

In 1985, Lenore Weitzman published a startling account of the economic devastation of women and children under California's no-fault divorce statute. In *The Divorce Revolution*, Weitzman reported that in the *first year after divorce*, women and children averaged a 73 percent decline in their standard of living, while men enjoyed a 42 percent rise.[11] Weitzman's work lit the flames of indignation, launching a flurry of commentary as observers struggled to explain the wildly disparate impact of divorce on men and women, and intensifying reform efforts in both the public and private sectors. Numerous other studies found a smaller but consistent disparity in standards of living one year after divorce—a 30 percent decline for women and a 10 percent increase for men.[12] Still other studies used a longer-range lens, measuring women's economic position *five years after divorce*, and finding a much smaller decline in living standard in general and an improved living standard for women who remarried.[13] In the end, Weitzman's figures proved to be exaggerated,[14] but few doubted that divorce disparately impacted women and men at least in the short term, and the reform momentum appeared unstoppable. The term "displaced homemaker" was popularized to signal the refugee-like status of caregivers who were exiled from their homes to face a sea change in income and status. The Displaced Homemakers Network (DHN), a grassroots organization formed in 1979, sought to provide financial support, counseling, and retraining opportunities for displaced homemakers, though its efforts were largely frustrated by inadequate funding. In its 1989 survey, the Census Bureau counted 15.6 million displaced homemakers, an increase of 12 percent over 1980 figures.[15] In 1990, the DHN reported that approximately 57 percent of former homemakers earned poverty or near-poverty incomes, a figure even higher for women of color.[16]

By 1991, at least twenty-six states had enacted legislation authorizing special programs for displaced homemakers, though minimal funding hampered the effectiveness of these programs.[17] In 1990, Congress responded to the plight of displaced homemakers by enacting the Displaced Homemakers Self-Sufficiency Assistance Act (DHSSAA).[18] The DHSSAA allocated funding for state programs that provided career counseling, training, and placement for displaced homemakers. In 1991, the DHSSAA authorized $35 million to "expand the employment and self-sufficiency options of displaced homemakers."[19] The DHN hailed the DHSSAA as "landmark legislation," but its reach was actually quite limited. The $35 million authorized in 1991, for example, would have provided less than three dollars for each of the 15.6 million displaced homemakers counted in 1989, most of whom lived in poverty. Even in 1991, three dollars couldn't buy much self-sufficiency.

Divorce thus left many displaced homemakers alone, with limited employment options, and without meaningful assistance. How could the compelling no-fault philosophy produce such horrendous consequences? The answer begins with a closer look at early no-fault statutes governing the economic consequences of divorce.

C. No-Fault Mistakes: Discretionary Justice and the Rehabilitation Illusion

No-fault reformers devoted much effort to selling the concept of no-fault, but gave little consideration to its economic consequences. Rather incidentally, the no-fault campaign inspired two visions of the economics of divorce. First, the parties' economic ties should be severed at divorce by a onetime division of marital property. Second, alimony (renamed "maintenance") should be avoided; if awarded at all, it should be temporary and for the purpose of rehabilitating a needy spouse. Each of these visions was underscored by the clean-break, fresh-start philosophy of no-fault and, as applied, each made divorce a financial catastrophe for long-term caregivers.

1. Property Distribution

No-fault reforms presumed that a onetime division of traditional property at divorce would equitably settle the parties' mutual rights and responsibilities. As an official comment to the UMDA explains, the intention is "to encourage the court to provide for the financial needs of the spouses by property disposition rather than by an award of maintenance."[20] The presumption that equity could be achieved through a property distribution alone soon proved to be wishful thinking.

A. MINIMAL ASSETS

While a substantial property award could ease the financial straits of a caregiver with low income potential, most marital estates were too small to make this option feasible. Lenore Weitzman's research, for example, found that half of the divorcing couples in Los Angeles County in 1978 had less than $20,000 in assets. In the worst-case scenario in which a couple's debts exceeded their assets, even the caregiver who received all of the marital property (a highly unlikely event) would still receive little or nothing. Prior to the 2008 economic downturn, a couple's only important asset was likely to be the equity in their home. Dividing the marital property thus required sale of the home, which would allow the equity to be split, but which also meant that a displaced homemaker would lose her home. Weitzman found that no-fault divorce eroded the long California tradition of awarding the family home to a wife with custody of children: in 1968, courts ordered sale of the family home in one case in ten; by 1977 this figure had risen to one in three.[21] By 1988, concern for the welfare of children had led California to enact legislation authorizing courts to defer sale of a home in which minor children were living.[22]

Over time, states increased the size of the marital pot by including nontraditional assets such as pensions and business goodwill. Most interesting were the efforts of a few courts to increase the size of the marital pot by expanding the definition of property to include a spouse's professional degree or license. Although courts in over half the states addressed this issue, only New York's highest court went so far as to classify a professional license as property, value the license, and distribute it between the spouses. The seminal New York case is *O'Brien v. O'Brien*, a 1985 case with hard facts.[23] Eighteen months after their wedding, the O'Briens moved to Mexico so the husband could attend medical school. During most of their nine-year marriage, the wife worked as a teacher to finance the husband's medical education. When the husband received his medical degree, he decided to divorce his wife instead of sharing his doctor's income with her. This left the wife in a hell of a spot. Since she appeared ineligible for alimony under New York law, given her ability to support herself (a disqualification we will take up later in this chapter), and the couple had not yet acquired significant traditional property, the wife's financial recovery depended on her ability to convince the court to reach beyond traditional definitions of property and award her a share of the husband's professional license. In an extraordinary departure from tradition, the court did just that, classifying the husband's medical license as marital property and awarding the wife 40 percent of its present value—the hefty sum of $188,800.

Outside New York, *O'Brien* remains an extraordinary case, and probably for good reason. As a practical matter, contorting degrees and licenses into traditional definitions of property raises significant concerns. High on this list is the rule that property distributions are ordinarily not modifiable. A sizable property order might thus effectively enslave a payor, limiting later career options and ensuring, for example, that the surgeon does not join the Peace Corps. In any event, since the typical divorcing caregiver has not supported a spouse through professional school, the *O'Brien* approach, even if it were more widely adopted, would provide an answer to the problem of the primary caregiver only in extraordinary cases.

Whatever the extent of marital property at the time of divorce, there was no guarantee that a caregiver would receive even half of it.

B. DISCRETIONARY DISTRIBUTION

The property distribution scheme in most states followed the UMDA lead in granting the divorce court broad discretion to divide property in a just, reasonable, or equitable manner. Most "equitable distribution" statutes identified relevant, nonexclusive factors, but left the ultimate decision of what is fair to a trial court's virtually unfettered discretion. Some states, like the UMDA, instructed a court not to consider marital fault, but other states declined to identify any inappropriate factors at all. Moreover, these statutes failed to specify the weight to be given any individual factor or to define a range of judicial choice. Equitable distribution statutes thus allowed courts to base the property division on nonstatutory factors consistent with a judge's internal code of fairness, or to give one listed factor, such as a spouse's greater financial contribution to the marriage, disproportionate or dispositive weight.

Weitzman's study suggests that judges vested with broad discretion were sometimes guided by curious assumptions. Some courts assumed that "it is fair to divide family income so that the wife and children share

one-third, while the husband keeps the other two-thirds for himself";
others frankly acknowledged a reluctance "to recognize the goodwill in
a profession because it would be too difficult for the husband to raise the
capital to 'buy back his wife's share'"; while many courts minimized the
difficulties faced by a long-term caregiver who had to raise capital to buy
out her husband's share of the home in order to keep it from being sold.[24]

The attitudes Weitzman observed were more widely documented in
studies reporting gender bias in the courts.[25] At least thirty states established task forces to investigate the possibility of such bias, and every study
that published its findings reported that gender bias detrimental to women
was rampant in divorce cases. A New Jersey task force, for example, concluded that despite efforts to achieve gender equity, "New Jersey women of
all ages may be the victims of a gender-based maldistribution of earnings
and resources at or after divorce."[26] A Michigan task force found that the
"resolution of economic issues is often premised on misconceptions about
the economic consequences of divorce for women" and that "[s]ome judges
and attorneys fail to recognize a spouse's loss of career or career potential as
a meaningful contribution to the economic partnership of the marriage."[27]
A New York task force reported a tendency among trial judges to under-
value caregiver contributions and to ignore the permanent economic loss
of women who forgo their own careers. As one legislator poignantly stated,

> [Male] perspective on family life has skewed decisions in equitable dis-
> tribution cases. The perception of most men—and the judiciary is mostly
> male—is that care of the house and children can be done with one hand
> tied behind the back. Send the kids out to school, put them to bed, and
> the rest of the time free to play tennis and bridge.[28]

To be sure, not all judges entertained such attitudes; sometimes a caregiver received fair treatment at the hands of a trial court. The financial
fate of a caregiver, however, should never depend on the goodwill or
prejudice of a particular trial judge. Because the stakes for caregivers
are so high, the frequency with which early no-fault judges dispensed
unfair treatment is deeply troubling.

To make matters worse, a caregiver could not expect critical appellate review of an unfair trial court decision. Broad judicial discretion
tends to frustrate appellate review; to prevail on appeal, a spouse must

establish that a trial court abused its discretion—a difficult task indeed when a statute vests a court with virtually unbridled discretion, and thus implicitly authorizes the court to rely on personal notions of fairness.

The minimal assets in many marriages, together with the broad discretion afforded trial courts under equitable distribution statutes and the widespread bias against homemaking women, made it unlikely that a onetime division of traditional property would alone fairly settle the rights of the parties. The Indiana judiciary's early application of its equitable distribution statute strikingly demonstrates this reality.

C. AN INDIANA STORY

Much like the UMDA, the Indiana equitable distribution statute as originally drafted simply directed a trial court to divide marital property in a just and reasonable manner.[29] A court was required to "consider" several UMDA-style factors, including the contribution of a spouse as caregiver. Applying this language in *Luedke v. Luedke*, the Indiana Supreme Court adopted a posture decidedly unfavorable to caregivers.[30] The trial court had awarded less than half the marital property to a stay-at-home mom of three children who had not been employed outside the home for nineteen years.[31] The disparity in the parties' earning abilities was extreme; the husband held a secure, high-paying executive position earning approximately $95,000 per year, while the wife had no income but hoped to earn $12,000 per year after training in respiratory therapy. Dissatisfied with the trial court's distribution of marital property, Shari Luedke appealed.

In an ill-fated attempt at critical review, the Indiana Court of Appeals held that the trial court abused its discretion in awarding the wife less than half the marital assets. The court reasoned that the equitable distribution statute required a "50–50 division of the property between the breadwinner and the caregiver, absent a determination by the court that one spouse has seriously neglected his or her role."[32] "This is perhaps a change in the law of this state," explained the court, "because in the past, on identical facts, one court might have divided marital property 60–40 and another court 40–60, and our standard of review would have left us little choice but to conclude that each division was within the trial court's discretion."[33] A 50–50 starting point, reasoned the court, would put bite in appellate review.

The Indiana Supreme Court, however, swiftly rejected the 50–50 starting point, observing that no language in the statute authorized it. The court added that although a judge perhaps ought initially to lean toward a 50–50 split, a judge could not be required to do so. Even before *Luedke*, Indiana appellate judges had complained that a divorce court's broad discretion frustrated meaningful appellate review of property divisions. After *Luedke*, one appellate judge charged that appellate review had become "little more than pretense."[34] In 1987, two years after the Supreme Court decision, the Indiana legislature amended its property distribution statute to require a trial court to "presume that an equal division of the marital property between the parties is just and reasonable."[35]

The Indiana story was encouraging in its demonstration that legislation could limit judicial discretion to award a caregiver less than half of marital assets, but disturbing in its implicit suggestion that in states without such legislation courts might continue to do so. Even when legislation deterred the worst abuses of judicial discretion, however, the no-fault assumption that a onetime division of property would afford equity between spouses was a mistake. The minimal assets in most marriages, together with the disparate earning abilities of a caregiver and a breadwinner, suggest that a caregiver should receive something in addition to a share of marital assets. No-fault compounded its first mistake, however, by discouraging a court from awarding alimony.

2. Alimony

Alimony was never intended to assure a perpetual state of secured indolence. It should not be suffered to convert a host of physically and mentally competent young women into an army of alimony drones, who neither toil nor spin, and become a drain on society and a menace to themselves.
—Samuel H. Hofstadter and Shirley R. Levittan, "Alimony—A Reformulation," *Journal of Family Law* 7 (1967): 55

Alimony has a terrible reputation. For many, the word triggers nasty visions of the abused male, as indolent young women enjoy a country-club lifestyle at the expense of their hardworking yet impoverished ex-husbands. Such visions, though largely mythical, seem close to the core of no-fault statutes that discouraged indefinite-term alimony.

A. DISCOURAGING ALIMONY

As the no-fault movement gained momentum, disdain for alimony was widespread, and not just among potential and current alimony payors. Some feminists of the day shunned alimony as a threat to female independence. As the no-fault reformer Herma Hill Kay argued, the law should not encourage women to make "economically disabling" choices that perpetuate "their traditional financial dependence upon men and contribut[e] to their inequality with men at divorce."[36] "Female dependency," said Kay, "should no longer be the necessary result of motherhood."[37] Kay explained that she would not go so far as to propose mandatory state laws requiring mothers to work or fathers to spend time with children, but insisted that the law must withdraw legal supports for gender-based family roles.

Not surprisingly, the no-fault scheme, as the UMDA explained it, was "to provide for the financial needs of the spouses by property distribution rather than by an award of maintenance."[38] At least in principle, alimony was out; property was in. No-fault laws thus did not eliminate alimony, but they gave it second-class status. Without much explanation, early no-fault alimony laws typically authorized trial courts to award alimony upon a finding that a spouse was *needy*—that is, without sufficient property and unable to support herself. The UMDA, for example, provides that a court may award alimony if it finds that the claimant "(1) lacks sufficient property to provide for his reasonable needs; and (2) is unable to support himself through appropriate employment or is the custodian of a child whose condition or circumstances make it appropriate that the custodian not be required to seek employment outside the home."[39]

Given no-fault's clean-break philosophy and the general disdain for alimony, one might have predicted that courts would limit alimony eligibility by magnifying the level of "need" necessary to qualify for an award. "Need," for example, might be defined to include only those alimony claimants on the brink of poverty or destitution, a definition that would shrink the pool of eligible claimants. It is not clear, however, that no-fault had this effect. Alimony has always been rare, and the number of awards seems not to have fallen dramatically under no-fault. From 1887 to 1922, less than 16 percent of divorcing wives received alimony.[40] At the turn of the century, alimony was awarded in only 9.3 percent of divorces.[41] In the 1970s and early 1980s, approximately 15 percent of the divorced women surveyed reported that they had been awarded alimony, as compared with 17 percent in 1989.[42] In her survey of state reports, Marsha Garrison found that in the 1980s, from 7 percent to 30 percent of divorced women received alimony.[43] In her study of the effects of no-fault divorce in California, Lenore Weitzman found that in 1968, 18.8 percent of divorced women were receiving alimony under California's fault-based divorce regime. After California's 1969 enactment of a no-fault divorce law, the figure dropped to 12.9 percent in 1972 and 16.5 percent in 1977.[44] Moreover, when alimony was awarded, it was not likely to be a sizable amount. While data on the size of alimony awards are hard to come by, the Census Bureau reported that the average annual alimony award in 1985 was $3,730.[45]

If no-fault's clean-break, fresh-start philosophy did not decrease the incidence of alimony, it probably shortened the duration of many alimony awards. In her study of the impact of no-fault in New York divorces, Marsha Garrison found a substantial decrease in the proportion of "permanent" alimony awards. Garrison reported that in the 1970s, approximately 80 percent of alimony awards in New York were permanent, but ten years later, only about 40 percent were permanent.[46] As we will see in chapter 4, the term "permanent alimony" is misleading, since it suggests an inflexible, lifetime award, when in reality alimony is freely modifiable and typically terminates upon the occurrence of certain events, such as a recipient's remarriage. For this reason, "indefinite-term" is used here to distinguish open-ended awards from "fixed-term" awards. For now, the point is that no-fault's clean-break philosophy invited courts to cast a claimant's "need" as a temporary rather than a permanent phenomenon, and so to limit alimony to a short, fixed period necessary for rehabilitation. Unlike longer-term alimony, rehabilitative alimony would thus delay, but not defeat, clean-break aspirations.

(1) The Rehabilitation Rainbow

Early no-fault courts were powerfully seduced by visions of spousal rehabilitation. Rehabilitative alimony seemed to offer a solution for everyone. If divorcing caregivers could be swiftly retrained, both spouses would soon be freed to begin new lives. Everyone would be happy—financially autonomous caregivers and their alimony-free ex-spouses, no-fault theorists advocating a clean break at divorce, and feminists shunning the need for male support. Inspired by such visions, many state legislatures added a provision for rehabilitative alimony to their no-fault statutes. By 1987, at least twenty-nine states had adopted legislation that either authorized rehabilitative alimony or authorized consideration of the length of time needed for education or training.[47]

Unfortunately, the infatuation with rehabilitative alimony ultimately proved to be wishful thinking. Those who worked with divorced caregivers began painting a bleak picture. "The saddest sight," lamented the DHN, "is the middle-aged woman who has been convinced she should go back to school and emerges two or four years older, a well-educated unemployable."[48] Indeed, some DHN programs declined to refer caregivers for federally subsidized retraining, since "even with the training they could earn little more than on welfare."[49] In a worst-case scenario, rehabilitative alimony merely delayed a caregiver's descent into poverty.

Even when retraining enabled a caregiver to become self-supporting, she had little hope of recapturing the lost earning capacity resulting from time spent in family labor. As we saw in chapter 1, primary caregiving has long been associated with market disinvestment and long-term losses in earning capacity. Curiously, evidence of the costs of caregiving was available for reformers, courts, and legislatures even in the early years of no-fault. In 1974, for example, Mincer and Polacheck reported that women who remained out of the labor market after the birth of their first child suffered a decline in earning capacity of about 1.5 percent per year and that women with advanced degrees suffered an even higher rate of depreciation.[50] Yet early no-fault courts seemed strangely unaware of the reality that a long-term caregiver's earning capacity would likely never match that of her spouse who participated in the job market without interruption. As the chimerical quality of the rehabilitation rainbow began to be understood, some feminists expressed regret for their earlier rejection of alimony. As Betty Friedan reminisced,

> The women's movement had just begun when the so-called divorce reform law was passed. At that time, we were so concerned with principle—that equality of right and opportunity had to mean equality of responsibility, and therefore alimony was out—that we did not realize the trap we were falling into.[51]

Even if rehabilitative alimony were a more realistic response to the costs of primary caregiving, it would raise troublesome conceptual concerns. The notion that a spouse who has labored in the home must be repaired so that she can begin a productive life unacceptably promotes a "blame-the-victim" perspective that devalues the caregiving role. Indeed, "rehabilitation" is an odd word choice, as if a woman were to be classed along with a criminal who, through rehabilitation, might be able to rise from vice to become a sound, productive citizen. Pretending that rehabilitative alimony could "repair" a "damaged" woman by turning back the clock and giving her the career opportunities she had before her marriage was a cruel, if convenient, illusion. Disdain for alimony and the attraction of the rehabilitation illusion had a powerful effect on some state legislatures, as the following story demonstrates.

(2) Another Indiana Story

The early Indiana no-fault statute authorized indefinite alimony only where a spouse either (1) was "physically or mentally incapacitated," or (2) lacked "sufficient" property and was the custodian of a child who was physically or mentally incapacitated.[52] The ordinary caregiver was ineligible for indefinite alimony under this statute, no matter how bleak her prospects for economic self-sufficiency or how great her spouse's income. Even in the extraordinary case of physical or mental incapacity of a spouse or child, alimony was not mandatory but depended on the discretion of a trial court.

Shortly after the Indiana statute was enacted, one concerned appellate judge suggested that a long-term caregiver is incapacitated by definition. "A spouse whose age, lack of education, inexperience and want of vocational skill or training renders him or her only marginally able to support himself or herself might appropriately be held to be 'incapacitated to the extent that the ability . . . to support himself or herself is materially affected.'"[53] This view, however, gained no momentum.

As originally enacted, the Indiana statute contained no other provision for alimony. In 1984, eleven years after implementing no-fault, Indiana amended its statute to authorize a discretionary award of rehabilitative alimony.[54] This amendment, however, limited rehabilitative alimony to a two-year period, which was extended to three years in 1987.[55] Because rehabilitative alimony was discretionary, not all Indiana caregivers received even this minimal support. Indeed, some Indiana trial courts denied rehabilitative alimony to long-term caregivers who could not demonstrate that their education was interrupted because of homemaking or child care responsibilities.[56]

Indiana offers a disturbing example of a no-fault alimony statute that carries the preference for short-term alimony to an extreme. Equally disturbing is the more typical early no-fault statute that authorized alimony for longer periods, but ultimately left the alimony decision to the broad discretion of a trial court.

B. DEFERRING TO DISCRETION

Unlike Indiana, most states' early no-fault statutes gave a trial court discretion to award indefinite alimony to a spouse in need. Most of these statutes were patterned after the UMDA, which as we have seen authorized (but did not require) courts to grant alimony upon a finding that a spouse was needy. The UMDA also left the amount of any alimony award to the discretion of a judge, who was to "consider" certain listed factors. Section 308(b) of the UMDA, for example, authorizes a court to order alimony "in amounts and for periods of time the court deems just, without regard to marital misconduct," after considering the following factors:

a. the financial resources of the party seeking maintenance . . . ;

b. the time necessary to acquire sufficient education or training to enable the party seeking maintenance to find appropriate employment;

c. the standard of living established during the marriage;

d. the duration of the marriage;

e. the age and the physical and emotional condition of the spouse seeking maintenance; and

f. the ability of the [paying] spouse . . . to meet his needs while meeting those of the spouse seeking maintenance.[57]

Many states patterned their no-fault alimony statutes after the UMDA model. The broad judicial discretion conferred by these statutes was sometimes exercised in ways surprisingly hostile to caregivers. Consider, for example, the following story.

(1) Judicial Hostility: A Minnesota Story

In 1969, Minnesota enacted a no-fault statute with property and alimony provisions similar to those of the UMDA.[58] Not surprisingly, the

Minnesota Supreme Court soon found within the new law a preference for short-term rather than indefinite alimony. In the 1980 case of *Otis v. Otis*, the court explained this preference in colorful equality rhetoric:

> In recent years, courts have retreated from traditional attitudes toward spousal support because society no longer perceives the married woman as an economically unproductive creature who is "something better than her husband's dog, a little dearer than his horse." Traditionally, spousal support was a permanent award because it was assumed that a wife had neither the ability nor the resources to become self-sustaining. However, with the mounting dissolution rate, the advent of no-fault dissolution, and the growth of the women's movement, the focal point of spousal support determinations has shifted from the sex of the recipient to the individual's ability to become financially independent. This change in focus has given rise to the concept of rehabilitative alimony.[59]

Applying this reasoning, the court in *Otis* affirmed an award of only four years of alimony to a forty-five-year-old caregiver who had not worked since the birth of the parties' child twenty-three years earlier. Although the parties had substantial assets, which were essentially split in half, they left the marriage on a decidedly disparate footing. The husband, a vice president of a major corporation, earned over $120,000 per year plus bonuses; with training, the wife could earn between $12,000 and $18,000 per year. A dissenting judge argued that the wife should receive indefinite alimony in view of her role in fostering her husband's career and the husband's insistence that she not work while raising a family.[60] The husband, it seems, had made clear that he was "not going to have any wife of mine pound a typewriter."[61]

Similar applications of the Minnesota alimony statute followed *Otis*. In *Napier v. Napier*, the Minnesota Court of Appeals affirmed a temporary alimony award to a forty-one-year-old caregiver who had only sporadic part-time employment during her nineteen-year marriage.[62] The husband earned $53,000 per year; the wife's most recent job paid six dollars an hour. The court declined to extend the alimony award, notwithstanding the fact that the wife had only an "outmoded undergraduate degree to present to potential employers" and would "probably never achieve the salary level that she might have had if she had been working full-time during the nineteen years she was married."[63]

Again in *Rohling v. Rohling*, the Minnesota Supreme Court affirmed a trial court's refusal to award indefinite alimony to a sixty-year-old caregiver of twenty-eight years with an eighth-grade education.[64] The Court noted that although it might have reached a different conclusion *de novo*, it was bound to affirm a decision with an "acceptable basis in fact and principle."[65]

Apparently in response to such egregious cases, the Minnesota legislature intervened, amending its alimony statute in 1985 to direct that "[n]othing in this section shall be construed to favor a temporary award of alimony over a permanent award, where the factors [listed] justify a permanent award."[66] As an added precaution, the legislature stated, "When there is some uncertainty as to the necessity of a permanent award, the court shall order a permanent award leaving its order open for later modification." This amendment had an immediate impact. Soon after its enactment, the Minnesota Supreme Court reversed a trial court's refusal to award indefinite alimony to a fifty-six-year-old caregiver of thirty-one years.[67]

The Minnesota experience with UMDA-style alimony provisions was unusual, not because of the hostile interpretation of its judiciary, but because of the intervention of its legislature. Unfortunately, in many other states, courts continued to apply similar alimony provisions in ways hostile to caregivers.[68] In some states, however, appellate courts acted without the aid of legislation to reverse hostile trial court application of alimony statutes. The following story from Wisconsin provides one such bright light in an otherwise bleak scene.

(2) Judicial Sympathy: A Wisconsin Story

Wisconsin's early no-fault statute, much like the UMDA, gave a trial court broad discretion to order alimony after considering a list of nonexclusive statutory factors.[69] In the 1982 landmark case of *Bahr v. Bahr*, the Wisconsin Supreme Court interpreted this statute to require a trial court to begin the alimony evaluation "with the proposition that the dependent partner may be entitled to fifty percent of the total earnings of both parties."[70] This 50–50 starting point enabled the court to reverse an award of only $1,500 per month indefinite alimony, where the husband's annual income was $313,000 and the wife's annual income was $5,000 or less. In another invocation of the 50–50 starting point, a Wisconsin appellate court reversed an order requiring a cardiovascular surgeon to pay only 4.6 percent of his income as alimony to his home-making wife.[71] While the Wisconsin Supreme Court's intervention to curtail trial courts' harsh treatment of caregivers was encouraging, trial courts in many other states continued to exercise their broad discretion to deny or severely limit alimony to displaced caregivers.

The history of alimony and property division under early no-fault statutes is a sad and troubling story of the well-intentioned clean-break philosophy gone awry, of displaced caregivers set free to bear most of the economic costs of their family role while primary breadwinners were set free to enjoy most of the benefits of their family role. The result was an economic disaster for many caregivers. How could courts have done such a thing? Judges are ordinarily not evil misogynists intent on the economic destruction of unwary caregivers. The explanation lies elsewhere, beginning with those gender bias studies of the 1980s that exposed judicial misconceptions about the contributions of caregivers and the economic consequences of divorce for women. Judges' broad discretion over the economics of divorce empowered these misconceptions, transforming them into life-altering sentences for caregivers. To understand this process, and to guard against a repeat performance, we take a closer look at the myths about caregivers, and about mothers in particular, that have seduced many a well-intentioned judge.

3

Alimony and Mother Myths

What was once thought can never be unthought.
—Friedrich Durrenmatt, *The Physicists*, trans. James
Kirkrup (New York: Grove, 1964), 92

When I was a child I didn't appreciate my mother. Actually, I don't recall much noticing her or the many things she did for me—at least not until I became a big girl and wished she would let me take care of myself. Now that I am a mother myself, I regret and am a little embarrassed by my childhood attitudes. I doubt however that they are unique and that is scary because if Durrenmatt is right, childhood thoughts about mothers are not easily shed; they are still with us and perhaps still capable of subtly shaping our views of mothers even when we should know better. Indeed, childhood perspectives seem to lie at the core of a curious set of myths about mothers—myths that are at once silly and dangerous. These myths are simple enough: *Mothering just happens. Mothering is free. Mothering is for babies.*

Taken together, mother myths ensure that the daily realities of mothers' work, the economic consequences of that work, and its value to the family do not receive serious attention. For real women who have lost

An earlier version of this chapter was published as "Mothers, Myths and the Law of Divorce: One More Feminist Case for Partnership," *William and Mary Journal of Women and the Law* 13 (2006): 203.

earning capacity because of family responsibilities, mother myths pose great danger, threatening to seduce even fair-minded divorce courts into peculiar notions of equity.

A. Mothering Just Happens: The Law of the Invisible Mother

The coolest mom I know who's not mine is Connor's. She plays soccer with him all the time. I don't think she has a job. She cooks.
—Amy Finnerty, "Status Is . . . for Middle-Class 8-Year-Olds: A Stay-at-Home Mom," *New York Times*, November 15, 1998 (quoting a six-year-old interviewee)

When I was a child, I was surrounded by evidence of my mother's labor. Underwear in drawers. Milk in the refrigerator. Dinner on the table. And sometimes, when I came home from school, oatmeal cookies— crispy ones made with real butter. Yet it never occurred to me that any of these things required much time or effort. In my world, these things were givens, dependably appearing, of mysterious and unimportant origin. Underwear in drawers just happened.

In the ordinary course of family life, mothers are invisible. The daily details of caregiving go largely unnoticed, drawing attention (and alarm) only when their absence becomes neglect. In a strange irony, it is thus the neglectful mother rather than the conscientious one who is seen. As Ann Crittenden observes, the "more skillful the caregiver, the more invisible her efforts become. Ideally, the recipients themselves don't even notice that they are being cared for."[1]

If mothers were paid for their work, their efforts would be more visible. Babysitters, nurses, housekeepers, launderers, cooks, tailors, and painters all earn paychecks in the marketplace; yet when they perform similar labors in their homes, they are considered unemployed. The invisibility of mothering thus stems not from the nature of the work, but rather from the fact that mothers are performing it in their own homes and for their own families. That gender plays a critical role in mothers' invisibility is suggested by the disproportionate attention paid to fathers who perform caregiving tasks. As Justice Bird noted long ago, a decision maker may glorify a father because he "often prepared the child's breakfast and dinner and picked her up from the day care center himself [though it] is difficult to imagine a mother's performance of these chores even attracting notice, much less commendable comment."[2]

Curiously, the myth that mothering just happens is sometimes shared by mothers themselves. Consider the case of Harriet Beecher Stowe, who confessed to being "constantly pursued and haunted by the idea that I do anything." And yet in the previous year (1849), Stowe "made two sofas, a chair, diverse bedspreads, pillowcases, pillows, bolsters, and mattresses; painted rooms; rearranged furniture; [gave] birth to her eighth child; [and ran] a huge household."[3]

At its most extreme, the myth that mothering just happens accounts for the popular if peculiar myth that full-time mothers are extinct, or almost extinct—swiftly disappearing relics of the 1950s Betty Crocker era. In its popularized form, the myth appears in the contemporary rhetoric of egalitarianism, the illusion that ours is a gender-neutral culture in which mothers and fathers co-parent, work full-time in the paid economy, and share equally, in their leisure time, the few family tasks that are really necessary. Accordingly, museum commentary references the "disappearance of full-time caregivers";[4] the popular press trumpets the demise of the traditional family;[5] and the American Law Institute explains that "universal adult labor force participation is both the empirical norm and the norm generally assumed" in the late twentieth century.[6]

Wait a minute. What about the 43.1 percent of married mothers with a child *under age one* who were not working for pay (or looking for paid work) in 2011; the 40.9 percent with a child *under age six* who were not working for pay (or looking for paid work); and the 29.5 percent with a child *age six to seventeen* who were not working for pay (or looking for paid work)?[7] As we saw in chapter 1, these stay-at-home moms are real and would no doubt be surprised to learn of their demise. The point is not that full-time caregiving is good or bad, wise or unwise, but only that it is really happening.

As we also saw in chapter 1, even when a married mother works outside her home, she is very likely to serve as the primary family caregiver, undertaking a disproportionately large share of household chores. In

2012, the Bureau of Labor Statistics reported that on an average day in 2011, 18.9 percent of men did housework—such as cleaning or doing laundry—compared with 47.8 percent of women.[8] That same year, 40.1 percent of men engaged in food preparation or cleanup on an average day, compared with 66 percent of women. In another study of married mothers and fathers, Bianchi, Robinson, and Milkie found that married mothers spent 19.4 hours weekly in primary housework activities in 2000, compared with 9.7 hours in primary housework for married fathers.[9]

Yet, despite overwhelming evidence to the contrary, the myth is that Betty Crocker[10] and soccer mom[11] have disappeared, and that family tasks are negligible, largely optional, and shared. If "[c]are of the house and children can be done with one hand tied behind the back,"[12] then stay-at-home moms (if they are real) must be lazy creatures. And so a divorce court charged with ensuring equity might, rather innocently, ask a stay-at-home mom,

"What have you been doing with all your time?"

The question, of course, is rhetorical, the mom's answer inescapable:

"I've been doing *nothing*, really—sitting on the sofa eating bonbons . . . (while the cooking, the cleaning, the shopping, the laundering, the tutoring, the grooming, the chauffeuring, the counseling, the disciplining and the stocking of underwear drawers just happened)."

The judicial response is predictable and unequivocal:

"Then shame on you. You need a kick in the butt to get you into a productive life."

And so a Wisconsin court explained a short-term alimony award to a full-time mother of three minor children:

I don't think she would want to sit around the rest of her life. My God, she will turn into a vegetable if she did that anyhow.[13]

Full-time caregiving turns mothers into vegetables? Mothering, it seems, requires little time or effort—surely not enough to interfere with a mother's responsibility to pursue a *real* job. So myth has it. The implication of such reasoning is clear enough: a divorcing mother, especially a stay-at-home mom, is probably a lazy, inferior creature who may generate pity, but who deserves no respect and no economic entitlements at divorce. Such a woman contributes no real value to the marriage and thus has earned no right to share in any economic fruits of the marriage. What she needs is a little rehabilitative alimony to return her to productive citizenship. The myth that mothering just happens further penalizes divorcing caregivers by contributing to the complementary myth that mothering is free.

B. Mothering Is Free: The Law of the Cost-Free Mother

[A]ny woman—no matter her age or lack of training—can
find a nice little job and a nice little apartment and conduct
her later years as she might have done at age 25.
—Lynn Hecht Schafran, "Documenting Gender Bias in the
Courts: The Task Force Approach," *Judicature* 70 (1987): 280,
285 (quoting a New York legislator's description of judicial
perspectives)

If mothering just happens, it must also be free. When I was a child it didn't occur to me that mothering imposed costs, that by doing the laundry, the shopping, the cooking, the cleaning, my mother invested time and energy that limited her opportunity to do other things. I am sure I never once considered the possibility that in the time my mother spent monitoring, stocking, and laundering my underwear she could have been reading a book or investing creative energy at the office. If mothering was costly, if it reduced my mother's earning capacity, she never told me. I thought mothering was free. So, evidently, do many judges. Consider, for example, the divorce judge who thought that after forty years as a stay-at-home mom Terry Hekker deserved only four years of alimony and a nudge to undertake job retraining at age sixty-seven.

The truth is that lost opportunities to invest in paid labor are pretty much unrecoverable at age sixty-seven. As we saw in chapter 1, primary caregiving exacts a significant price from mothers in the form of lost market opportunities and ultimately decreased earning capacity. Simply put, time spent laboring in the home is not spent laboring in the market, and as mothers limit their investment in a job or career, their ability to generate income decreases. Ultimately, opportunities are lost altogether. The realities of declining human capital impact many types of caregivers: stay-at-home moms, who forgo market employment altogether; gappers, who periodically drop out of the job market; and the many primary caregivers who daily compromise their market engagement in order to assume the majority of family responsibilities.

Notwithstanding massive evidence of the human capital costs of primary caregiving, no-fault divorce law invites judges to entertain the myth that mothering is free. This invitation is fundamentally grounded in the clean-break philosophy of no-fault divorce. As we saw in the last chapter, no-fault rejects old notions of divorce as a remedy for a wronged spouse, taking the more pragmatic, less moralistic position that divorce is merely legal recognition that a marriage has died, if not of its own accord, at least without any identified fault by either party. Free of blame, each spouse is thus entitled to begin life anew, free of the shackles of a dead marriage. To the extent these shackles include economic entanglements, these too must be severed. So the no-fault script reads.

In practical terms, this clean-break principle encourages judges to settle all equities between the spouses through a onetime division of property and to deny or severely limit alimony. If alimony is unavoidable, it should be limited to the smallest amount necessary for a spouse's retraining—that is, for rehabilitation to enable the damaged spouse to become a productive citizen this time around. More extensive alimony would inappropriately and unnecessarily prolong the agony of a dead marriage. The critical alimony question is thus "How much time will it take to repair an economically dependent caregiver?" Myth supplies an easy answer: "Very little time, since mothering is free." Alimony is thus rare and, when it is ordered, likely to be short-term.

The clean-break principle and its supporting mother myth pose significant danger for caregivers. Most obviously, judges are tempted to overlook disparate economic positioning resulting from marital roles, to ignore the reality that a mother who has been working exclusively or primarily in her home is not likely to be the market equal of her spouse who has more fully invested in paid employment. For if disparate positioning really exists, it spoils everything. If there is not enough property to equitably address disparate earning capacities, which usually there is not, then a court is hard-pressed to achieve equity through a onetime order that terminates economic ties. Much easier to pretend caregiving has not imposed market costs than to reconcile caregiving-induced income disparities with clean-break principles. Easier to insist that if income disparity exists, it is the product of a mother's poor work ethic or intellect, or of society's bias. A mother's predicament is thus her fault or society's fault and therefore appropriately ignored by a divorce judge charged with ensuring interspousal equity. In the end, it has been easier for a court to pretend that a sixty-seven-year-old caregiver can be "retrained" than to violate the wildly popular clean-break principle. Not surprising, then, are those gender bias studies that, as we saw in chapter 2, disclosed widespread misconceptions about the economic consequences of divorce for women.

Indeed, as we have seen, the history of no-fault divorce law is a sad tale of denial of the costs of mothering, of judges freeing even long-term caregivers to begin new lives—with limited property and limited earning capacity, as if they were twenty-five and could actually start over again. Some commentators claim that the law is moving toward more realistic and more humane treatment of displaced homemakers, and hopefully they are right. But the continuing vitality of the clean-break philosophy suggests that no-fault divorce laws have not altogether escaped their history. Indeed, even as the law may be moving toward more realistic views of the cost of long-term caregiving, it appears stubbornly resistant to evidence that primary caregivers who combine market and family work also experience lost earning capacity. A primary caregiver's market participation may be exaggerated and her home efforts minimized in order to create the illusion of a fully egalitarian marriage that facilitates conscience-free application of the clean-break principle. Even after divorce, however, this younger mother's market losses will continue to accrue as she undertakes primary caregiving responsibilities,[14] often with less help from the children's father than before the divorce. While such a mother may benefit incidentally from child support, such support will not compensate her for the diminished earning capacity caused by market disinvestment. Child support, by definition, aims to provide for children, not for the mother who cares for them.

The temptation to ignore the costs of mothering, especially in the case of younger mothers, is made more compelling by the law's traditional reluctance to recognize lost opportunities as compensable losses. Contract law generally does not award damages for the lost opportunity to have contracted with a more reliable partner, or to have entered a more lucrative contract. Though contracting parties understand the reality of lost opportunities, the law traditionally has viewed them as too speculative to warrant recovery.[15] A mother's claim that she lost market opportunities because of mothering may trigger this traditional response, for until her child care years end, her diminished earning capacity will be partly or fully hypothetical, and therefore easy to deny. Even when a mother's diminished earning capacity is evident, determining the extent of that loss will be difficult or impossible, for rarely will there be a comparative baseline against which to measure a mother's best alternative opportunity—that is, what she would have become but for caregiving. Primary caregivers may indeed be "just a man away from poverty,"[16] but because they are not *yet* in poverty, it is easy to pretend mothering is free.

To be sure, the myth that mothering is free is not universal. To its credit, the American Law Institute, in its *Principles of the Law of Family Dissolution*, has attempted to shatter this myth, warning that the costs of primary caregiving are "both significant and common" and "cannot be ignored by the law."[17] But until the myth that mothering is free is fully slain, caregivers will continue to be vulnerable to judges seduced by egalitarian illusions of caregivers' economic opportunities and tempted by the compelling clean-break philosophy to set them free.

C. Mothering Is for Babies: The Law of the Excessive Mother

Now that I have them, . . . they shan't escape me.
—Wicked Witch, upon the approach of Hansel and Gretel,
Grimms' Fairy Tales by the Brothers Grimm, trans. Mrs. E.
V. Lucas, Lucy Crane, and Marian Edwardes (New York:
Grosset and Dunlap, 1945), 337

Fundamentally, we know that excessive mothers exist. Take, as an extreme example, the wicked witch in the fairy tale "Hansel and Gretel," who was an excessive cookie baker indeed, having constructed an entire house of gingerbread, evidently for the very bad purpose of enticing and consuming children:

> Once her gingerbread house accomplished its purpose and lured Hansel and Gretel, the wicked witch continued her mothering: "Ah, dear children, who brought you here? Come in and stay with me. You shall come to no harm." She took them by the hand and led them into the little house. A nice dinner was set before them: pancakes and sugar, milk, apples, and nuts. After this she showed them two little white beds into which they crept, and they felt as if they were in heaven.[18]

Little steps in the witch's larger plan to eat the innocent, tasty children. Such an excessive mother is terrible indeed. But wicked witches are generally easy to spot—they have red eyes and a keen sense of smell.

Too often family law, searching for the excessive mother, mistakes "unemployed" mothers of two-year-olds for wicked witches. The story begins with the normative vision of marriage as an egalitarian, companionate relationship in which both spouses make equal contributions to the market and the home. From this foundation flows the natural conclusion that all mothers either are or should be at work in the market, with perhaps a limited exception for mothers of very young children. This understanding of the-way-things-are-supposed-to-be is dramatically evident in the laws governing imputation of income in child support cases.

In all states, child support is calculated according to guidelines that generate a presumptively appropriate amount of support based on various factors. When a residential parent's income is one of the guideline factors and that parent has limited her market employment in order to care for children, the law may impute income to her for purposes of calculating child support. This income imputation effectively reduces the amount of child support and thus creates an incentive for the unemployed or underemployed residential parent to find appropriate employment. Or so the theory goes. Of course, the effect of imputing income to a residential parent who does not respond by beginning or increasing her market work is simply to reduce the amount of support available to a child, a result that is starkly inconsistent with family law's general goal of protecting the best interests of children. Such is the price for guarding against excessive mothering.

So when do a child's needs allow a residential parent's increased employment and thus justify income imputation to a mother who is inappropriately underemployed? Early on, say some states. Deference to a caregiver's employment decision is appropriate, says Idaho, only until a child is *six months old.*[19] *Two years old,* say Alaska[20] and Mary-land.[21] *Two and a half years old,* says Colorado.[22] *Three years old,* say Kentucky,[23] Maine,[24] and North Carolina.[25] *Five years old,* says Louisiana.[26] *Six years old,* says New Mexico.[27]

Once a child reaches this identified age, income may be imputed to "enable" the gainful employment of a mother who has misjudged how much mothering is appropriate. Of course, not every court will impute income to every mother of a child beyond the threshold age. Still, the law's message is disturbingly clear: after a child reaches the age of six months, six years, or some age in between, a judge should assess whether a mother's decision to limit her market investment in order to mother is warranted in view of her market opportunities. At worst, a judge begins this cost/benefit appraisal of a mother's decision with the assumption that if a mother *can* earn more, she *should* earn more, since the law has already disqualified her from the statutory deference granted mothers of younger children.

The danger to mothers posed by the myth that mothering-is-for-babies is not limited to child support. The same reasoning that leads a court to reduce child support in order to coax a mother out of the home may lead a court to deny or limit alimony toward the same end. Consider the case of the long-term, full-time caregiver who has been out of the job market for many years. If mothers should be working in the paid economy once a child reaches age six months or six years, how can this caregiver justify the time she spent in full-time caregiving beyond her children's early years? Surely, she must be an excessive mother. Lazy. Self-indulgent. Superfluous. At any rate, for some reason she has behaved inefficiently, inappropriately, and therefore, any market costs that flow from such behavior are her fault and her responsibility. No long-term alimony for such an excessive mother, who needs a kick in the pants to get her off the sofa and into real, meaningful labor.

Similar reasoning endangers the younger mother who has compromised her market investment to care for children, either by temporarily dropping out of the market or by working part-time or seasonally, perhaps in the secondary-job market in order to accommodate her caregiving. Unlike the long-term Betty Crocker, this mother has her most potentially productive career years ahead of her. Ample time for a judge to set her on the path to productive citizenship by enabling her to become gainfully employed—that is, by denying her alimony, or awarding her just enough to facilitate her education or retraining. Clearly, an alimony award sufficient to allow her to persist in excessive mothering would be very bad. The law of alimony, like the law of child support, thus invites judges to determine how much mothering is "appropriate" or "excessive"—a frightening prospect for a mother facing a judge who thinks mothering is for babies.

In its *Principles of the Law of Family Dissolution*, the ALI warns that "[d]uring a child's minority, the interests of all parties are generally best served by enabling the gainful employment of the residential parent." "When the child has grown up," warns the ALI, "it is in the residential parent's interest to have maximized the quality and quantity of past labor-force participation."[28] No doubt Terry Hekker, that stay-at-home mom of five whose husband of forty years divorced her, now wishes she had "maximized" her labor force participation while her children were growing up. But it is the law that makes Terry regret her decision to parent full-time; the law that casts her decision as the wrong choice; the law that authorizes a divorce court to throw her under the bus; the law that punishes Terry for failing to understand that mothering is for babies. Is this good policy? Should family law be coaxing mothers to spend more time in the labor market and punishing those who resist the "right choice" to maximize labor force participation?

The initial question must be whether mothering beyond infancy confers a benefit at all. Surely, as mothering becomes less necessary, it does not necessarily become valueless. As children outgrow the need for diapers, rational mothers do not persist in diapering them, but direct their efforts elsewhere—into planning and preparing family meals, helping with math and English homework, transporting children to ballet and basketball and soccer practice, raising money for football helmets, and cleaning, laundering, shopping, and stocking underwear drawers. If a mother performed these labors for an employer, no one would question whether the employer received a benefit. When she performs similar labors for her family, benefits are also conferred, whether or not they are actually necessary. The point here is certainly not that mothers *should* do these things, but only that doing them confers a benefit on the family.

Of course, not all that is beneficial is valuable in the economic sense. The real concern may not be that post-infancy mothering confers no benefit, but rather that it is inefficient. And so the question becomes, At what point on the continuum of a child's life do the costs of mothering exceed its benefits? When do the inefficiencies of work directed at an individual family (that doesn't actually *need* much mothering) warrant the conclusion that a mother should focus on the market instead (that is, get a job or a job with more hours), and that her failure to do so must be a product of excessive mothering? Difficult questions follow: What are the costs (to a mother, to her family, to the community, to society at large) of mothering? Of market engagement in lieu of mothering? What are the benefits (to a mother, to her family, to the community, to society at large) of mothering? Of market engagement in lieu of mothering? What are the costs and benefits (to a mother, to her family, to the community, to society at large) of a mother's "balancing" home and market labor in various ratios? Obviously, some costs and benefits are easier to quantify than others. Consider Jane Lazarre's account of the fictional Mr. and Ms. Weber, sojourners at a small shelter for the homeless in Gramercy Park East:

> It is a cold night in the middle of the winter of 1987. Sleet is falling in a thick film and the streets are deserted. . . .
>
> "I come here with my wife," [Mr. Weber] says, nodding in the direction of a small, dark woman still engaged in preparing her belongings for the night. She takes a blue bathrobe from her shopping bag, folds it in her lap, then pulls one out for her husband and lays it across the pillow, which she fluffs up before turning down the sheet. Carrying two white towels and a large plastic bag filled with soaps and creams, she walks out of the room as if she is alone and busy in her own home, as if there are not a dozen people seated at tables, many of them watching her intimate preparations for the night.[29]

Ms. Weber's acts are small things: fluffing a husband's pillow, turning down his sheet, laying out his bathrobe. What are the costs and benefits of such actions? Not much cost, evidently, Ms. Weber's efforts requiring only a few minutes. Unless, of course, she has arthritis or passed up work at McDonald's or Macy's to be there with her husband. As for benefits, Mr. Weber is hardly a baby; he is not even a child and he certainly doesn't need anyone to fluff his pillow. And maybe he doesn't appreciate his wife's efforts much, having grown accustomed to them. But if she had forgone her attentions this night, would costs have followed? Would Mr. Weber have been saddened by her absence or her inattentiveness? If there is not much benefit here, maybe there is still enough to outweigh the negligible cost.

But something is lacking in this analysis, something market tools seem hopelessly inept at capturing—the powerful intuition that even small acts of mothering can confer great benefit. Grandma bringing tea in a flowery china cup to soothe my tummy ache. If Grandma had been at work, she wouldn't have been there to see my pain. Was she an excessive grandma? As a teenager I may have thought so, but even then I was taking in something from her attention—you-are-valuable, this-is-how-you-care-for-others—little lessons that build on one another and persist much longer than Grandma's cup of tea. Market analysis seems an awkward tool with which to value the efforts of mothers, and grandmas, and Ms. Webers.

One thing seems clear, however, even without the help of market analysis. When Bobby boards the school bus for the first time, his mother's mandatory workload declines. But does Bobby's absence from 9:00 a.m. to 2:00 p.m. necessarily mean that his mother should take a job from 9:30 a.m. to 1:30 p.m.? From 8:00 a.m. to 5:00 p.m.? What if the physical and emotional stress of being on her feet all day or fighting office back-stabbing or appeasing angry customers makes Bobby's mother less efficient (and less caring) at home? How much time and energy does it take to mother well? To nurture a child? To build a haven from the nastiness outside? Is a minimalist answer better than a generous one? Is there a one-size-fits-all answer?

If we cannot answer such questions with confidence, maybe it is wise to defer to a family's judgment about how much mothering is appropriate. Who can better understand what efforts will benefit the family, and how much time those efforts require? A mother may be wrong in her assessment, but who has a better shot at being right? Not Bobby. And not third parties seduced by the myth that mothering is for babies.

Until myths about the reality, the costs, and the value of mothering are debunked, divorce judges vested with broad discretion will continue to penalize mothers who prioritize caregiving over market labor. And things could get worse. As we will see in chapter 4, alimony guidelines are becoming increasingly popular, and there is no reason to believe that the drafters of these guidelines are less susceptible to mother myths than judges. At worst, state-wide statutory guidelines will memorialize these myths, creating modernized, bright-line divorce regimes that punish mothers with even greater certainty than the discretionary regimes of current law.

PART II

Alimony Mechanics

Alimony is a concrete thing around which all the feelings
concerning the divorce or separation are likely to gather.
—Catherine Groves Peele, "Social and Psychological Effects
of the Availability and the Granting of Alimony on the
Spouses," *Law and Contemporary Problems* 6 (1939): 283

As we have seen, despite the rhetoric of gender equality, the reality in
many U.S. homes is that one spouse, usually a mother, serves as a primary
family caregiver. This role often leads caregivers to disinvest in market
labor, a move that over time reduces a caregiver's earnings and ultimately
her earning capacity. We have also seen that most divorcing couples have
little property, which leaves alimony as the only judicial tool for addressing income disparities linked to marital roles. Early no-fault divorce laws
gave courts broad discretion to award alimony, but no-fault's clean-break
philosophy simultaneously discouraged courts from doing so.

 This part explores some of the changes in the law of alimony since
the beginning of no-fault divorce forty years ago. Of these changes,
the most significant is the alimony guideline movement, which has
recently been energized by alimony reform groups dedicated to halt-
ing "alimony abuse." These groups have sprung up in several states to
popularize alimony horror stories and push for state guidelines that
limit the duration and amount of alimony awards. Their efforts have
begun to pay off, and the guideline movement in the United States is in
danger of being co-opted by a new generation of anti-alimony fervor.

This politically charged atmosphere stands in sharp contrast to the careful and thoughtful approach taken by the Canadians, who launched a national project to identify a rationale and formula for quantifying alimony. Led by two family law scholars, the Canadian project recently culminated in a set of nonmandatory alimony guidelines that have proven influential in that country. The Canadian experience, along with that of a few other countries, provides a useful baseline for judging our own success in developing a rational law of alimony.

4

The Contemporary State of Alimony

Alimony remains broken—without a rationale, unpredictable, uncertain, and uncommon. In 2006, the Census Bureau counted 9,261,000 divorced women aged eighteen or older.[1] That same year, only 382,000 persons (male or female) aged fifteen or older were receiving alimony income.[2] The rarity of alimony is partly a testament to the continuing dominance of no-fault's clean-break, fresh-start philosophy; to alimony's terrible reputation; to the broad judicial discretion over alimony decision making that invites judges to rely on personal codes of fairness driven by misconceptions about primary caregiving; and to a new movement to limit alimony that is curiously reminiscent of the anti-alimony attitudes of forty years ago. If much remains unchanged since the dawn of no-fault, much has changed, and so we take a closer look at the contemporary state of alimony law.

A. Alimony Mechanics
1. Alimony and the Distribution of Property

As we saw in chapter 2, the no-fault scheme is to limit alimony and rely on property distribution as the preferred tool for addressing any economic inequities between divorcing spouses. This basic scheme continues. Unfortunately, property distribution fails in its idealized role today for much the same reasons it failed at the dawn of no-fault.

Like their early no-fault counterparts, property distribution statutes in all common-law states and most community property states generally vest trial courts with broad discretion to distribute property "equitably."[3] State statutes typically provide lists of nonexclusive, relevant factors to guide judicial decision making, but leave the ultimate determination of what is fair to an individual court.[4] Many state equitable distribution statutes now include a reference to the contributions of a homemaker, although if read literally, this factor is sometimes limited to a homemaker's contribution to the "acquisition" of marital property.[5] While some homemakers will presumably be able to show that the hours they spent washing dirty clothes contributed to acquisition of the family car, many other homemakers will find such proof difficult.

The judicial task of crafting a fair distribution of property is complicated by the conflict between the two basic principles that underscore equitable distribution factors: first, that property should be allocated according to spousal *contribution*, and second that property should be allocated according to spousal *need*.[6] An emphasis on contribution will support a larger award for a primary wage-earner, while an emphasis on need will support a larger award for a primary caregiver who is less financially well-positioned. Should contribution trump need or vice versa? Equitable distribution statutes offer no answer to this question, exacerbating the already difficult task of determining equity.

In one important respect, however, contemporary equitable distribution regimes depart from their early no-fault counterparts. Increasingly, courts are directed to presume or at least to begin their search for fairness with an assumption that marital property should be split equally.[7] A 50–50 presumption has much intuitive appeal. Indeed, "as any group of schoolchildren dividing a bag of candy know, the default meaning of fair is 'equal.'"[8] An equal split of marital property is also consistent with the partnership metaphor that so attracted the drafters of the 1970 Uniform Marriage and Divorce Act, which, as we saw in chapter 2, inspired many a state to authorize no-fault divorce.

The usefulness of a 50–50 starting point, however, is limited by the unfortunate reality that most divorcing couples have little or no property to divide. Prior to the 2008 downturn, if a couple had a significant asset at all, it was probably the equity in the marital home. In 2002, for example, the median net worth of married couples in the United States was $101,975, but when home equity was excluded, net worth was only $25,950.[9] With the most recent recession, the net worth of many couples has fallen. Overall, median household net worth declined 35 percent between 2005 and 2010, from $102,844 to $66,740.[10] The housing bust has made home equity less likely; indeed, many couples are upside-down on their home mortgage. Since 2007, "about 39 percent of all Americans have been foreclosed upon, unemployed, underwater on a mortgage" or are more than two months behind on their mortgage payments.[11] Retirement plans too have been hard-hit by the recession. No matter how well-crafted the property distribution tools, a skimpy or empty property pot gives a court little or nothing to work with. What all this means is that alimony remains important. As we saw in chapter 1, family roles often leave divorcing spouses with disparate earning capacity, and in these cases alimony is likely to be the only available tool for avoiding a lopsided, inequitable divorce outcome.

2. General Alimony Statutes: Discretionary Equity

Most contemporary alimony statutes, much like the UMDA model of the early 1970s, vest trial courts with broad discretion to determine alimony eligibility and to fix the amount and duration of an alimony award. Many statutes distinguish between indefinite-term and fixed-term awards. Indefinite alimony that specifies no duration is sometimes termed "permanent" or "lifetime" alimony. These latter two labels are misleading, however, since even a "permanent" award generally terminates upon the death of either the recipient or payor, is modifiable upon a substantial change in circumstances,[12] terminates automatically upon a recipient's remarriage, and in many states is suspended or terminated upon a recipient's cohabitation. Fixed-term alimony generally specifies the award's duration (e.g., five years), and sometimes also identifies the purpose of the award. Massachusetts, for example, recognizes four types of alimony:

- "General term alimony" is support for an "economically dependent" spouse.
- "Rehabilitative alimony" is support for a spouse "who is expected to become economically self-sufficient by a predicted time."
- "Reimbursement alimony" compensates a spouse for contributions to the other spouse's education or job training.
- "Transitional alimony" is meant to transition the recipient to "an adjusted lifestyle" after divorce.[13]

Alimony statutes typically offer courts a laundry list of nonexclusive factors relevant to the alimony decision, but leave the ultimate decision as to whether to award alimony and the size and duration of any award to the court's discretion. A 2010 survey found that forty-two state alimony statutes contain lists of relevant factors;[14] in the remaining states, relevant factors appear in case law. The Illinois alimony statute is typical:

> (a) In a proceeding for dissolution of marriage . . . the court *may* grant a temporary or permanent maintenance award for either spouse *in amounts and for periods of time as the court deems just*, without regard to marital misconduct, in gross or for fixed or indefinite periods of time . . . after consideration of all relevant factors, including:
>> (1) the income and property of each party, including marital property apportioned and non-marital property assigned to the party seeking maintenance;
>> (2) the needs of each party;
>> (3) the present and future earning capacity of each party;
>> (4) any impairment of the present and future earning capacity of the party seeking maintenance due to that party devoting time to domestic duties or having forgone or delayed education, training, employment, or career opportunities due to the marriage;
>> (5) the time necessary to enable the party seeking maintenance to acquire appropriate education, training, and employment, and whether that party is able to support himself or herself through

appropriate employment or is the custodian of a child making it appropriate that the custodian not seek employment;

(6) the standard of living established during the marriage;

(7) the duration of the marriage;

(8) the age and the physical and emotional condition of both parties;

(9) the tax consequences of the property division upon the respective economic circumstances of the parties;

(10) contributions and services by the party seeking maintenance to the education, training, career or career potential, or license of the other spouse;

(11) any valid agreement of the parties; and

(12) any other factor that the court expressly finds to be just and equitable.[15]

The Illinois statute, like statutes in many other states, authorizes but does not require judges to award alimony after considering all relevant factors. (Note the word "may" in the first sentence of the statute.) If a court decides to award alimony, the amount and duration of the award again depend on judicial discretion—that is, on what the judge thinks is "just." In making her decision, a judge is directed to "consider" the eleven identified factors, but also invited (in factor 12) to consider anything else she thinks is a "just and equitable" factor.

Alimony factors vary from state to state, but the dominant theme is the same—the claimant's need. To the extent she is "needy," a claimant is a "good" candidate for alimony, and if a court decides to award alimony, her "need" will be a factor in determining the size and duration of the award. The first five factors in the Illinois statute, for example, all aim to identify need by examining the spouses' relative income and property, the needs of each party, the spouses' present and future earning capacity, any impairment of the claimant's earning capacity, and the time needed for the claimant to acquire "appropriate employment." The eighth factor also relates to need—the parties' age, and physical and emotional condition. But nowhere does the statute suggest *why* need should be so central to alimony decision making. A claimant's need does not "provide any satisfactory explanation for placing the obligation to support needy individuals on their former spouses rather than on their parents, their children, their friends, or society in general."[16] Need thus serves as an alimony trigger rather than an alimony rationale, perpetuating a view of alimony as a handout, mandated in the discretion of a judge who is assumed to be wise and fair-minded and to whom we have delegated the task of determining whether a handout is appropriate in any particular case.

Making need-based alimony even more unpredictable is the fact that "need" has no consistent definition. Because we cannot explain why need is the primary alimony trigger, we cannot choose, in a principled way, among the many possible definitions of need. Is a spouse needy only if she is living in poverty or near poverty? Below the middle class? Below the standard of living during the marriage? Below some line that seems reasonable in the view of a particular judge? Ultimately, states leave the definition of need to an individual trial court. "The result is that the meaning of 'need'—the most fundamental issue created by [alimony] statutes—is hopelessly confused."[17]

While need is a dominant alimony determinant, the duration of the marriage is a close second. For reasons that may seem intuitive, the length of the marriage is an important factor in determining alimony eligibility, and in quantifying any alimony award. There is no consistent explanation, however, for why marriage duration has been assigned this important role, an issue to which we will return in chapter 6, on alimony theory.

Since the early years of no-fault, some states have added homemaker references to their lists of relevant alimony factors. Factor 4 of the Illinois statute, for example, recognizes the potential costs of caregiving, authorizing courts to consider "any impairment of the present and future earning capacity of the party seeking maintenance due to that party devoting time to domestic duties or having forgone or delayed education, training, employment, or career opportunities due to the marriage." The Tennessee alimony statute takes a broader approach, recognizing that "the contributions to the marriage as homemaker or parent are of equal dignity and importance as economic contributions to the marriage."[18]

The overall design of general alimony statutes is thus to defer to the discretion of an individual judge. While long lists of relevant factors offer courts some guidance, the statutes typically suggest no range of choice or weight for any of these factors, and generally authorize courts to consider anything else that seems relevant. No surprise, then, that alimony decisions remain uncertain and unpredictable. There is, however, an important exception to this picture of discretionary decision making. In some states, Illinois included, courts are specifically directed *not* to consider one potentially relevant factor—marital misconduct.

3. The Fault Factor: Eating Cookies in Bed and Other Marital Sins

The issue of marital fault is not an easy one, and there is a great temptation to allow "hard cases" to make "bad law." Consider, for example, a couple of worst-case-scenario law school hypotheticals. First, there is the stay-at-home mom who, after thirty years as a stellar parent and wife, has a onetime fling with the tennis pro, which she immediately and profoundly regrets. Should she be denied alimony? Should she be allowed to defend, or at least explain, her behavior, perhaps by pointing to her husband's emotional or physical abuse? Should it matter that her act of infidelity has broken her husband's heart and left him unable to trust again? Should the mom's fault constitute a line in the sand—no excuses, no explanations, no mercy?

While the story of the long-enduring, temporarily straying mom may illustrate the harsh results that can come from allowing marital fault to play a determinative role in alimony decision making, other hypotheticals illustrate the inequity that can result when judges ignore marital fault. Consider the case of the husband who conspires to murder his wife or who infects her with a sexually transmitted disease, perhaps an incurable one. Should such a husband receive alimony? Or should his very bad behavior be reason enough to deny his alimony claim? Should it matter that the husband has otherwise been a devoted partner and parent, tending to the couple's twelve children and giving up an opportunity to become a brain surgeon?

With such worst-case scenarios in the background, it is easy to understand why the issue of marital fault inspires passion and controversy and why states disagree about its appropriate role in alimony cases. In a 2010–2011 survey, Linda Elrod and Robert Spector counted twenty-six states that make marital fault relevant to alimony decision making.[19] A North Carolina statute, for example, *prohibits* a court from ordering alimony on behalf of a "dependent spouse" who "participated in an act of illicit sexual behavior," and *requires* a court to order a "supporting spouse" guilty of the same conduct to pay alimony.[20] A Virginia statute disallows "permanent" alimony for a spouse who committed adultery or other marital fault except when that denial would "constitute a manifest injustice, based upon the respective degrees of fault during the marriage and the relative economic circumstances of the parties"[21]

Other states follow the UMDA lead in instructing courts to disregard "marital misconduct" in the alimony decision.[22] The Illinois alimony statute, for example, directs the court to make the alimony decision "without regard to marital misconduct."[23] Of course, a statutory directive to disregard marital fault will not always preclude *sub rosa* considerations of marital fault by courts aware of it, but presumably a directive to disregard such fault will dissuade many other courts from considering it.

Those objecting to consideration of marital fault point to its inconsistency with the spirit of no-fault divorce, the inappropriateness of asking judges untrained in family dynamics to gauge marital misconduct, and the troubling question of whether defenses to marital fault should be allowed. For these reasons and others, the *ALI Principles* strongly urge a pure no-fault approach to divorce, rejecting any role for marital fault—as a ground for divorce or as a factor in the distribution of property or alimony. The ALI notes the difficulty of defining "fault" for couples with varying moral standards and emotional sensitivities, and reasons that if fault is relevant, fairness requires an opportunity for the "guilty" spouse to offer a justification or at least an explanation for his/her offense, a process that can trigger a downward spiral of spousal finger pointing and entangle judges in decision-making challenges they are ill-equipped to handle. As the ALI explains,

> Some individuals tolerate their spouse's drunkenness or adultery and remain in their marriage. Others may seek divorce if their spouse grows fat, or spends long hours at the office. . . . And the complexity of marital relations of course confounds the inquiry. The fading of affective ties makes spouses less tolerant of one another. So determining the "cause" of a marital failure requires establishing the reason for the loss of affection. One cannot otherwise decide, for example, whether it is the complainant's apparently unreasonable intolerance that is the cause of the marital failure, rather than conduct of the other spouse that prompted the complainant's loss of affection (and which in turn encouraged the intolerance). . . . Was the mental breakdown in Marriage One caused by one spouse's adultery or the other's emotional insensitivity? In Marriage Two, by the first's adultery or the second's failure to keep fit?[24]

The ALI's concern with the challenge of identifying marital fault was starkly captured by a Michigan justice who, in a dissenting opinion, insisted that marital fault should not be relevant to the distribution of property. As Justice Levin warned,

> The majority's analysis makes even "cookie crumbs" relevant. Under the majority's construction of the 1971 no-fault statute, the judge might consider, might even be obliged to consider, in deciding the division of property—to be sure *only* as a "factor"—whether a party did indeed eat cookies in bed.[25]

Slippery-slope definitions of marital fault, together with the broad discretion that invites divorce courts to rely on definitions of fault consistent with internal moral codes, are powerful arguments against assigning marital fault a role in alimony cases.

Wait a minute. Doesn't this overstate the problem? Eating cookies in bed may be crumby marital behavior, but surely it lies outside the spectrum of general understandings of "marital fault." Just as surely, the spouse who conspires to murder a mate or infects a mate with an incurable sexually transmitted disease is guilty of marital misconduct.[26] The point is that some marital fault is egregious, easy to identify, indefensible, and, unlike cookie eating, renders a spouse an inappropriate candidate for alimony. Yes, this is a moral judgment, but it is one consistent with marital norms and general social understandings of appropriate spousal behavior. At least at the extremes of marital behavior, lines can indeed be drawn.

In the end, the best response to the fault question may lie in a compromise that authorizes a court to consider marital fault only if it rises to the level of unconscionable behavior. This is not a perfect solution, but it may be the best the law can do. Some states do just this. A New Jersey statute, for example, provides that "[n]o person convicted of Murder, Manslaughter, Criminal Homicide, Aggravated Assault, or a substantially similar offense . . . may receive alimony if: (1) the crime results in death or serious bodily injury . . . to a family member of a divorcing party; and (2) the crime was committed after the marriage or civil union."[27] The statute further provides that "[a] person convicted of an attempt or conspiracy to commit murder may not receive alimony from the person who was the intended victim." The statute adds that its provisions are not intended to "limit the authority of the court to deny alimony for other *bad acts*."[28]

To be sure, the identification of "bad acts" will not always be easy. Limiting such acts to those that rise to the level of unconscionable conduct will sometimes provide an easily applied standard. At one end of the unconscionability spectrum is something that "shocks the conscience"—conspiring to murder a spouse, for example. At the other end of the spectrum is eating cookies in bed. As for conduct in between these two extremes, some guidance can be found in the law of contracts, which has long trusted courts to identify the unconscionable.

The heated debate over the relevance of marital fault is but one more factor that complicates the already complex discretionary alimony regimes. Broad judicial discretion, long lists of nonexclusive, unweighted relevant factors, and the absence of a contemporary rationale for alimony all contribute to a scheme that leaves divorcing spouses uncertain as to the outcome of an alimony contest. This is an especially untenable situation for a primary caregiver who is likely to have few resources to finance a risky litigation proposition. Dissatisfaction with the discretionary alimony regime has led some states and local entities to experiment with alimony guidelines in an attempt to inject a modicum of certainty into alimony decision making.

B. The Guideline Movement: In Search of Certainty

Alimony guidelines are not new, but in recent years they have morphed in two significant ways. First, guidelines are taking on more importance, shifting from local to state-wide application, and from optional guidance to statutory presumptions. Second, guidelines have assumed a new goal: in addition to increasing the certainty and predictability of alimony awards, guidelines are increasingly advanced as a means to *limit* alimony eligibility, duration, and value. Much of the energy of the contemporary guideline movement comes from grassroots alimony reform groups, state-by-state organizations composed largely of alimony payors (and sometimes their new spouses) who aim to end "alimony abuse." In a movement eerily reminiscent of the early days of no-fault, today's reformers are inspiring a new wave of disdain for alimony and new statutory restrictions on its availability. To better understand this reform movement, we begin with a look at the operation of alimony guidelines.

1. Guidelines at Work: Who? How Long? How Much?

Alimony guidelines typically focus on one or more of three fundamental questions:

1. Who qualifies for alimony? (alimony eligibility)
2. How long should alimony last? (alimony duration) and
3. How much alimony should be awarded? (alimony value)

Guidelines may be far-reaching, operating as statutory presumptions throughout the state, or they may be quite limited in application, operating as optional rules of thumb on a county-by-county basis.[29] Local, nonstatutory guidelines are by far the more common.

A. NONSTATUTORY GUIDELINES

Early alimony guidelines operated at the county level and provided guidance to divorce judges who, at least in theory, were free to disregard them. Many guidelines continue to operate in this fashion. One of the earliest alimony guidelines was developed in 1977 in Santa Clara, California.[30] These guidelines proved popular and have now been adopted by many California counties, including Alameda and Marin. The Santa Clara guidelines offer a formula for quantifying the value of a temporary (*pendente lite*) alimony award, which applies during the pendency of divorce proceedings. Under this formula, temporary alimony is generally calculated by (1) identifying each party's net income, (2) subtracting the amount of any child support order from the payor's net income, and then (3) subtracting a percentage of the payee's net income from a percentage of the payor's net income and adjusting for tax consequences. The percentage of each party's net income used in step 3 varies by county. In Santa Clara County, the guideline formula subtracts 50 percent of the payee's net income from 40 percent of the payor's net income. The Santa Clara formula also includes guidelines for the duration of alimony. For marriages that lasted less than ten years, the duration of an alimony award is equal to one-half the length of the marriage; for marriages that lasted between ten and twenty years, the duration gradually increases until it matches the length of the marriage. Factors justifying deviation from the guidelines include the underemployment of either party, any additional payments the payor is making for children, and any disparately large share of marital debt the payor has assumed.

Since 1981, the Fairfax County, Virginia, Bar Association and Circuit Court have used alimony guidelines, primarily to calculate the value of a temporary alimony award.[31] The guidelines were developed from hundreds of case notes collected from family attorneys and are intended to reflect rather than reform alimony practice. These guidelines use a quantification formula similar to the one developed in California, but substitute different percentages. Generally, alimony is calculated by subtracting 50 percent of the payee's income from 30 percent of the payor's net income. In cases in which child support is being paid, the percentages are 58 percent of the payee's income and 28 percent of the payor's income. In New Mexico, guidelines originating in Bernalillo County closely resemble the Fairfax County formula.

In Kansas, the Johnson County Bar Association developed guidelines that generally quantify alimony based on the parties' income differential.[32] Under the guideline formula, the parties' gross income differential is first calculated. Alimony is equal to 25 percent of any differential (up to $50,000) if there are no minor children and 20 percent of any differential if there are minor children. Twenty-two percent of any income differential over $50,000 is then added. The duration of an alimony award depends on the length of the marriage. For marriages that lasted five years or less, alimony should not exceed the number of years of marriage divided by 2.5. For marriages that lasted more than five years, alimony should not exceed two years plus one-third of the number of years of marriage.

The Maricopa County, Arizona, Family Court has published guidelines that take a different approach.[33] Under the Arizona guidelines, if a marriage lasted over five years and the payee's income is no more than 75 percent of the payor's income, alimony is calculated by taking the difference in the parties' incomes and then multiplying that difference by the duration factor. The duration factor equals the length of the marriage multiplied by .015, with a maximum of .50. The length of an alimony award is set as a range equal to the length of the marriage multiplied by .3 and .5. Alimony extends for an indefinite term if the marriage lasted twenty years or more and the payee is over fifty years old. As we shall see in chapter 7, the Arizona guidelines are largely patterned after the American Law Institute's proposal for alimony reform—not surprising, since the chief reporter of the *ALI Principles,* Ira Mark Ellman, is a professor at Arizona State.

Other guideline formulae calculate alimony by assigning weight and/or points to various factors. Michigan provides a good example of this approach. The Michigan guidelines originated in Washtenaw County (Ann Arbor), and have been endorsed by the Family Law Section of the State Bar of Michigan.[34] These guidelines rely on numerous factors, including the income, age, and education of the payee and the number of children. Based on these and other factors, computer software assigns an alimony score under which 0 signals "absolutely no case" for alimony and 100 signals "a lock for permanent alimony."

This description of nonstatutory guidelines is representative, but not exhaustive. Guidelines are also at work in many other states, including Arkansas, Kentucky, Oregon, and Nevada. Less commonly, states have incorporated guidelines into their alimony statutes.

B. STATUTORY GUIDELINES

As the guideline movement has gained momentum, states have increasingly included guidelines in their alimony statutes. These guidelines sometimes impose an eligibility requirement based on the length of a marriage or limit the duration of an alimony award. When a statute provides more—a guideline for calculating the value of an award—the formula often applies only to temporary alimony.

Statutes in Maine and Texas, for example, disallow alimony after marriages of "short" duration. Under Maine's alimony statute, general alimony is presumptively disallowed if the marriage lasted less than ten years.[35] In these "short" marriages, Maine allows only rehabilitative alimony.[36] Texas, which until 1995 did not authorize alimony at all, now limits alimony, except in exceptional circumstances, to marriages that lasted ten years or longer.[37]

State statutes may also impose caps on the duration of an alimony award. Maine's alimony statute, for example, creates a rebuttable presumption that general alimony may not be awarded for a period longer than one-half the length of the marriage. This presumption does not apply to marriages that lasted more than twenty years.[38] The Delaware statute imposes a similar cap, limiting alimony duration in marriages of under twenty years to one-half the length of the marriage.[39] Utah is more generous, capping the duration of an alimony award at the number of years of marriage, with an exception for extenuating circumstances.[40] Texas caps alimony duration according to a sliding scale based on the length of the marriage—after a ten- to twenty-year marriage, alimony is limited to a maximum of five years; after a twenty- to thirty-year marriage, alimony is limited to a maximum of seven years; and after a marriage of thirty years or longer, alimony is limited to a maximum of ten years.[41]

It is important to note that none of these durational caps *require* a judge to extend alimony for the full period specified; the caps rather impose *limits* on a judge's ability to extend alimony beyond the specified period. The onus remains on the alimony claimant to establish that alimony should extend for the maximum period allowed under the statute.

Less frequently, but increasingly, state alimony statutes address the *value* of an award. In the simplest case, a statute may cap the value of an award. The Texas statute, for example, caps an alimony award at *the lesser of* $5,000 per month or 20 percent of the payor's average monthly gross income.[42] In other states, alimony statutes include a guideline formula for quantifying the value of an alimony award. The guideline formula is usually limited to temporary alimony, after which alimony depends on a more traditional discretionary alimony regime. As a practical matter, however, a temporary award may carry over into a post-divorce award by establishing a status quo that offers a default position for judges eager to finesse the difficult task of determining equities de novo.

The Pennsylvania alimony statute, for example, has long required judges to base temporary alimony on a guideline formula. The formula is not contained in the statute itself, but rather in Uniform Support Guidelines, established under rules promulgated in 1989 by the Pennsylvania Supreme Court. The statute aims to ensure that "persons similarly situated shall be treated similarly," and to this end requires that guideline figures operate as rebuttable presumptions.[43] The Pennsylvania statute further requires that the guidelines be based on the "reasonable needs" of the claimant and the ability of the payor to meet those needs. As promulgated, the guidelines provide that temporary alimony should equal 40 percent of the difference in the monthly net incomes of the payor and payee. If the payor has a child support obligation, the income differential is reduced by the amount of child support and then multiplied by 30 percent.[44] Deviation from these sums is permitted upon written or specific findings on the record that the guideline would produce an "unjust or inappropriate" result based on criteria established by the Supreme Court.[45]

In Colorado, a guideline formula appears in the state's alimony statute itself.[46] The guideline deals only with temporary alimony and applies only to cases in which the spouses' combined gross annual income is $75,000 or less. In these cases, temporary alimony is presumptively calculated by subtracting 50 percent of the payee's income from 40 percent of the payor's income. A court may deviate from the guideline figure upon a finding that the result would be "inequitable or unjust." Deviation requires a written statement of reasons. If the spouses' combined income exceeds $75,000, the statute reverts to a discretionary regime, authorizing but not requiring a court to award temporary alimony after considering a short list of typical, nonexclusive alimony factors. The statute is careful to state that the guideline formula for temporary alimony shall not be used to calculate post-divorce alimony and shall not prejudice the rights of either party as to such post-divorce orders.

In New York, as in Colorado, a guideline formula appears in the text of the alimony statute.[47] The New York guideline was adopted in 2010, a little-noticed part of the widely publicized statutory amendments that authorized unilateral no-fault divorce. The guidelines identify presumptive values for temporary alimony. Deviation is permitted if a court determines, after considering a statutory list of typical discretionary factors, that the presumptive award would be "unjust or inappropriate." Any deviation from the guideline must be supported by a written order stating the reasons for deviation.

In its oversimplified version, the New York guideline formula generally provides that where the payor's income is $500,000 or less (the income cap), temporary alimony should be the lesser of (1) 30 percent of the payor's income minus 20 percent of the payee's income or (2) 40 percent of the parties' combined income minus the payee's income. A spouse whose annual earnings are $500,000, for example, would presumptively pay $140,000 per year to a spouse whose annual earnings are $50,000.[48]

Where the payor's income exceeds $500,000, the statute directs the court to first calculate alimony under the above formulae and then determine any additional alimony based on a long list of nonexclusive factors.

As originally drafted, New York's alimony guideline would have applied to post-divorce alimony, but the bill was changed at the eleventh hour to apply only to temporary alimony. Legislators cast the new law as an experiment and a possible forerunner of guidelines for post-divorce alimony. New York's guideline experiment has proven controversial. Some charge that awards under the statute are too high, especially in cases where a payor is also paying child support. The result, say some, is a "redistribution of income" that leaves payors with less disposable income than payees.[49] And while the New York guidelines allow courts to deviate from guideline figures, some observers worry that clogged court dockets will lead courts to simply follow the statutory guideline rather than take the time to explain a deviation.

So which guideline is the "right" guideline? Is there a best-practices guideline choice?

2. What Is "Equity"? Which Guideline Is the "Right" Guideline?

As we have seen, guideline formulae vary widely. Just how widely was made clear in a recent article by Victoria M. Ho and Jennifer J. Cohen, who applied five different alimony guidelines to the facts of five actual Florida cases.[50] The outcomes under the guidelines of Arizona, California, Kansas, Kentucky, and Pennsylvania varied considerably, and none mirrored the results in the actual Florida cases. In this section we explore three of these Florida cases.

The first case involved a marriage of twenty-six years.[51] At the time of the divorce petition, the husband was fifty-two years old and the wife forty-eight. The couple had three children, all of whom were adults. During the marriage the husband, an attorney, was the primary wage-earner. The wife was the primary caregiver and worked part-time. The husband's monthly earnings at divorce were $16,750, and the court imputed $1,000 in monthly income to the wife. A Florida court awarded the wife $8,000 per month in "permanent" (indefinite-term) alimony, a sum that would be reduced after two years and again after four years, in anticipation of the wife's increased income. Ho and Cohen figured the value of a monthly alimony award under guidelines in Arizona ($6,143), California ($6,200), Kansas ($3,590), Kentucky ($7,875), and Pennsylvania ($6,300). Quite a range—from $3,590 to $7,875 per month. As a practical matter, this means a payor living in Kentucky will be around $51,000 poorer each year than one living in Kansas; a payee $51,000 richer. Who is right? Kentucky or Kansas, or a state in between?

The second case involved a marriage of thirty-two years.[52] At the time of their divorce, the parties were both fifty-three, and had two adult children. The husband was a doctor and the wife a practical nurse. The husband's gross monthly earnings at divorce were over $11,000. The wife was earning eight dollars an hour in temporary work while pursuing training as a registered nurse, but in the month prior to the final hearing, she grossed $914. A Florida court awarded the wife $4,000 a month in "permanent" alimony. Ho and Cohen calculated the value of a monthly alimony award under guidelines in Arizona ($4,841), California ($3,943), Kansas ($2,344), Kentucky ($5,043), and Pennsylvania ($4,043). Again, quite a range—from $2,344 to $5,043. For the payor and payee, living in Kentucky versus Kansas has significant consequences. In Kentucky the payor will be around $32,400 poorer each year than one living in Kansas; the payee $32,400 richer. Who is right? Kentucky or Kansas, or a state in between?

One more example will suffice. This case involved a marriage of fourteen years.[53] The parties had one child, who attended private school. The husband's monthly income was over $7,000, while the wife's monthly income was $1,760. A Florida court ordered the husband to pay "permanent" alimony of $600 per month and child support of $797 per month. Based on these facts, Ho and Cohen calculated the value of a monthly alimony award under guidelines in Arizona ($1,100), California ($1,601), Kansas ($1,048), Kentucky ($1,823), and Pennsylvania ($1,333). A payor living in Kansas will thus be $9,300 poorer each year than one living in Kansas; a payee $9,300 richer. Who is right? Kentucky or Kansas, or those states in between?

So which guideline is the most fair to the payor? Which most fair to the payee? Which is most equitable? Is there a best-practices guideline formula? In 2007, the prestigious American Academy of Matrimonial Lawyers answered this question with a guideline formula of its own.[54] Based on a survey of alimony guidelines throughout the United

States, the AAML identified two common denominators: income of the spouses and duration of the marriage. Drawing on these factors, the AAML approved a simple formula that quantifies alimony in the absence of specified deviation factors. The value of an award is calculated "by taking 30% of the payor's gross income minus 20% of the payee's gross income," capped at "40% of the combined gross income of the parties." The duration of an award is a function of the length of the marriage, and in the absence of deviation factors is calculated "by multiplying the length of the marriage by the following factors: 0–3 years (.3); 3–10 years (.5); 10–20 years (.75), over 20 years indefinite-term alimony." Is the AAML guideline formula an improvement over the formulae at work in Arizona, California, Kansas, Kentucky, and Pennsylvania?

The answer to this question depends on the purpose of an alimony award, which in turn depends on alimony's rationale. Unfortunately, as we have seen, there is no consistent answer to the question of *why* anyone should be forced to share income with a former spouse. The absence of a contemporary rationale for alimony makes it impossible to choose among the many formulae that have been offered to define alimony eligibility, duration, and value, making it impossible to identify, in any reasoned way, the "right" formula. The guideline movement continues to gain momentum, however, without much thought to alimony's rationale. Not surprisingly, given the absence of any agreed-upon justification for alimony, the guideline movement is increasingly becoming a movement to limit alimony rather than simply to make it more predictable. This new focus is dramatically evident in the recent revision of the Massachusetts alimony statute.

3. The Massachusetts Story

In 2011, Massachusetts dramatically rewrote its alimony statute, incorporating guidelines that limit the duration and value of post-divorce alimony awards. The new law became effective in 2012 and, as the president of the American Academy of Matrimonial Lawyers stated, it represents an about-face that is sure to "reverberate across the country."[55]

The Massachusetts story began in 2009 with the appointment of a legislative task force to explore the state's alimony law. The task force was composed of family law attorneys and advocates, including the president and founder of Massachusetts Alimony Reform, a grassroots group largely composed of alimony payors. Task force members quickly agreed that the Massachusetts alimony scheme was broken, and their mission became a search for ways to repair it. Their work culminated in statewide reforms, which have been hailed as the end of "lifetime alimony" and denounced as "mean-spirited and Draconian" "craziness." Understanding the controversy surrounding the new law begins with a look at the statute itself.

A. THE DETAILS

The 2012 Massachusetts alimony statute begins with a broad definition of "alimony" as a payment to a spouse "in need."[56] This definition continues the early no-fault focus on spousal need as the basis of alimony. As we have seen, the statute recognizes four familiar types of alimony: *general term alimony* (payments to an "economically dependent" spouse), *rehabilitative alimony* (support for a spouse "who is expected to become economically self-sufficient by a predicted time"), *reimbursement alimony* (support to compensate a spouse for contribution to the financial resources of the payor), and *transitional alimony* (support "to transition the recipient spouse to an adjusted lifestyle or location").

Some provisions of the new statute are unsurprising. Reimbursement and transitional alimony are authorized only in marriages of five years or less, are not modifiable, and may extend for only limited periods— no more than five years in the case of rehabilitative alimony and no more than three years in the case of transitional alimony. Rehabilitative alimony and general term alimony may be modified upon a material change of circumstance, and terminate upon the recipient's remarriage. General term alimony "*shall* be suspended, reduced or terminated" if the recipient cohabits for a continuous period of at least three months, terminates when the payor attains full retirement age, and shall not be reinstated if the recipient's remarriage ends. The new statute also provides that the income and assets of a payor's spouse shall not be considered in actions to modify alimony.

Most controversial are two sections of the new statute that impose caps on the duration and value of a general, post-divorce alimony award. The statute strictly limits a court's ability to award indefinite-term alimony, specifying that general alimony must terminate on a "date certain" unless the marriage lasted more than twenty years or "the interests of justice" require otherwise. The statute then sets durational caps based on the length of the marriage. If the marriage lasted five years or less, general term alimony shall not continue for a period longer than 50 percent of the number of months of marriage; if the marriage lasted between five and ten years, alimony shall not continue for a period longer than 60 percent of the number of months of marriage; if the marriage lasted between ten and fifteen years, alimony shall not continue for a period longer than 70 percent of the number of months of marriage; if the marriage lasted between fifteen and twenty years, alimony shall not continue for a period longer than 80 percent of the number of months of marriage. These durational caps do not, of course, *require* a court to extend an alimony award for the designated period, but rather *limit* the court's ability to extend alimony beyond this period. The statute authorizes deviation from the durational cap upon a written finding that deviation is necessary.

The new law is retroactive. It anticipates a series of modification actions brought by current payors seeking to terminate alimony obligations that extend beyond the new durational caps. Presumably to avoid judicial overload, the statute sets out a timetable for these modification actions. Alimony payors who were married to the payee for five years or less may file a modification action as of March 1, 2013; those who were married five to ten years must wait until March 1, 2014; those married for ten to fifteen years must wait until March 1, 2015, and those married for fifteen to twenty years must wait until September 1, 2015. Payors who have reached full retirement age get special treatment: they may file a modification action (to end their alimony obligation) on or after March 1, 2013, no matter the length of their marriage.

The second controversial section of the overhauled Massachusetts statute imposes a cap on the value of alimony awards (except reimbursement alimony). Under the statutory formula, "the amount of alimony should generally not exceed the recipient's need or 30% to 35% of the difference between the parties' gross incomes." As with the durational cap, a court may exceed this value cap upon written findings that deviation is necessary. Another section of the statute provides that when determining income, the court shall exclude "gross income which the court has already considered for setting a child support order."[57] In practical effect, this section appears to disallow alimony where a payor with income under $250,000 is paying child support.

B. THE CONTROVERSY: FOR BETTER OR WORSE

Supporters of the new Massachusetts law hailed it as the end of an archaic and dangerous alimony regime that "put a lot of people in the poor house" and "made people never able to retire." An article in the *New York Times* described the new law as "sharply curbing lifetime alimony."[58] "The previous system," said the author, "allowed judges to award lifelong alimony after both short and long marriages, in contrast to the practices of most states." Steve Hitner, president of Massachusetts Alimony Reform, praised the new law, which he expected would prevent a recurrence of alimony stories like his own. Hitner, it seems, spent $250,000 in legal fees in an unsuccessful effort to obtain a reduction in his $45,000 annual alimony payment, after which he went into bankruptcy.

Other observers were outraged by the new law. Critics charged that the supposed abuse of "lifetime alimony" under the old Massachusetts law was myth. Prior to the 2012 reforms, the Massachusetts statute was typical of early no-fault discretionary alimony regimes. Judges applying the prior statute already disfavored "lifetime alimony"—a misnomer for indefinite-term alimony. Consequently, lifetime alimony was rare. One Massachusetts divorce lawyer observed that in the course of her six-teen-year career, she had seen a judge grant "lifetime alimony" in only a few unusual cases—where a spouse was living in a homeless shelter, where a husband had been hiding assets.[59]

Critics further charged that the durational caps in the new statute would have distorting effects, exerting pressure on victims of domestic abuse to stay in the marriage through a durational marker (e.g., five years, ten years, fifteen years) and creating incentives for potential payors to divorce before a durational marker. Critics also worried about the harsh effects of the Massachusetts reforms on caregivers. On CNN.com, the adjunct law professor and former visiting Harvard scholar Wendy Murphy called the new law "craziness" and worried that it would hurt women who drop out of the paid labor force to care for their families by ignoring the career costs they face.[60] A former president of the International Academy of Matrimonial Lawyers expressed concern that the law would hurt those who make sacrifices in marriage and described the bill as "mean-spirited and Draconian."[61]

Murphy warned other states to beware. "Lawmakers motivated to please special interest groups," she charged, "would be wise to remember they represent the public interest, not only the interests of wealthy men with lobbyists."[62] States should take heed of Murphy's warning, for there is much to be wary of.

4. Guidelines, Hype, and Déjà Vu: At What Price Certainty?

Alimony guidelines are dangerous. Even as guidelines can make alimony more predictable, they can make it more inequitable, entrenching inequity with even greater certainty than discretionary regimes. Guideline formulae must be carefully chosen so that they ensure not only uniformity, but equity as well. Yet gauging the efficacy of a formula is complicated by the absence of any agreed-upon understanding of the purpose of alimony. Because alimony has no contemporary rationale, alimony guidelines and the numbers that populate them vary widely, and there is no principled basis for preferring one guideline over another, no metric for determining whether a given guideline is likely to produce more equity than inequity. Guidelines cannot finesse the need for a theory of alimony, a topic to which we will return in chapters 7 and 8.

The absence of a rationale also makes alimony vulnerable to hype—to impassioned cries for new limits on alimony based on anecdotal, aberrational stories of alimony atrocities. There are stories of cuckolded men driven into bankruptcy and their parents' basements, of men never able to retire because of huge lifetime alimony awards, of an Alzheimer's patient who cannot get a reduction in his alimony obligation. The horror stories are compelling, partly because alimony cannot easily defend itself. Indeed, alimony cannot even explain its existence. And so the stories of alimony abuse abound, feeding on each other, inspiring myths and misconceptions, disdain for alimony, and an energized new wave of anti-alimony reform efforts. Lobbying efforts have been intense, as alimony reform groups have sprung up in various states and labored hard to publicize tales of alimony abuse. Never mind that alimony is rare, typically short-term, freely modifiable, and generally disfavored in the law. Never mind that alimony reform groups are demanding protection for primary wage-earners while ignoring the effect on primary caregivers. The hype is irresistible.

To be sure, in a broadly discretionary legal system, there will be outliers—cases in which a court awards alimony, and for a longer period and in a larger amount than most observers would think equitable, cases in which a judge refuses to modify an alimony award even when the circumstances calling for modification seem strong. Take, for example, the story that sounds like a worst-case scenario: the Alzheimer's patient who could not get his alimony obligation reduced.[63] Looking only at the facts in the *USA Today* article, we may wonder what explains this case. Not the statute itself, for we know that general alimony statutes give judges broad discretion to do the right thing after considering the facts of a particular case. If the statute is not to blame, maybe it is the judge—a man-hater perhaps, or at least someone who is misguided, for who else would require an Alzheimer's patient to pay alimony? Or maybe we just don't know all the facts. Toward the end of the story is a brief reference to the fact that the payor was married to his first wife for *thirty-six years*. Thirty-six years? What else don't we know? Maybe nothing. Maybe the Alzheimer's case and the many other alleged alimony horror stories are true outliers, wrongly decided cases. And that is indeed an awful prospect for a payor and his/her new spouse. But the many publicized cases of supposed alimony abuse must be considered dispassionately and with due regard for all their facts. Not every publicized story of alleged alimony abuse is a true outlier. Sometimes we just don't know all the facts.

Even more importantly, true outlier cases—and surely such cases exist—must be put in perspective. Alimony is rare, usually short-term, and freely modifiable. There is an obvious danger in drawing general conclusions from aberrational cases, danger in reform inspired by those angry over the aberrational who seek to reform the general, danger in reform efforts led by those unaware of history and seduced by hype. The wise response to cases of real alimony abuse is not statutory reform that entrenches new inequities for everyone else. The answer is not to let the tail wag the dog. But this is exactly what hype tends to do.

One gets an eerie sense of déjà vu when examining the contemporary anti-alimony movement; there is something familiar about the horrific visions of hardworking, impoverished, abused ex-husbands supporting "alimony drones who neither toil nor spin, and become a drain on society and a menace to themselves."[64] These are old myths about alimony, the same myths that fueled anti-alimony sentiment in the early days of no-fault divorce, the same myths that led to the severe limits on alimony in those early regimes. Anti-alimony sentiment found its ideological counterpart in the compelling clean-break philosophy of no-fault divorce, which aimed to give both spouses a fresh start on life free of the shackles, economic or otherwise, of a dead marriage. So compelling was the clean-break philosophy in the early years of no-fault that courts often denied or severely limited alimony even for long-term caregivers whose years of family labor had reduced their earning capacity beyond any reasonable hope of repair. Then, as now, there was little recognition of the reality and costs of family caregiving. Judges of the day bought into misconceptions about the prospects for "rehabilitation" of long-term caregivers. In the words of one legislator, the perception was that "any woman—no matter her age or lack of training—can find a nice little job and a nice little apartment and conduct her later years as she might have done at age 25."[65] No need for alimony.

As we saw in chapter 2, in the years following enactment of no-fault, word of the terrible economic consequences of divorce on long-term caregivers slowly spread, culminating, most alarmingly, in Lenore Weitzman's 1985 book *The Divorce Revolution*. As one indignant California court proclaimed, no-fault divorce "may not be used as a handy vehicle for the summary disposal of old and used wives."[66] The first modern alimony movement began, and it was a movement to sidestep the clean-break philosophy of divorce and encourage judges vested with broad discretion to award long-term or indefinite-term alimony to displaced homemakers. Until recently, the trend has been away from the "no-alimony" or limited rehabilitative alimony philosophy of early no-fault and toward increased recognition that indefinite-term alimony is sometimes appropriate, especially after a long marriage.

Today's second wave of alimony reform represents a return to the anti-alimony perspectives of forty years ago, perspectives that drove the limitations on alimony that proved so disastrous for caregivers. Once again, after the supposed recognition of the realities and human capital costs of family caregiving, a movement is afoot to protect primary wage-earners against the abuses of long-term alimony. At worst, today's primary caregivers will face the same danger as their displaced homemaker mothers and grandmothers, as divorce once again becomes a "handy vehicle for the summary disposal of old and used wives." Only this time around, anti-alimony sentiment will guide decision making with even greater certainty than under the old discretionary regimes, as disdain for alimony is entrenched in statutory presumptions that judges are hard-pressed to resist.

Alimony needs reform—no doubt about it. But reform by the historically ignorant, the forgetful, and the self-interested is a dangerous prospect indeed. Reform without an underlying rationale for its objective is dangerous for both alimony payors, who risk involuntary servitude, and for alimony payees, who risk being thrown under the bus after years of family service. Reform with integrity requires that we first identify the "Why?" of alimony. The Canadians provide a noteworthy example of the powerful role of theory in the formulation of alimony guidelines.

5

Alimony in Context

A Comparative Perspective

Alimony law draws on the culture it serves. Its role in any particular place is thus part of a larger picture of cultural views of the meaning and duration of intimate commitment and of individual versus community responsibility for dependency. A glimpse of alimony in other countries can broaden our perspectives of possibilities for alimony in the United States and enrich any discussion of alimony reform. With this thought, we take a brief look at the law of alimony in a few select countries and at the *Principles of European Family Law regarding Divorce and Maintenance between Former Spouses*. We then take a more extensive look at the fascinating evolution of alimony law in Canada, culminating in the adoption of national alimony guidelines.

A. Alimony from Ireland to Samoa
1. Ireland

The story of alimony in Ireland begins with that country's long refusal to recognize absolute divorce.[1] Until 1995, the Irish Constitution prohibited divorce. By a slim majority, the Irish people voted in November

1995 to remove the constitutional ban on divorce. The next year Ireland adopted a no-fault divorce regime, which became effective in 1997. The new divorce law, however, did nothing to displace the long-standing Irish tradition that the spousal duty of mutual support is a lifetime obligation. Concerned that no-fault divorce would negatively impact caregiving mothers, Ireland rejected the clean-break model of divorce that underscored no-fault reforms in the United States. Under Irish law, the spousal duty of mutual support survives divorce, terminating only on the payor's death or the recipient's death or remarriage. Ireland's rejection of the clean-break model has been hotly criticized,[2] and there is some suggestion that the Supreme Court is rejecting the clean-break model less enthusiastically than it once did. As the Supreme Court stated in 2011, "Irish law does not establish a right to a 'clean break.' However, it is a legitimate aspiration."[3]

The amount of an alimony award is left to the court's discretion. As in the United States, courts are directed to consider a nonexclusive list of statutory factors, which include actual and potential financial resources; financial needs, obligations, and responsibilities; standard of living; age of spouses and the length of the marriage; disability; spousal contributions; earning capacity; and conduct. The reference to "conduct" authorizes courts to consider marital fault, though in practice this factor holds little weight unless there is a serious imbalance in the spouses' respective misconduct. Irish law also authorizes courts to compensate a spouse for lost earning capacity related to marital responsibilities—a recognition of the continuing reality and costs of the role of full-time homemaker, which many Irish women continue to assume.

2. Malaysia

Malaysia has a split legal system, under which the applicable law governing marriage and divorce is determined by a couple's religion.[4] If the couple is Muslim, the Islamic Family Law Act or Enactment (IFLA) governs. These laws vary from state to state. If the couple is non-Muslim, the Law Reform (Marriage and Divorce) Act 1976 (Act 164) (LRA) governs.

Both the IFLA and the LRA authorize women to claim alimony and child support. A threshold requirement is that the claimant prove she is the legal wife of the respondent by showing that the marriage is registered and valid under Malaysian law. Without such proof, the court has no jurisdiction to hear her petition for alimony. The LRA provides that an order of support for a former wife or child should be set according to the means and needs of the parties.

If a wife does not claim alimony, her right does not lapse, but rather becomes "a debt due from the husband to the wife." The wife can claim unpaid alimony as a debt recoverable from a husband who is cast as a defaulter. The LRA gives her three years to make this claim.

3. Russia

Article 90 of the Russian Family Code recognizes three types of former spouses who have a right to claim alimony:

> a. A former spouse who lacks essential means and the capability to work because of a disability which has occurred before or within one year after the dissolution of the marriage (or, in the case of a long-term marriage, if he or she has reached the age of retirement within five years after the divorce);
> b. A former wife during pregnancy, if the pregnancy has commenced before the dissolution of the marriage, and thereafter until the common child has reached the age of 3 years;
> c. A needy former spouse, effectuating care for a disabled common child of the ex-spouses before it reaches the age of 18 years; or an adult common child of the ex-spouses with a disability of the first degree irrespective of its age.[5]

Under Russian law, a claimant's need is thus not sufficient to establish a claim to alimony. More is required—a disability (established by the Socio-Medical Expert Commission) or old age (in 2002, fifty-five for women and sixty for men) that renders the claimant unable to work; or special circumstances relating to pregnancy or the care of a disabled common child. As Masha Antokolskaia notes, this strict limitation on alimony reflects the Soviet adage that "he who does not work, shall not eat."[6] The rationale for alimony in this limited system is based on a duty of spousal support that survives divorce rather than on any notion that one must compensate a spouse for income loss linked to marital roles.[7] Indeed, as Antokolskaia explains, the vision of a full-time caregiver dependent on a full-time wage-earner is foreign to Russian thinking, as the vast majority of Russian women have been in the full-time labor force for three generations.[8]

4. Samoa

The story of alimony in Samoa is a striking example of the critical link between alimony and the culture it serves.[9] In 2010, Samoa enacted the Divorce and Matrimonial Causes Amendment Act 2010 (DMCA 2010), which replaced Samoa's old fault-based divorce law with a pure no-fault regime. Divorce in Samoa is thus available only on the ground of an irretrievable breakdown of the marriage and, absent domestic violence, after a twelve-month separation. Also in 2010, the Maintenance and Affiliation Amendment Act 2010 (MAAA 2010) changed the Samoan law of alimony. Prior to 2010, the Maintenance and Affiliation Act 1967 gave courts broad discretion to award alimony in a reasonable amount, but offered no guidance as to how a court might determine what amount is reasonable. In an effort to guide judicial discretion, the MAAA 2010 includes a list of relevant alimony factors. Lalotoa Mulitalo and Jennifer Corrin summarize these factors as follows:

a. the needs of the applicant having regard to their age and any special needs;

b. the financial resources of the applicant, disregarding the financial resources of any other person unless the court considers this relevant in the special circumstances of the case;

c. the financial resources of the defendant;

d. the commitments of the defendant for their own support or the support of any other person that the defendant has a duty to maintain; and

e. any special circumstances which would result in injustice or undue hardship to any person.[10]

These alimony factors come as no surprise to any observer of U.S. alimony law; indeed, as we saw in chapter 4, their thrust is typical of many alimony statutes in this country. The factors' primary focus is the *need* of the alimony claimant (the applicant) and the *resources* (ability to pay) of the potential alimony obligor (the defendant). As Mulitalo and Corrin observe, however, these factors are culturally inappropriate in Samoa. Most Samoans live in a communal setting on "customary land" and do not receive individual income or own individual property. Everyone in Samoa has access to land through immediate or extended family. "Needs" and "resources" are thus awkward concepts for most Samoans. The new statute's reliance on these factors may thus produce unintended consequences—disallowing alimony where it would have been allowed under prior law because of difficulties in establishing the spouses' relative resources.

Factor d of the MAAA 2010 injects another awkward concept into alimony decision making in Samoa. This factor directs the court to consider the potential payor's commitment to support third parties to whom he or she owes a "duty to maintain." In Samoan culture, such commitments are broad indeed. As Mulitalo and Corrin point out, a Samoan's commitment to others includes extended family, the community at large, and the church—a group that is so large that if the statutory language were literally applied, it would render most potential obligors unable to pay alimony to a former spouse.

Fortunately for alimony claimants in Samoa, a court may avoid these outcomes by turning to another provision of the MAAA 2010. Section e authorizes a court to consider "any special circumstances which would result in injustice or undue hardship to any person." Mulitalo and Corrin anticipate that this catchall section may allow courts to reach more appropriate decisions than the statute would otherwise produce. The Samoan example makes clear that there can be no culturally blind, one-size-fits-all answer to the question of a best-practices alimony statute.

B. European Principles of Alimony: The Commission on European Family Law

Ireland's rejection of the clean-break model of divorce conflicts with the view of much of the rest of Europe. Understanding the law of alimony in Europe has been greatly facilitated by the work of the Commission on European Family Law (CEFL). Formed in 2001, the CEFL is an international group of scholars whose goal is the harmonization of family law within Europe based on both "common core" and "better law."[11] The CEFL's first focus was laws governing access to divorce and alimony (termed "maintenance"). This effort began with the drafting of comprehensive national reports on the law governing access to divorce and alimony in specific countries. These reports are available on the CEFL website, and each report is helpfully organized as a series of responses to a set of 105 detailed questions.[12] In December 2004, the CEFL published its *Principles of European Family Law regarding Divorce and Maintenance between Former Spouses* (hereafter *European Principles*).[13]

The *European Principles* begin with the general proposition that "each spouse should provide for his or her own support after divorce," a proposition familiar to students of the clean-break philosophy of no-fault divorce in the United States. Eligibility for alimony depends on "the creditor spouse [the alimony recipient] having insufficient resources to meet his or her needs and the debtor spouse's [the alimony payor's] ability to satisfy those needs." The *European Principles* identify several factors that deserve particular attention in determining the appropriateness of alimony: "the spouses' employment ability, age and health; the care of children; the division of duties during the marriage; the duration of the marriage; the standard of living during the marriage and any new marriage or long-term relationship." Again, with the possible exception of the last factor addressing new relationships, the factors relevant to alimony decision making are quite similar to the factors in a typical U.S. alimony statute. Additionally, in an apparent recognition of the relevance of marital fault—or at least egregious marital fault—the *European Principles* provide that "[i]n cases of exceptional hardship to the debtor spouse [the payor] the competent authority may deny, limit or terminate maintenance because of the creditor spouse's [the recipient's] conduct." As for the duration of an award, alimony will ordinarily extend for a limited period, but in exceptional cases may extend for an indefinite term. Alimony ends if either party dies or if the recipient "remarries or establishes a long term relationship."

In an interesting provision addressing the issue of subsequent families, the *European Principles* direct alimony decision makers to "(a) give priority to any maintenance claim of a minor child of the debtor spouse; and (b) take into account any obligation of the debtor spouse to maintain a new spouse." The latter directive in particular is consistent with the general proposition of the *European Principles* that former spouses should be self-supportive after divorce and thus, by implication, able to take on new family commitments disentangled from lingering obligations to a former spouse. This premise is consistent with the position of alimony reform groups in the United States who argue that alimony should not interfere with a payor's ability to remarry and start a new family. As we have seen, however, the clean-break philosophy underscoring this position can impose severe hardship on primary caregivers, especially after a long marriage.

C. Alimony and the Canadian Guideline Experiment

In 2008, Canada took the dramatic step of implementing national alimony guidelines.[14] These guidelines are nonlegislated and nonmandatory, but since their promulgation have been influential in directing negotiations and mediation, in setting a range of choice for trial judges' discretion, and in making alimony decision making more certain and predictable. The story of Canada's national alimony guideline experiment begins with a brief look at the Canadian system of family law and with three major cases on alimony (termed "spousal support") decided by the Supreme Court of Canada. Each of these cases had a profound effect on the law of alimony in Canadian jurisprudence, and each offers a compelling narrative of the evolution of alimony in Canada.

1. The Canadian System of Family Law

Family law in Canada is determined under a federal system in which legislative power is split between the federal government and the governments of ten provinces. Section 91(26) of the Canadian Constitution confers jurisdiction over marriage and divorce on the Parliament of Canada.[15] In exercise of this broad constitutional authority, the Canadian Parliament enacted a comprehensive Divorce Act in 1968, which sets the grounds for divorce and the rules governing custody, child support, and spousal support that arise in the context of divorce. The current Divorce Act is a 1985 iteration. In a more recent exercise of federal constitutional power over marriage, the federal government redefined marriage in 2005 to include same-sex marriage.

Provincial governments also have considerable power over issues related to the family. Section 92(13) of the Canadian Constitution confers authority on provincial legislatures to make laws regarding "property and civil rights in the province." Provincial laws thus govern the distribution of property at divorce, and also govern issues of custody, child support, and spousal support that arise outside the context of divorce.[16]

Federal and provincial laws on spousal support are very similar, and are all based on a model of marriage as a partnership of equals. Section 15.2(6) of the Divorce Act identifies four objectives of alimony. Under this section, an order of spousal support should

> a. recognize any economic advantages or disadvantages to the spouses arising from the marriage or its breakdown;
> b. apportion between the spouses any financial consequences arising from the care of any child of the marriage over and above the obligation apportioned between the spouses pursuant to [the child support order];
> c. relieve any economic hardship of the spouses arising from the break-down of the marriage; and
> d. in so far as practicable, promote the economic self-sufficiency of each spouse within a reasonable period of time.

Section 15.2(5) of the Divorce Act makes marital misconduct irrelevant to spousal support. Section 15.2(4) identifies factors relevant to both spousal and child support:

> In making an order . . . the court shall take into consideration the condition, means, needs and other circumstances of each spouse and of any child of the marriage for whom support is sought, including
>
> a. the length of time the spouses cohabited;
> b. the functions performed by the spouse during cohabitation; and
> c. any order, agreement or arrangement relating to support of the spouse or child.

Under Canada's unitary judicial system, superior court judges decide spousal support issues arising under both federal and provincial laws. Appeals from these decisions are heard by provincial courts of appeals and then by the Supreme Court of Canada, which is the ultimate authority on the law of spousal support under both federal and provincial governments. Canada's guideline project was preceded by three significant Supreme Court decisions on spousal support that recognized vague principles of entitlement, but gave judges little direction in exercising their broad discretionary power to decide support issues.

2. The Supreme Court of Canada and the Law of Spousal Support

Pelech v. Pelech[17] was one of three spousal support cases handed down by the Supreme Court of Canada in 1987.[18] Each of the cases in this *Pelech* trilogy involved a spousal support obligation that had terminated under a separation agreement. The former wives, who were all unemployed and financially hard-pressed, asked the court to vary or set aside the agreement and apply the spousal support provisions of the Divorce Act. Courts refused each of these requests. Although the *Pelech* trilogy involved settlement agreements, the Court's opinion reflected a clean-break vision of spousal support that greatly influenced courts in other cases. Lower courts drew from *Pelech* a "causal connection" test for spousal support, under which support is appropriate only to address needs caused by the marriage. In interpreting the new 1985 Divorce Act, lower courts applied a narrow version of the causal connection test, defining "need" in terms of necessities rather than the marital standard of living, and limiting spousal support to short-term, transitional awards, sometimes even after long-term, traditional marriages. This clean-break goal of early Canadian no-fault law is familiar, for it closely parallels the aim of early no-fault divorce law in the United States. As we saw in chapter 2, this law set many displaced homemakers free to begin new lives, with limited assets, minimal job experience, and little hope of ever recapturing the earning capacity losses caused by their years of family labor. A "fresh start" is not always a prize.

The 1992 decision of *Moge v. Moge* changed the direction of spousal support in Canada.[19] The Moges had been married for sixteen years when they separated; seven years after their separation, Mr. Moge filed for divorce. Ms. Moge was awarded custody of the children and Mr. Moge was ordered to pay $150 per month in combined child and spousal support. Sixteen years after the couple's separation, and after their youngest child had reached majority, Mr. Moge sought to terminate his support obligation. At the time, Mr. Moge was earning $24,000 annually while Ms. Moge was earning $800 per month. The lower court granted Mr. Moge's request, reasoning that Ms. Moge had enjoyed ample time to become self-sufficient in the sixteen years since the parties' separation. An appellate court disagreed, reinstating the $150 per month support order on the ground that Ms. Moge continued to suffer economic disadvantages from her marital role as the children's caregiver. Mr. Moge appealed to the Supreme Court of Canada. He lost. The Court dismissed Mr. Moge's appeal, leaving intact the $150 per month support order (which Ms. Moge did not seek to increase). In the process the Court offered a dramatic new vision of spousal support.

In a powerful opinion penned by Justice Claire L'Heureux-Dubé, the Supreme Court of Canada rejected the clean-break model of support that dominated under the *Pelech* trilogy, offering in its place a new and expanded compensatory model of support. The Court objected to the tendency of post-*Pelech* courts to overemphasize the goal of spousal self-sufficiency while neglecting other relevant factors listed in the Divorce Act. Spousal support, said the Court, should focus on the "effect of the marriage in either impairing or improving each party's economic prospects."[20] *Moge*'s broad compensatory principle thus cast support as a tool for ensuring the equitable distribution of the economic consequences of a failed marriage. Key to the *Moge* decision was the Court's recognition of the persistence of gender roles within marriage, its acknowledgement of the human capital costs of family labor, its concern with equity for primary caregivers, and, in a retreat from the strict test of causation common after *Pelech*, its willingness to assume that economic disadvantage is linked to roles within marriage. The Court thus rejected Mr. Moge's argument that Ms. Moge would have been cleaning houses even if she had not married him.

Not surprisingly, after *Moge*, spousal support in Canada became more important—more generous in amount and more likely to be imposed for an indefinite term. But all was not well in this post-*Moge* world. While the broad principles articulated in *Moge* shifted the focus of lower courts away from the clean-break model, these principles offered little guidance as to how courts should implement the new expanded compensatory model of support. *Moge* gave courts no tips on how to measure a claimant's loss. Measuring the economic loss caused by participation in a failed marriage is no easy feat. Quantification of such loss requires comparison of a claimant's present situation with the situation she would have been in but for the marriage, a task that is inherently speculative and expensive. Canada's lower courts attempted to finesse the challenge by developing a proxy measure of loss—typically, a claimant's "need" as measured against the marital standard of living. This approach had an unintended consequence. As Carol Rogerson observed, "the compensatory model of spousal support started to collapse into something that resembled a more traditional support model where governing concepts were need and standard of living."[21] Moreover, the focus on loss associated with marital roles seemed to provide no basis for spousal support in the case of disabled spouses whose disability did not arise from the marriage. Some lower courts thus denied spousal support to disabled spouses even after long-term marriages. Other courts returned to *Moge*'s broad language of compensation, expanding the compensatory principle to include loss of access to the other spouse's income, reasoning that loss of this access could be cast as an economic disadvantage of the marital breakdown.[22]

In 1999, the Supreme Court of Canada responded to these concerns by recognizing a new basis for spousal support in addition to the compensatory model set out in *Moge*. The case—*Bracklow v. Bracklow*—involved a disabled wife who sought "permanent" spousal support.[23] The couple's relationship lasted seven years—four years of cohabitation followed by three years of marriage. The couple had no children and led financially independent lives. At the time of their divorce, the husband earned approximately $44,000 annually and the wife received a government pension of $787 per month. The husband paid interim support, but at divorce the lower court denied the wife's request for permanent support, finding no compensatory basis for her claim since her disability was the product of an illness rather than the marriage. An appellate court affirmed. The Supreme Court of Canada took a different view, concluding that the wife was entitled to spousal support on the basis of her need. Having concluded that the wife was entitled to support, the Court remitted the case to a new trial judge for quantification of the award. The trial judge cut a compromise, ordering the husband to pay $400 per month for five years—something less than the "permanent" support the wife sought, but more than the husband hoped to pay.

Like *Moge*, *Bracklow* changed the direction of spousal support in Canada. Unlike *Moge*, however, the *Bracklow* Court offered little theoretical explanation for its needs-based model of support, noting simply

that section 15.2(6)(c) of the Divorce Act recognizes that spousal support may relieve financial hardship resulting from breakdown of the
marriage. Nor did *Bracklow* offer lower courts any practical guidance
for applying this new model. In the end, *Bracklow* gave lower courts
only a vague directive to award spousal support on the basis of a claimant's need, but left the definition of "need" and decisions about the
appropriate amount and duration of an award to the broad discretion
of individual trial courts. As Carol Rogerson observes, the result was
a return to historical notions of spousal support based on need and
dependency in which "needs and means" dominated decision making
and judges vested with broad discretion acted on individualized understandings of spousal support.[24] Across the country, spousal support
became increasingly unpredictable and uncertain.

3. The Guidelines

By 2001, dissatisfaction with the broad discretionary support regime that
followed *Bracklow* led the Canadian Department of Justice to organize a
project to explore the possibility of spousal support guidelines.[25] In the
years following *Bracklow*, a significant disparity in the spouses' incomes
at divorce came to signal an entitlement to support, which left the amount
and duration of a support order as the most troublesome questions.[26] The
guideline project thus represented an effort to aid lawyers, judges, and
others in determining the size and duration of a spousal support award.
The guideline project was designed to reflect current practice rather than
to reform it, and was grounded on an assumption that despite the uncertainty and unpredictability of support decisions, there were dominant patterns that could be identified and incorporated into advisory guidelines.

Professors Carol Rogerson and Rollie Thompson were named co-
directors of what became a seven-year project. A draft version of the
Spousal Support Advisory Guidelines (SSAG) was released in 2005, followed by a final version in 2008. As Carol Rogerson notes, the guidelines
are "complex," filling 166 pages, and yet do not attempt to resolve many
of the toughest questions about spousal support—what to do about the
payor's income increases, retirement, or responsibility for a new family, and what to do about the recipient's remarriage or repartnering.
Moreover, the guidelines do not precisely quantify support, but rather

generate wide ranges for the value and duration of support awards, leaving the ultimate choice to the discretion of a trial court based on the facts of a particular case. Still, the Canadian support guidelines are impressive. Alimony is itself complex, and Canada has succeeded on a national level in making these difficult decisions *more* certain and predictable, if not completely so. The Canadian guidelines are organized into two basic formulae—one for marriages *without* minor children at the time of divorce and another for marriages *with* minor children.

A. WITHOUT CHILDREN: THE SPOUSAL SUPPORT ONLY FORMULA

When divorcing couples have no minor children, either because they have never had children or because their children are no longer minors, the Canadian guidelines apply a "Without–Child Support Formula." Under this formula, the *value* of a spousal support award begins with calculation of the disparity in the spouses' gross incomes. This disparity is then multiplied by a percentage, which ranges from 1.5 percent to 2 percent for each year of cohabitation, up to a maximum of 50 percent. The maximum range is capped at income equalization.

If, for example, the parties were married for ten years, and A's income at divorce was $100,000 and B's income was $40,000, support ranges from $9,000 to $12,000 annually. The income disparity, $60,000, is multiplied by either 15 percent (1.5 percent times ten years) or 20 percent (2 percent times ten years). Fifteen percent of $60,000 is $9,000 per year ($750 monthly). Twenty percent of $60,000 is $12,000 per year ($1,000 monthly).

If A and B cohabited for twenty years, support ranges from $18,000 to $24,000 annually. The income disparity, $60,000, is multiplied by either 30 percent (1.5 percent times twenty years) or 40 percent (2 percent times twenty years). Thirty percent of $60,000 is $18,000 per year ($1,500 monthly). Forty percent of $60,000 is $24,000 per year ($2,000 monthly).

The *duration* of spousal support is based on the length of the marriage—from one-half to one year of support for each year of cohabitation. Duration is indefinite (unspecified but not necessarily lifelong) in either of two cases: (1) the marriage lasted twenty years or more, or (2) the marriage lasted at least five years and the number of years of marriage plus the age of the recipient total sixty-five or more ("the rule of sixty-five"). To return to our previous example, if the parties cohabited for ten years (and the rule of sixty-five does not apply), A would pay between $9,000 and $12,000 per year in spousal support for a period of between five and ten years. If the parties cohabited for twenty years and the rule of sixty-five applies, A would pay between $18,000 and $24,000 per year for an indefinite period. As Carol Rogerson and Rollie Thompson explain, the without-children guideline formula is based on the principle of merger over time, a rationale we will explore more fully in chapter 8.

B. WITH CHILDREN: THE CHILD SUPPORT
PLUS SPOUSAL SUPPORT FORMULA

When divorcing couples have minor children, the spousal support formula takes into account the child support obligation and so is more complex, employing multiple formulae and relying on computer software for computation. The basic formula applies when the higher-income spouse pays both child support and spousal support, and the lower-income spouse is the primary residential parent after divorce. Under this formula, the *value* of a spousal support award begins with calculation of each parent's "individual net disposable income" (INDI)—the income remaining for each parent after deducting child-support obligations. The INDI computation includes factors such as taxes and government credits and benefits. The with-children formula then calculates the amount of spousal support that will leave the recipient with between 40 percent and 46 percent of the parents' combined INDI. Like the without-children formula, the with-children formula generates a range of values. In an example from Rogerson and Thompson involving a mother who is the primary residential parent of two children, the father's payment of child and spousal support would leave the mother's household with between 52 percent and 57 percent of the net household income and the father with 48 percent to 43 percent.

The *duration* of an initial spousal support order under the with-children formula is indefinite, but the guidelines offer "soft" durational limits.[27] The guidelines offer two tests for estimating duration: a length-of-marriage test and an age-of-children test. Whichever formula produces the longer duration under these two formulae trumps. The length-of-marriage formula mirrors the durational formula for support in divorces without children—one-half to one year of support for each year of marriage (cohabitation). The age-of-children formula sets a durational range between (1) when the youngest child starts full-time school and (2) when the youngest child completes high school. By way of example, Rogerson and Thompson offer the case of a couple with two children (ages eight and ten) who were married for eleven years. In this case, the length-of-marriage test suggests a duration of between 5.5 and 11 years. The age-of-children test suggests a duration of between 0 and 10 years. Because duration under the length-of-marriage test is longer, that formula trumps. As previously noted, however, the initial spousal support order has an indefinite duration, with the formula offering only a suggested range for subsequent variations (modifications). As Carol Rogerson and Rollie Thompson explain, the with-children guideline formula is based on the principle of "parental partnership," a rationale we will explore more fully in chapter 8.

C. AN ASSESSMENT

Early reaction to the Canadian spousal support guidelines was mixed. While most lawyers and some judges welcomed the practical guidance, critics objected that the guidelines intruded on judicial discretion, had no statutory basis, and reflected a "hidden agenda."[28] The guidelines received a major boost in 2005 with the decision of the British Columbia Court of Appeal in *Yemchuk v. Yemchuk*.[29] The *Yemchuk* court described the guidelines as a "useful tool" that reflected current law.[30] As project directors Rogerson and Thompson report, "[i]mmediately, *Yemchuk* gave legitimacy to the [guidelines] throughout British Columbia, one of Canada's largest provinces, . . . and had a radiating effect upon submissions by counsel across Canada."[31] Appellate courts in New Brunswick and Ontario subsequently endorsed the guidelines,[32] and courts in six other Canadian provinces used the guidelines in varying degrees.[33] The Quebec Court of Appeal, however, criticized the guidelines in a 2006 case, ending their use in that province.[34]

Rogerson and Thompson report that the guidelines have dramatically changed the Canadian law of spousal support, altering both the calculation of support and perspectives on support outcomes. They observe that the guidelines have improved Canadian support law by shaping client expectations, setting a starting point for negotiation, reducing the number of litigated cases, simplifying resolution of typical cases, permitting calculation of lump-sum awards of support, identifying "outlier" decisions and forcing courts to explain or change them, forcing gender-neutrality in support outcomes, establishing a standard for appellate review, and providing a structure for the exercise of judicial discretion that makes decisions more logical and transparent.[35] At the same time, Rogerson and Thompson frankly acknowledge several problems that have arisen from use of the guidelines, including the unthinking use of the guidelines by lawyers who claim the low guideline figure for payors and the high guideline figure for recipients, and by judges who default to the midrange; the failure to consider exceptions to the guideline ranges; the failure to consider the facts of atypical cases; more frequent claims for retroactive spousal support; and the inaccessibility of the computer-driven with-children formula to unrepresented litigants.[36]

While the Canadian guidelines are no panacea, they are a laudable effort to make alimony more predictable, more certain, and more equitable. As we will see in the next chapter, the success of the Canadian experiment with guidelines is due partly to its identification of an underlying rationale for alimony that provides the basis for the guideline numbers. Absence of such a rationale has hampered efforts in the United States to develop consistent guidelines among the states and generally to rethink the law of alimony. It is to this issue that we now turn.

PART III

Alimony Theory

It would be so nice if something would make sense for a change.
—*Alice in Wonderland* (Walt Disney Productions, 1951)

As we have seen, the absence of a contemporary rationale for alimony is more than an abstract concern. Without any answer to the question of *why* someone should be compelled to support an ex-spouse, judges vested with broad discretion are given free rein to determine equity according to internal codes, influenced by the widespread disdain for alimony and by myths and misconceptions about the reality and costs of family labor. As a result, general alimony awards are unpredictable, uncertain, and rare. The absence of a contemporary rationale for alimony also confounds efforts to choose among the many guideline formulae that have been offered to quantify alimony, and leaves alimony vulnerable to hype—to impassioned cries for new limits on alimony enflamed by anecdotal, aberrational horror stories that characterize a new wave of anti-alimony reform efforts.

The absence of a contemporary rationale for alimony imposes yet another cost, and it is a significant one. Because alimony cannot explain itself, it cannot provide a reasoned answer to the divorcing spouse who is hard-hit by an alimony decision—to the spouse who is ordered to pay alimony, or to the spouse who is denied alimony. This inability to offer

legitimate reasons for decisions, which sometimes inflict brutal consequences, suggests an arbitrariness and capriciousness that undermine
the integrity of the legal system. A dramatic example lies in the near-
universal rule that alimony terminates upon a recipient's remarriage.

6

Reasons Matter

Alimony, Intuition, and the Remarriage-Termination Rule

Here we go again
She'll break my heart again
I'll play the part again
One more time.
—Ray Charles, "Here We Go Again," in *Modern Sounds in
Country and Western Music* (Rhino Records, 1988)

Marriage is a wildly popular institution—so popular that failure of a
first marriage usually does not deter spouses from marrying again.
Approximately 75 percent of divorcing women remarry within ten
years, 54 percent within five years.[1] These second marriages are at least
as likely to fail as first-time marriages.[2]

For some who marry a second time, marriage demands a hefty admis-
sion price not imposed on first-timers: any alimony claim against a former spouse will likely terminate. The intuition of most observers is that
this is the right result—an ex-husband should not pay alimony to a former wife who is married to someone else.[3] Indeed, the vast majority
of states, either through case or statutory law, provide that a recipient's
remarriage automatically terminates alimony, or at least creates a prima
facie case for termination. Notwithstanding the near-universality of the
remarriage-termination rule, and its recent endorsement by the American Law Institute (ALI), the rule has no conceptual basis in contemporary

Much of this chapter was previously published as "One More Time: Alimony, Intuition, and
the Remarriage-Termination Rule," *Indiana Law Journal* 81 (Summer 2006): 971.

understandings of alimony. As the ALI acknowledges, the underlying rationale for the remarriage-termination rule is "remarkably unclear."[4]

Intuition is not enough to sustain a rule with such a brutal impact. Consider, for example, the case of Helen and Anthony, who divorce after a twenty-six-year marriage.[5] During marriage, Helen worked as a full-time homemaker and caregiver of the couple's children while Anthony pursued a career. At divorce, Anthony earned $158,000 annually as a bank executive while Helen, who "qualified for only unskilled, entry level positions at minimum wage," began work as a part-time medical assistant earning $90 a week. A divorce decree divided the spouses' marital property, ordered Anthony to pay $500 a week in alimony, and set Helen and Anthony free to begin new lives as single persons. One and a half years later, Helen married again. Her new husband earned $28,000 annually, $7,800 of which he paid in child support. Nevertheless, upon Anthony's petition, a court terminated Helen's alimony.

If this scene sounds no equitable alarms, it may be because the frame has been artificially frozen in time. But of course Helen's story does not end with her remarriage. Suppose that her second marriage, sadly, also ends in divorce, as many remarriages do. Unable to qualify for alimony based on a short second marriage, Helen is left to fend for herself, armed with two years of undergraduate work, $90 a week in earnings, and a twenty-six-year history as a caregiver for the family she and Anthony once shared. Helen's brief remarriage has freed Anthony to enjoy all the career rewards of his role as family breadwinner and left Helen alone to bear all the career costs of her role as family caregiver. It is not much of a stretch to suppose that Helen feels mistreated by a law that evidences such indifference to her past contributions and present economic straits.

What is the answer to Helen's sense of unfairness? Can the law honestly tell her that termination of Anthony's alimony obligation is fair to her, painful as it may be? Or, if not fair to her, that the remarriage-termination rule is a necessary part of the way things must be—part of a broader scheme of social justice? Helen and other alimony recipients deserve an explanation. It is hardly a sufficient answer to point out that if Anthony's payments had been part of the division of property, perhaps installments on a buyout of Helen's interest in the marital home, rather than alimony, her remarriage would have had no effect on Anthony's obligation. Why is Helen's right to a buyout of her interest in a house, a Mercedes, or a yacht more deserving of protection than her right to compensation for her lost career opportunities or to a buyout of her interest in the marital partnership? Helen deserves an answer.

A. The Remarriage-Termination Rule

The remarriage-termination rule begins with the general principle that an alimony award, unlike a division of property, is modifiable. Often, judicial authority to modify alimony is specifically granted by statute. The Uniform Marriage and Divorce Act (UMDA), for example, allows modification "only upon a showing of changed circumstances so substantial and continuing as to make the terms unconscionable."[6] Ordinarily, the changed circumstances that trigger modification involve economics—a reduction in the payor's resources, for example, or an improvement in the recipient's financial status—that warrant a decrease in alimony. When an alimony recipient remarries, however, a different rule applies: alimony is not merely modified, but *terminated*, usually with no possibility of revival, and without regard to the financial impact of the recipient's new marriage. Remarriage alone is thus the termination trigger, typically without regard to any other factors usually relevant to modification. Whether it appears in statutory or case law, this notion that alimony should terminate upon a recipient's remarriage is a baseline of contemporary American law.

1. Statutory Termination Rules

The majority of states provide by statute that alimony terminates automatically upon a recipient's remarriage. One court's survey classified automatic termination statutes into three rough categories: (1) immediate termination on remarriage;[7] (2) termination upon petition and proof of remarriage;[8] and (3) termination unless an agreement or decree provide otherwise.[9] A typical statute in the last category, which is the most common, might provide as follows:

> Unless otherwise agreed in writing or expressly provided in the decree, the obligation to pay future [alimony] is terminated on the death of either party or the remarriage of the party receiving [alimony].[10]

Such language leaves little room for equitable entreaties that alimony should survive remarriage in the absence of an agreement or decree requiring it. Moreover, establishing such a continuation provision may be no easy matter, as some courts require exceedingly explicit language to avoid termination. A California court, for example, determined that an agreement making alimony "non-modifiable for any reason whatsoever" did not prevent alimony termination on the wife's remarriage, since "nonmodifiable" does not mean "nonterminable."[11]

A few statutes authorize but do not require termination of alimony upon a recipient's remarriage, leaving the termination decision to trial court discretion. An Oklahoma statute, for example, requires a court to terminate alimony on remarriage unless the recipient (1) petitions for continuance within ninety days of remarriage and (2) demonstrates that "support is still needed and that circumstances have not rendered payment . . . inequitable."[12] As one Oklahoma court explained, however, even this language "envisions termination after remarriage in ordinary circumstances."[13]

2. Judicial Termination Rules

In the absence of a statute specifically addressing remarriage, courts have generally adopted one of three views: (1) remarriage automatically terminates alimony; (2) remarriage creates a prima facie case for termination; or (3) remarriage is a factor to consider in determining whether modification is warranted. Clearly, the impact of remarriage is most dramatic under the first view and least significant under the last.

A few courts have endorsed the hard-line rule that alimony terminates automatically upon a recipient's remarriage without regard to financial impact. Alaska courts, for example, have held that a recipient's remarriage "requires the termination of alimony as a matter of law."[14] The Alaska Supreme Court applied this automatic-termination rule to cut off alimony to a wife who had remarried, notwithstanding a provision in the divorce decree that alimony "remain in full force and effect until such time as [the wife] gets in a position to support herself."[15]

The majority of courts have taken a less draconian position, adopting a rule that remarriage creates a prima facie case for termination, but allowing for continuance in cases of extraordinary circumstances. Contrary to general alimony modification principles, which require a party dissatisfied with the status quo to prove that circumstances justify change, this prima facie rule requires the party resisting change to prove that extraordinary circumstances justify the status quo. This evidentiary shift places a heavy burden on the alimony recipient, "affirm[ing] the general principle that alimony should terminate on . . . remarriage."[16]

Courts do not always agree on what constitutes extraordinary circumstances. While many courts have determined that a second spouse's inability to support an alimony recipient at the standard of living of the first marriage does not establish extraordinary circumstances, a few courts have reached contrary conclusions under extreme facts. Proof that the first marriage was long or the recipient's caregiving contributions extensive is unlikely to establish extraordinary circumstances. Some courts have treated annulment of a recipient's remarriage as an extraordinary circumstance justifying continuation of alimony, especially if the second "marriage" was very brief,[17] though other courts have disagreed.[18]

Finally, in the absence of a controlling statute, a few courts have taken the position that remarriage is simply a changed circumstance to be considered, along with other factors, in determining whether termination is appropriate. Of the three judicial approaches to remarriage, this final approach is clearly most consistent with general alimony modification rules, which require the party seeking modification to bear the burden of proving changed circumstances. Of course the result of an inquiry into whether changed circumstances warrant modification may depend on a particular court's attitude toward the baseline view that alimony should not survive a recipient's remarriage. Given the dominance of the remarriage-termination rule, one might expect that even judges applying general modification principles will terminate alimony on remarriage, though not every court has done so.

One developing distinction in the remarriage cases requires mention. Some courts have held that modification rules, including the remarriage-termination rule, do not apply to cases of nontraditional alimony, such as reimbursement alimony. As we have seen, reimbursement alimony aims to compensate a spouse for past financial contributions, typically to the other spouse's education or training. One difficulty with this tiered approach, however, is that reimbursement alimony is not always clearly distinguishable from other forms of alimony, especially when a decree or agreement fails to label the award or to specify its function. Nevertheless, the willingness of some courts to link the remarriage-termination rule to an alimony rationale such as reimbursement for educational expenses is a welcome retreat from the knee-jerk reaction to remarriage that underlies the baseline rule.

3. The ALI Termination Rule

In its recent *Principles of the Law of Family Dissolution* (*ALI Principles*), the ALI endorses the majority statutory rule that alimony should end automatically at the remarriage of the recipient.[19] The *Principles* are intended to provide a template for state law and, given the prestige of the ALI, have the potential to direct the course of law reform. Like many statutory remarriage-termination rules, the ALI recognizes that parties may contract out of the automatic-termination rule. In an apparent concession to the judicial prima facie rule, the ALI also authorizes continuation of alimony where termination "would work a substantial injustice because of facts not present in most cases."[20] The ALI intends an exceedingly narrow definition of the unusual facts necessary to avoid termination, noting that only "rare cases" will fall within this exception and giving a decidedly peculiar example of such a case: after a thirty-year marriage, a wife "marries" a bigamist who dies one month later.[21] If these facts are an indication of the frequency of the kind of facts that will justify continuation of alimony beyond remarriage, the ALI's exception will be rarely invoked indeed.

Drawing an analogy to case law on reimbursement awards, the ALI also recognizes that the small proportion of alimony orders that are based on restitution should be nonmodifiable.[22] These restitutionary awards will generally involve short marriages and unusual circumstances.[23]

The persistence of the remarriage-termination rule in statutes, case law, and now in the *ALI Principles* does not, of course, itself justify the rule. But neither does the rule's harsh impact on alimony recipients necessarily make it inconsistent with principles of social justice. If the remarriage rule is to continue as a baseline of divorce law, however, it must have an articulable, legitimate rationale. The search for this rationale begins with a look at some of the rationales that have been offered to explain the purpose of alimony.

B. Unraveling Intuition: Alimony Rationales and the Remarriage-Termination Rule

If alimony has served its purpose, it should end; if that purpose has not been served, however, the case for termination becomes more difficult. Identifying the purpose of alimony is thus an essential first step in assessing the legitimacy of the remarriage-termination rule.

1. Historical Rationales: Lifetime Support and Fungible Husbands

As we saw in chapter 2, the rationale for alimony was once simple enough: upon marriage a husband undertook a lifetime obligation to support his wife. While he could obtain a legal separation, rarely could he fully sever marital ties. The husband's duty of support thus continued throughout the wife's life, and alimony was the tool for enforcing his obligation. An integral part of this vision was the system of coverture, under which a married woman's identity merged into that of her husband. As Blackstone explained, "the very being or legal existence of the woman is suspended during the marriage, or at least is incorporated and consolidated into that of the husband under whose wing, protection, and cover, she performs everything."[24]

If these visions of limited divorce and lifetime support sound peculiar to contemporary ears, they do one thing quite well—they explain the remarriage-termination rule. However a husband's support obligation managed to survive divorce, that obligation is surely cut off when a new man takes on the task of supporting her. Upon remarriage, a new man becomes the ex-wife's protector and provider, taking her under his wing and finally releasing the first husband from responsibility for her. This vision is neat enough: a "husband has a lifetime obligation to keep his wife from need until the obligation [is] assumed by another."[25] To take this reasoning a step further, allowing a woman to be the beneficiary of two husbandly duties of support would amount to polygamy, or at least to prostitution. The implication of such reasoning is that while a wife requires a husband's support, the law does not much care *which* husband supports her. One husband is enough, and any husband will do. The remarriage-termination rule thus seems historically grounded in an unsettling view of husbands as necessary, if fungible, providers.

2. Fault-Based Rationales: Damage Awards and the Ultimate Betrayal

If the appearance of absolute divorce undercut alimony's rationale, fault-based divorce sometimes supplies a new one. Cast as the remedy of an innocent spouse against a guilty one, divorce under a fault-based regime depends upon proof of marital wrongdoing, such as adultery, cruelty, or abandonment. As we saw in chapter 2, the no-fault reforms of the 1970s did not entirely eliminate fault from judicial decision making. Many states simply added a no-fault ground to their existing fault-based laws. Even among states that disallow fault as a ground for divorce, marital fault may affect the economic consequences of divorce.

Fault may indeed explain alimony—at least in some states and in some cases. An adulterous spouse, for example, might be required to pay alimony as damages for breach of the marriage contract. Of course such a fault-based rationale would require only guilty spouses to pay alimony to innocent spouses; that is, no innocent spouse would ever pay alimony and no guilty spouse would ever receive alimony. Because such a limitation does not describe the law of alimony, fault can at best provide a partial rationale.

If alimony is cast as a damage award against a guilty spouse, what explains the remarriage-termination rule? Drawing further on the contract analogy, alimony might be designed to give an injured wife the benefit of her bargain—that is, to put her in the position she would have been in had her husband shared his income with her, for life according to traditional views of marriage. Nothing in this analogy to contract, however, explains why alimony should terminate upon a wife's remarriage. Certainly, in contract generally, a party's good fortune subsequent to a damage award does not require her to forfeit her damages. Even when a wife's remarriage amounts to good fortune, it is difficult to see why her improved financial footing should absolve a former husband of liability for the wrongdoing that triggered the alimony award. A contracting party who wins the lottery need not return a damage award. And of course not every remarriage is a winning lottery ticket. Yet the remarriage-termination rule cuts off alimony, good fortune or no.

An analogy to mitigation of damages is unhelpful. The mitigation principle ensures that a court "ordinarily will not compensate an injured party for loss that that party could have avoided by making efforts appropriate, in the eyes of the court, to the circumstances."[26] If applied to alimony termination, mitigation principles would suggest the peculiar conclusion that a wife should remarry in order to mitigate her losses and save her ex-husband money. Mitigation principles are also awkward because the timing is wrong. Opportunities to mitigate loss will ordinarily serve to decrease a damage calculation before it is reduced to judgment. In the case of divorce, however, a wife *cannot* avoid loss through remarriage at the time alimony is initially calculated, since she is not yet divorced. While it is true that alimony is modifiable and thus theoretically capable of repeated recalculation, mitigation principles would at most support a reduction in alimony commensurate with a wife's improved financial status, yet the remarriage rule usually applies without regard to financial consequence and completely *eliminates*, rather than *proportionately reduces*, alimony.

Neither can principles of novation or renunciation explain the remarriage-termination rule. Novation occurs when a creditor (the ex-wife) takes a third party's promise to pay (the new husband's support obligation) in satisfaction of a debt (the ex-husband's alimony obligation). Under this analogy, the new husband's support obligation would substitute for the ex-husband's alimony obligation, thus discharging the ex-husband. The difficulty with this reasoning is that novation requires the agreement of the original parties—that is, both the ex-husband *and* the ex-wife. Novation thus explains the remarriage-termination rule only if the wife's remarriage constitutes her implicit agreement to forgo alimony, a strained interpretation of remarriage given the negative economic consequences of termination and, in the end, an interpretation that begs rather than answers the question of why alimony terminates on remarriage. The failure of an ex-wife to expressly forgo alimony similarly undercuts any rationale for termination based on renunciation of rights, since renunciation also supposes a voluntary agreement to forgo alimony. Contract principles simply cannot explain the remarriage-termination rule.

Is it possible that this analogy to contract disappoints because it fails to consider *all* the contracts between the ex-spouses? Has the wife breached some unarticulated post-divorce contract with her ex-husband that entitles him to an offset against his alimony obligation? If this is the theory that explains alimony termination, it is difficult to identify the precise nature of the ex-wife's broken promise. Is it a promise of loyalty and good faith, of sexual fidelity, a promise to remain unattached to another man? Does a wife's remarriage thus constitute the ultimate betrayal of her former husband—a betrayal egregious enough to justify termination of his alimony obligation? Surely not.

3. No-Fault Rationales: Handouts and Masked Need

Central to the no-fault movement was a new vision of divorce as an opportunity for a fresh start and a clean break—a vision that leaves little room for alimony. As we have seen, general no-fault alimony statutes give courts discretion to award alimony on the basis of a spouse's "need," though "need" is not defined. Moreover, "need" alone provides no rationale for alimony, for it fails to explain why a former spouse should be responsible for a claimant's need.

Can a need-based alimony model explain the remarriage-termination rule? Not by a long shot. If need triggers an alimony handout, then termination of alimony should depend on the elimination of need (or a payor's inability to meet need). Yet the remarriage-termination rule commonly applies without regard to need. Under the automatic-termination rule and, except in extraordinary cases, also under the prima facie rule, alimony terminates upon a recipient's remarriage whether or not her financial position has improved.

Even when an alimony recipient marries someone of sufficient earnings or assets to maintain or improve her standard of living, this economic improvement may be only temporary. Should her second marriage also end, an alimony recipient may be just as needy as she was prior to her remarriage, especially when the second marriage is short and she therefore can qualify for little or no new alimony. This is an especially serious concern for older women who remarry after a long-term first marriage. Advancing age is an irreversible impediment to a second long-term marriage and thus a counter-indicator of significant alimony the second time around. Moreover, the job or career opportunities available before a first marriage may not spontaneously reappear when a second marriage ends. The education, career, and personal life choices available at age twenty-five may simply not be available ten or twenty or thirty years later. The point is that while remarriage may mask need, it does not necessarily eliminate it. At most, a need-based alimony model can support suspension or reduction of alimony during remarriages that improve a recipient's financial status, but a need-based model provides no basis for—and in fact clearly contradicts—a rule that terminates alimony on remarriage without regard to the financial consequence of remarriage.

4. The ALI Rationale: Perpetuating the Inexplicable

The *ALI Principles* propose a dramatic recharacterization of alimony as "compensation for loss rather than relief of need," a rationale we will explore in the next chapter. Whether or not a loss-allocation model is the best the ALI could have done, its rigorous rethinking of alimony is a critical step toward understanding the proper role of alimony in a gender-neutral, no-fault regime. Yet the ALI's careful crafting of a rationale for alimony and healthy scrutiny of current law abruptly end as it confronts the remarriage-termination rule. Without much fanfare and without much discussion, the ALI endorses a version of the automatic termination rule for its primary alimony awards.

What explains the automatic termination of alimony under the ALI's loss-allocation model? Elimination of a recipient's loss is clearly not the answer, since alimony ends automatically and almost always without regard to the financial impact of remarriage. Acknowledging that "[t]he modern explanation for the traditional remarriage rule is remarkably unclear given its universality,"[27] the ALI halfheartedly casts about for an explanation and comes up with three possibilities.

First, says the ALI, although the recipient's loss may not end on remarriage, the payor's responsibility for that loss does end. This statement of course rephrases but does not answer the question of *why* the payor's responsibility ends.

Protecting the integrity of the second marriage is the ALI's next rationale. Noting that personal and financial exclusivity are an essential part of marriage, the ALI claims that termination of alimony is necessary to protect the integrity of a recipient's new marriage. "To require support of the second marriage by the first spouse," says the ALI, "would cast doubt on the second marriage's authenticity."[28] This reasoning sounds suspiciously like historical rationales for alimony termination: a wife can belong to only one husband at a time. A married woman needs a husband's support, but only until she finds a new husband to support her—one husband at a time, please. To allow a wife to be the beneficiary of two husbandly support obligations would smack of bigamy, and since bigamy is forbidden, the second "marriage" would be void. Is this what the ALI means by "cast[ing] doubt on the second marriage's authenticity"?[29]

Equally perplexing is the ALI's failure to consider the gender-neutral implications of its second-marriage-authenticity principle. If termination of alimony is necessary to ensure the authenticity of an alimony recipient's (a wife's) remarriage, why isn't it also necessary to ensure the authenticity of an alimony payor's (a husband's) remarriage? That is, why doesn't alimony terminate automatically upon a payor's remarriage? Just as a wife can have only one husband, a husband can have only one wife. Under this reasoning, no husband should be required to support two wives at one time. While suggestions of this view do indeed appear in anti-alimony rhetoric that seeks to preserve an ex-husband's opportunities for remarriage, alimony obligations do not terminate automatically upon a payor's remarriage.

Finally, the ALI suggests a rationale for termination based on recovery of psychic loss. "The most important loss on divorce," it observes, "may be the failed expectation of having a close and caring lifetime companion."[30] Because such loss ordinarily cannot be measured, it is necessarily disregarded at divorce. "Remarriage," however, "presumptively solves this measurement problem, for the inference naturally arises that the obligee derives great nonfinancial rewards from the new relationship overall, whatever its financial component."[31] The ALI then reaches the curious conclusion that "[c]ontinuing compensatory payments after the obligee's remarriage would make overcompensation likely because the obligee could combine the first spouse's earnings with both the personal and financial qualities of the second spouse."[32] The message is that an alimony recipient's presumed joy on remarriage should trigger financial loss in order to avoid her overcompensation. What? If the ALI is serious about this psychic-loss rationale, shouldn't it have explained why no one would ever think that alimony payments should *increase* with a payor's remarriage, which has presumptively brought him psychic joy? In the end, the ALI's rhetoric is an effort to rationalize intuition rather than a rigorous attempt to provide a real rationale for the remarriage-termination rule. Courts enforcing the rule have done no better.

C. Dressing Up Intuition: Judicial Reasoning and the Remarriage-Termination Rule

Judicial attempts to provide a rationale for the remarriage-termination rule are few in number and disappointing in substance. Efforts to explain termination come disproportionately from early courts, contemporary courts being more prone to enforce the rule than to justify it. Judicial rationales for the remarriage-termination rule fall into three rough categories: (1) unseemliness, (2) election, and (3) untidiness.

1. Unseemliness

By far the most common explanation for the remarriage-termination rule is the conviction that to allow a woman to collect support from two men—her ex-husband and her current husband—would be positively unseemly. In a much-cited case from 1930, a Connecticut court explained that to continue alimony beyond a wife's remarriage

> would offend public policy and good morals. It is so illogical and unreasonable that a court of equity should not tolerate it. Well has it been characterized as *legally and socially unseemly*.[33]

In a much-quoted passage from 1968, a Nebraska court agreed:

> [I]t is against public policy that a woman should have support or its equivalent during the same period from each of two men. . . . *Aside from positive unseemliness, it is illogical* and *unreasonable*.[34]

Other courts have opted for language of distaste and repugnance. As a Kansas court explained in 1967,

> It is *distasteful* to permit a divorced wife to hold both her former husband under a decree of alimony and her present husband under the marital duty of support which inheres in every marriage contract. . . . It is *repugnant* to a sense of justice for one man to be supporting the wife of another who has recently assumed the legal obligation for her support.[35]

While later courts have sometimes taken up the rhetoric of unseemliness, more often they have softened their prose, opting for the less disdainful and less colorful language of unreasonableness. "To permit a spouse to elicit the support of two spouses simultaneously," said the Alaska Supreme Court in 1982, "would be *unreasonable*."[36] The Massachusetts Supreme Court agreed, explaining in 1995 that ordinarily it is "'*illogical and unreasonable*' that a spouse should receive support from a current spouse and a former spouse at the same time."[37] Also in 1995, the Kansas Supreme Court opined that it is "*against public policy* to allow a payee to hold a claim against his or her former spouse for maintenance and hold a claim against his or her current spouse for the marital duty of support."[38] Speaking in 1981, an Alabama court seemed more alarmed by the possibility of continuance of alimony beyond remarriage. "Such is *unconscionable*," said the Court. "[It] is *very inequitable*."[39]

What explains this judicial intuition that continuing alimony beyond a recipient's remarriage would be unseemly, repugnant, unconscionable, or at least unreasonable? While dramatic adjectives signal a conclusion rather than an explanation, the sense of impropriety evident in judicial prose hints at a familiar theme: a virtuous woman cannot have two husbands at once, and since alimony evidences a husband's support obligation, it must end when a woman takes a new husband. Under the historical model of alimony, a wife needs and deserves her husband's protective cover only until a new man takes on the obligation to support her. No woman can or should have the support of two men at the same time, for this would amount to polygamy, or at least to prostitution, both of which are positively unseemly. The problem with such reasoning, of course, is that it reflects nineteenth-century views of marriage that have little in common with contemporary notions of marriage as a partnership of equals.

2. Election

Another popular explanation for the remarriage-termination rule is that the wife who chooses to remarry has thereby elected to relinquish her alimony. As the Nebraska Supreme Court explained in 1968, an alimony recipient has a "privilege to abandon the provision made by the decree of the court for her support . . . and when she has done so, the law will require her to abide by her *election*."[40] "If the dependent spouse has entered into a new marital relationship," said the Alaska Supreme Court, "we think that the remarriage should serve as an *election* between the support provided by the alimony award and the legal obligation of support embodied in the new marital relationship."[41] "The policy behind terminating sustenance alimony after remarriage is that the wife has *elected* to be supported by a new husband," reasoned the Ohio Supreme Court.[42]

The election rationale does not depend on whether a second spouse is actually able to provide support, as one court acknowledged in terminating alimony upon a recipient's remarriage to a man whose income consisted of social security and minimal retirement benefits.[43] The low income of the wife's new husband, said the court, "in no way diminishes the choice she voluntarily made to share her living expenses with him."[44]

Closely tied to the election rationale is the proposition that upon remarriage the second husband substitutes for the first. As a Nebraska court explained in 1956, "[t]he reason for the discontinuance of alimony allowance upon the recipient contracting another marriage is that, in that event, the legal obligation of the second husband supplants that of the first."[45] "Absent extraordinary circumstances," said the Massachusetts Supreme Court in 1995, "the former spouse should not be required to pay alimony when another person has assumed the support obligation."[46]

At the core of the election rationale is the dubious assumption that remarriage necessarily implies a choice to forgo alimony. What explains this assumption? Is it the historical view of alimony as a husband's obligation to sustain his wife, from which it must naturally follow that only one man at a time can owe a woman this obligation? *Why* must an alimony recipient choose between remarriage and alimony? Why can't she choose remarriage *and* alimony? Rather than offering a reasoned explanation for this forced choice, the election rationale merely describes the consequence of the remarriage-termination rule. It is thus the remarriage-termination rule, rather than any reasoned rationale for it, that forces the recipient to choose between remarriage and alimony. The circularity of the election rationale makes it wholly unconvincing.

3. Untidiness

A final termination rationale comes from courts concerned with the possibility of multiple divorces and multiple alimony awards. As one judge described the problem,

> Jane Doe is married to John Doe; they are divorced and he is required to pay alimony. Jane then marries John Smith; he must support her by state law and the trial judge, when they are divorced, orders alimony. Jane now receives alimony from two different men. Enter Fred Smith. He marries Jane but, alas, alack, this third marriage goes awry and they are divorced. Yes, the trial court orders alimony as Fred is very well-to-do and is convinced Jane should have support (alimony) money. Where will this cycle of repetitive alimony (support) end? It should end with the first remarriage.[47]

"[G]ood housekeeping," said another court, "would suggest that when a recipient of alimony remarries, an appropriate order recognizing that fact, and the cessation of the alimony obligation, should be entered."[48] This concern for tidiness surely overstates the risks and costs of multiple alimony awards. Alimony is only rarely ordered, and long-term awards are the exception rather than the rule. Moreover, a significant factor in determining the duration and value of an alimony award is the length of the marriage. How many significant-term marriages can one spouse have?

Assuming arguendo that multiple, long-term alimony orders are likely, the question becomes whether the costs of such untidiness outweigh the benefits of continued alimony. If alimony is an entitlement rather than a handout, as contemporary alimony models suggest, and an entitlement of significant economic importance to those who receive it, a concern for tidiness will rarely outweigh the benefits of continuing alimony beyond remarriage.

D. Helen

So where does all this leave Helen? It leaves her with no alimony and no satisfactory explanation for why, after twenty-six years as a caregiver for the family she and Anthony once shared, her brief remarriage (to a man with little income) should terminate Anthony's alimony obligation.

Because she has fallen in love and made a new intimate commitment, the law has freed Anthony to alone enjoy all the career rewards of his role as family wage-earner and left Helen to alone bear all the career costs of her role as family caregiver. Why does Helen's new life trigger such significant consequences, while Anthony's new life is largely irrelevant to the law? Helen deserves an explanation, yet the law has none.

Only historical models of alimony grounded in coverture can explain the remarriage-termination rule, and these models are starkly inconsistent with modern understandings of gender equality and no-fault divorce. Other rationales—from fault-based damage awards to no-fault need models to the ALI's loss-sharing model—provide no explanation for termination of alimony upon remarriage and, in fact, provide compelling arguments against termination. The sense of impropriety and indignation that infuse occasional judicial efforts to explain the rule only confirm the suspicion that the roots of the remarriage-termination rule lie in archaic models of alimony, which cast a wife not as a marital partner, but rather as a man's burden, dependent on her husband for protection and survival until the next man comes along to relieve him of the task. This vision of burdened men and incapacitated women makes a dispiriting statement about husbands and wives and about the institution of marriage itself.

Yet the inability to explain the remarriage-termination rule has not deterred the law from applying it—brutally in cases such as Helen's. Helen and others like her have been sacrificed to an intuition without a reason. A law with integrity owes her more. Perhaps theories of alimony offered by contemporary scholars can help, and it is to these theories that we now turn.

7

The Search for a Contemporary Rationale

Alimony is complex. Nowhere is this complexity more evident than in the search for a conceptual basis for alimony in contemporary marriage. Numerous commentators have proposed theories of alimony that aim to answer a simple question: Why should anyone be forced to share income with a former spouse? If divorce severs the tie between spouses, if each spouse is entitled to a clean break and a fresh start as no-fault laws teach, what is the rationale for alimony? Contemporary commentators have long struggled to explain alimony in an age of easy divorce and equality rhetoric, but there is still no consensus on the answer to these questions.

In extreme cases, the pragmatic justification for alimony is simple enough: alimony protects the state from the job of supporting a divorced spouse who without alimony would be thrust into poverty. Indeed, as we saw in chapter 4, state statutes typically identify a claimant's need as

An earlier version of this chapter was published as "Alimony Theory," *Family Law Quarterly* 45 (2011): 271.

an alimony trigger. But need alone does not explain why one's ex-spouse rather than one's children, siblings, parents, or community should be responsible for meeting need. Moreover, trial courts are given broad discretion to define "need," and state self-interest does not explain cases in which need is defined in ways that have little to do with avoiding poverty. Nor can pragmatism alone answer the many questions surrounding an alimony award: How much? How long? On what grounds modification or termination?

The law's inability to articulate a justification for alimony is more than an abstract concern. The broad discretion vested in judges to determine alimony eligibility, duration, and value, in the absence of a theory to guide decision making, has produced an alimony regime marked by unpredictability, uncertainty, and confusion. Some legal actors have responded to the dysfunction of current alimony law by endorsing alimony guidelines, but the lack of consensus on an underlying theory of alimony confounds efforts to identify a mathematical formula for generating the numbers that populate these guidelines. If guideline numbers are predictable, they are not necessarily equitable or consistent across jurisdictions. The absence of an underlying theory also leaves alimony vulnerable to myth, misconception, and hype—all of which characterize a new, energized anti-alimony reform movement that has reignited sentiments popular forty years ago. Alimony is at a crossroads. If it is to survive, it must have a rationale.

But first a threshold point. If alimony has no rationale consistent with contemporary understandings of marriage, maybe it shouldn't survive. Indeed, some have argued that alimony is an outdated remedy, a relic of coverture that has outlived its time. The problem with this response is that alimony is often the only available tool for addressing inequities in the spouses' financial positioning at divorce. As we have seen, most divorcing couples have minimal property. If marital roles have disparately affected the spouses' individual earning capacity—a common scenario in the many homes in which one spouse serves as primary caregiver—divorce will set one partner free to enjoy most of the long-term benefits of marital teamwork while the other bears most of the costs. For many alimony theorists, establishing the inequity of this scenario is a first step in formulating a rationale for alimony.

A. Alimony's Work: Addressing the Disparate Impact of Teamwork

Many theorists have argued that a divorcing caregiver's reduced earning capacity is the *couple's* responsibility rather than the sole responsibility of the individual caregiver. Their reasoning begins with the point that, as we have seen, caregiving is not free. As Elisabeth Landes explained in 1978, wives' prioritization of household production (family labor) generates costs in the form of forgone earnings and "loss of market earning power through depreciation of market skills previously acquired, and forgone opportunities to invest in market skills."[1]

In 1982, the human capital theorists Elizabeth S. Beninger and Jeanne Wielage Smith cast the wife's lost earning capacity as the product of a joint marital decision.[2] "[A] wife," they reason, "forgoes the opportunity to develop her own career when a *couple makes the community decision* to allocate her time to housework and child care, and . . . this decision limits her earning potential."[3] Such a wife "is willing to forgo investment in her own career because she anticipates sharing her husband's future increased earnings."[4] If the parties divorce, however, "the husband obtains the full benefit of his increased earning power and the wife sustains the full burden of the opportunity cost of her years spent in nonmarket labor."[5]

Other theorists expanded this marital script to include primary caregivers who work outside their homes but forgo job opportunities in order to take on the lion's share of family labor. As Margaret Brinig and June Carbone observe, "the longer the marriage, the more likely even working women are . . . to have sacrificed to some degree their own financial future to further the marriage."[6] If such a marriage ends, "the benefiting spouse retains the advantages of an enhanced career or properly raised children, while the contributing spouse suffers a unilateral loss."[7] Jana Singer adds that because divorce courts "generally do not recognize career assets as marital property, . . . the husband . . . is permitted to keep most of the assets accumulated during marriage, while the wife who has invested in her family and her husband's career is deprived of a return on her *marital investment*."[8]

In his 1989 article "The Theory of Alimony," Ira Mark Ellman reasons that the division of labor in many marriages is rational.[9] Such "specialization" makes sense, Ellman writes, for "[i]f the spouses view their marriage

as a *sharing enterprise*, they will usually conclude that they are both better off if the lower earning spouse spends more on their joint domestic needs, and allows the higher earning spouse to maximize his or her
income."[10] If the parties divorce, however, "the spouse who has specialized in domestic aspects of the marriage—who has invested in the marriage rather than the market—suffers a disproportionate loss."[11] Ellman
observes that "divorce typically burdens the wife more than her husband
for two reasons: She has more difficulty finding a new spouse, and she
suffers disproportionate financial loss because of her domestic role."[12]

In 1993 Joan Williams added a powerful interpretation of the marital script to reform discourse, although her goal was not to explain or
endorse alimony. As Williams states, the "dominant family ecology"
consists of "an ideal-worker husband" supported by a flow of domestic
services from his "marginalized-caregiver" wife, whose services support
his performance as an ideal worker while simultaneously marginaliz-
ing her own market participation.[13] This specialization allows the couple to have it all—children who are cared for and a *family wage*. "The
ideal-worker's salary," Williams reasons, thus "reflects the work of two
adults: the ideal-worker's market labor and the marginalized-caregiver's
unpaid labor."[14] At divorce, however, the spouses' sharing abruptly ends
as the ideal worker's paycheck is taken from the family and assigned to
one spouse as his alone. On this reasoning, both the primary caregiver's
earning capacity losses and the primary wage-earner's earning capacity
gains are the product of marital teamwork.

In 2002 the American Law Institute (ALI) offered a vision of marital teamwork reminiscent of the one described by Beninger and Smith
twenty years earlier. In its *Principles of the Law of Family Dissolution*
(*ALI Principles*), the ALI explains that "wives continue in the great
majority of cases to care for their children, in reliance upon continued
market labor by their husbands," and that these caretaking responsibilities "typically result . . . in a residual loss in earning capacity that
continues after the children no longer require close parental supervision."[15] The ALI reasons that in such cases the caregiver has fulfilled
the couple's "*joint responsibility* for their children's care," allowing the
other parent "to have a family while also developing his or her earning
capacity." At divorce "the primary wage earner retains both that earning capacity and the parental status, while in the absence of any remedy

the primary caretaker loses any claim upon the other spouse's earnings." Two years later, in 2004, Carolyn Frantz and Hanoch Dagan warned that "excluding earning capacity from the marital estate . . . exploits the spouse whose acceptance of burdens on behalf of the *communal endeavor* is transformed by the law into self-sacrifice."[16]

As Alicia Kelly explains, the rhetoric of marital community envisions marriage as something more than a mere association of two separate individuals who happen to live together.[17] Phrases like "community decisions," "marital investments," "sharing enterprises," "the family wage," "joint responsibility," and "communal endeavors" all paint a picture of marriage as a collaborative venture in which spouses work together for the common good and expect to share the gains and losses of their teamwork. Indeed, this is the essence of contemporary marriage—a commitment to an intimate partner to share life together as a couple and the ups and downs, the costs and benefits of that life.

Marriage, of course, is much more than a financial collaboration. As Nancy Cott observes, "Marriage is like the sphinx—a conspicuous and recognizable monument on the landscape, full of secrets."[18] From a normative perspective, marriage joins parties on emotional, psychological, spiritual, sexual, and social levels in ways that vary with individuals and with time. But marriage also joins spouses on a financial level, and it is this aspect of marriage that the law is fit to address. For over thirty years, scholars from Beninger and Smith to Kelly have recognized that marriage is, among other things, a joint financial endeavor. This vision is the first step in identifying a rationale for alimony. We turn now to a series of alimony theories that build on this foundation.

B. Contemporary Theories of Alimony

Most theories of alimony focus primarily on one of three interests: (1) a claimant's contributions to the other spouse (contribution theory); (2) a claimant's expected gain (gain theory); and (3) a claimant's loss (loss theory). These foci are familiar to any student of contracts, for they suggest the three classic contract interests of restitution, expectation, and reliance. Few reformers, however, embrace a contract metaphor for marriage. This resistance to contract is part of an old debate that informs the search for a contemporary theory of alimony.

1. Shunning Contract

Early efforts to identify the nature of the marriage relationship focused on whether marriage is a contract or a status. The debate was sometimes heated. As Hegel declared, "To subsume marriage under the concept of contract is thus quite impossible; this subsumption—though shameful is the only word for it—is propounded in Kant's *Philosophy of Law*."[19]

At the heart of this dispute is the very practical question of who should fix the terms of the relationship—the parties, the church, or the state. The state ultimately won. As the U.S. Supreme Court observed in 1888, "[m]arriage as creating the most important relation in life, as having more to do with the morals and civilization of a people than any other institution," is "something more than a mere contract."[20] Marriage, the Court concluded, "is, rather, a social relation, like that of parent and child, the obligations of which arise not from the consent of concurring minds, but are the creation of the law itself."

This view of marriage as something more than a purely consensual relationship afforded the necessary basis for extensive state regulations. Such regulations prescribed the age, race, sex, and number of marital partners, the incidents of solemnization and licensing, and the rights and obligations of the parties. Even the parties' ability to terminate their relationship was strictly regulated through laws that limited divorce to cases of serious marital fault. Little was left to party autonomy.

In the years following World War I, traditional reverence for the institution of marriage began to yield to a new emphasis on individual fulfillment. This new emphasis seemed at odds with extensive state regulation of marriage, and seemed especially inconsistent with fault-based divorce laws, which limited individual choice. This uneasy tension, together with the equality rhetoric of the emerging women's movement, signaled the need for a new model of marital commitment.

As we saw in chapter 2, the Uniform Marriage and Divorce Act (UMDA) offered this new model in the early 1970s in the form of no-fault divorce, which presaged a new deference to private decision making about the duration of marriage. The UMDA acknowledged the old contract-status debate by defining marriage as a "personal relationship between a man and a woman arising out of a civil contract to which the consent of the parties is essential."[21] This definition of marriage as a status arising out of a contract seems to incorporate rather than resolve the contract-status debate. More helpful is the drafters' brief reference, in a prefatory note, to a partnership model for divorce.[22] Although its rationale is not fully described, the UMDA suggests a view of marriage as a consensual relationship, the dissolution of which, in the absence of an agreement otherwise, should be governed by legislatively supplied rules similar to those of partnership law, a model we will explore more fully in the next chapter.

To be sure, marriage is more than an ordinary contract. But in addition to the "mores," marriage is also a contract. And, as we shall see, contract principles and rules can be very useful in identifying a rationale for alimony. Yet contemporary commentators often assume that contract is an inappropriate metaphor for marriage. There are three primary reasons for this rejection of contract, none of which is convincing.

The first objection is that contract is too crass a model for an institution as venerable as marriage. A contract model, the reasoning goes, promotes an alienated, cynical view of marriage that debases its intimate nature. A contract model of marriage, however, hardly accomplishes this insidious result. A contract is simply "a promise or set of promises, that the law will enforce or at least recognize in some way,"[23] a definition that accurately, if generally, describes the marital relationship. Marriage vows are simply promises, and a couple's decision to formalize their promises by obtaining a state-issued marriage license signals an intent to enter a legally recognized relationship. Indeed, couples who marry choose a relationship that the law will recognize over one the law will *not* recognize; the latter alternative is cohabitation.

Secondly, the availability of no-fault divorce has led some to assume that marriage has become an at-will relationship, which makes a contract metaphor inapt. Actually, no-fault tends to affirm marriage's status as a contract rather than undercut it. Easy access to divorce demonstrates a deference to private ordering—a principle that lies at the core of the law of contract. Marriage may be a forever commitment—marriage licenses don't designate a term other than life—but like contracts in general, it is not an inescapable commitment. Those who marry may "choose [a] life partner and enter with the person into a committed, officially recognized, and protected family relationship,"[24] but this doesn't mean they cannot change their minds and walk away. As any first-year contract student knows, I can break a promise at any time and for any reason, and if I do, the law ordinarily will not compel me to do what I promised or punish me for changing my mind or even ask me why I walked away.

Finally, a contract model for marriage has been rejected on the ground that it would require conceptualizing alimony as damages for breach of contract, an analogy that appears inconsistent with no-fault divorce. Damages, however, are not the only obligation that may arise when a contractual relationship ends. In some cases, parties may agree that termination triggers a duty of alternative performance, such as a buyout, quite apart from damages. In the absence of an agreement requiring a buyout, such a duty might be imposed by statute, as, for example, where partnership default rules require the buyout of a departing partner, an important analogy to which we will return in the next chapter.

Moreover, an analogy to contract damages is not as inconsistent with no-fault principles as some have supposed. No-fault does of course undercut an analogy that casts alimony as damages intended to punish a spouse who commits marital fault or who unilaterally wants to end the marriage, but such an analogy would also be inconsistent with general principles of contract law. Damage awards do not ordinarily aim to punish a party for changing her mind and breaking her promise. The law's goal is rather to impose an exit price designed to protect the interests of the other party—the expectation interest, or sometimes the reliance or restitution interest—which, as we will see in the next section, is the goal of many alimony theorists. Alimony could thus be analogized to an exit price designed not to punish or assign blame, but rather to protect the party who has not broken the marriage promise.

So in the case of marriage, what is the promise that is broken at divorce, and who breaks it? The answer begins with the marriage promise—the commitment to a life partner to share the ups and downs, the costs and benefits of life together. This commitment has many layers, and one of those layers involves money—a promise to share the financial costs and benefits of life together. This promise is not insignificant. As the court in *Goodridge* observed, marriage imposes "weighty . . . financial . . . obligations."[25] Divorce may occasion the breaking of the financial promise, and if it does, the law should impose an exit price. To take an easy example, consider what has now become a familiar case: the divorcing couple whose roles during marriage, as primary caregiver and primary wage-earner, have left them with disparate earning capacity at divorce. If one spouse walks away with all the benefits of marital team-work (in the form of enhanced earning capacity), that spouse has bro-ken the marriage promise to share the financial benefits of marriage. Another example involves couples who have together generated a pool of marital human capital, a scenario we will take up in chapter 8. Mar-riage, of course, occasions much more than a financial promise, but it is this promise, rather than the promise to be a best friend, or to love and nurture a mate, that the law is capable of addressing.

The challenge, of course, is to identify an exit price that is consistent with no-fault principles—a price that does not depend on who files for divorce, or who commits adultery or some other traditional act of mari-tal fault; and a price that does not punish a spouse who wants out or compel specific performance of the marriage promise. In chapter 8 we take up this challenge and explore a compelling new conceptualization of alimony as an exit price loosely analogized to a partnership buyout. For now, the goal is to defend the much-maligned contract metaphor for marriage and set the stage for the many theories of alimony that employ contract remedies.

2. The Theories

Even scholars who resist a contract metaphor often focus their alimony theories on protection of an interest familiar to the law of contract. These theories can be loosely categorized as (1) contribution theory, (2) expectation theory, and (3) reliance theory.

A. CONTRIBUTION THEORY

Contribution theory is the most modest effort to explain alimony. Based on principles of restitution, contribution theory aims to protect a promisee's "interest in having restored to him any benefit that he has conferred on the other party."[26] As Joan Krauskopf explains, "The basic requirements are that one person has received a benefit at the expense of another, and that as between them it would be unjust for the recipi-ent to retain the benefit without compensation to the other person."[27] By way of analogy, an alimony theory based on restitution measures the contributions a claimant made to her spouse and then asks whether justice requires that she be reimbursed.

Contribution theory is helpful in explaining alimony in extraordinary cases. Where, for example, one spouse supports the other's education or training, contribution theory provides a rationale for requiring the student to reimburse his/her mate—for tuition, books, lab fees, and perhaps even living expenses. The *ALI Principles*, for example, recognize a restitution-based rationale for alimony that applies to short marriages in which one spouse supported the other's education or training, which was completed within a limited number of years before divorce and "substantially enhanced" the student's earning capacity.[28]

The reach of contribution theory beyond these extraordinary cases is limited by the principle that benefits conferred gratuitously are not unjustly retained and thus need not be returned. Ordinary benefits conferred by spouses on each other during marriage are generally viewed as gifts—that is, they are conferred with donative intent, and thus do not unjustly enrich the beneficiary. On this reasoning, only benefits extraordinary enough to suggest non-donative intent are reimbursable. Even in these extraordinary cases, contribution theory supports only a limited recovery (reimbursement) that may grossly undercompensate a supporting spouse who expects to share the return on the parties' joint marital investment—that is, the student's enhanced earnings.

Contribution theory might broaden its reach by expanding the concept of contribution to include family labor, but this is a dubious option for a primary caregiver. Even if an individual caregiver's past family labor over the course of a marriage could be tallied—year by year, month by month, day by day—and then assigned a market value, her contributions would not be reimbursable unless they exceeded those of the primary wage-earner. Indeed, if the primary wage-earner's financial contributions to the marriage exceeded the market value of the caregiver's contributions, justice might require the primary caregiver to reimburse the wage-earner—a curious result and one inconsistent with most observers' understandings of equity.

Even more problematic is contribution theory's tendency to undermine contemporary norms of marriage as a partnership of equals. As June Carbone observes, restitution is appropriate "only if the courts are willing to abandon the presumption that both spouses contribute equally to an ongoing marriage and, instead, total up and compare their individual contributions"[29]—a high price to pay for a theory of alimony.

B. GAIN THEORY

Gain theory offers a more generous compensation rationale for the divorcing spouse who finances her mate's education or training. Early human capital theorists reasoned that the nonstudent who serves as both primary caregiver and primary wage-earner forgoes opportunities to increase her human capital through educational or other time-intensive investments. Meanwhile, the student works to enhance his personal human capital, forgoing opportunities for immediate remunerative employment. In such cases, the marital unit makes an investment in the student's human capital, both parties expecting that this joint investment will generate a return—the student's enhanced earnings—that the *marital unit* will enjoy. If the parties divorce, the nonstudent is thus entitled to a share of her expected gain—that is, to a return on her marital investment. As Joan Krauskopf reasons, "the court should consider not only restitution for the monetary contribution, but also fulfillment of the expectation of return in proportion to the amount of investment."[30] Krauskopf suggests an award based on "the amount of capitalized earnings attributable to the additional education."

Since most alimony claimants have not supported their spouses through school, if gain theory is to offer a satisfactory rationale for alimony, it must also address more ordinary cases. In 1978, Elisabeth Landes laid the groundwork for a more expansive view of marital investment. Landes reasons that "[b]y spending more time in household production, a wife directly frees some of her husband's time to the market, increasing both his current market earnings and his incentive to invest in earnings-augmenting skills."[31] As Landes explains, "one of the returns from the wife's investments in household production . . . is the augmentation of the husband's earning capacity. The marriage contract transforms a purely general investment, the productivity of which is independent of the marital state, into marriage-specific capital."[32]

Other theorists have expanded on Landes's reasoning, offering rationales for post-divorce income sharing, although their proposals are not always labeled "alimony." Joan Williams, for example, offers a compelling vision of the "dominant family ecology"—an ideal worker and a marginalized caregiver working together to support a family with children and together generating a family wage to which each is entitled—which suggests the kind of teamwork and entitlement to returns on joint labor that signals gain theory, although she shuns the notion of "alimony."[33] Jana Singer reasons that each spouse makes "an equal (although not necessarily identical) investment in a marriage,"[34] which entitles each divorcing spouse to "an equal share of the fruits of the marriage." Singer stresses that "the emphasis of such an investment partnership model is not on formal *equal treatment* of the spouses at the time of divorce, but on each spouse receiving *equal benefits* from the marriage."[35]

Other theorists have added interesting twists to gain theory. Stephen Sugarman, for example, reasons that spouses' human capital merges over time. The longer the parties are married,

> the more their human capital should be seen as intertwined rather than affixed to the individual spouse in whose body it resides. This idea is consistent with the notion that human capital needs constant renewal—a regular tune-up, repair, and parts replacement model, if you like. After a while, one can less and less distinguish between what was brought into the marriage and what was produced by the marriage.[36]

Sugarman reasons that at divorce each spouse is entitled to a share of what has become a collective resource.

Another version of gain theory comes from Robert Kirkman Collins, who calls for "an equitable sharing of the residual economic benefits from work done during the marriage."[37] By way of example, he offers the vision of a couple pedaling a tandem bicycle:

> [The bicycle] will not come to a screeching halt the moment that one or both riders stops pedaling; while current efforts may cease, the momentum from their prior work continues to carry the pair forward at a gradually decreasing pace until the effects of friction (of the sort known to physicists, as opposed to that found in disintegrating marriages) eventually cause the bicycle to stop. How long the two riders will continue to coast forward will be a direct function of how fast they were going—that is, how great their momentum had been when the joint efforts stopped.

Collins thus characterizes alimony as "a decreasing share of marital residuals."[38]

Gain theory offers straightforward and workable quantification models. In its most radical form, a gain-based formula might require lifetime income sharing, as Jane Rutherford has proposed, on the theory that homemakers expect to share income for life.[39] Gain formulae are usually more modest, limiting income sharing to a period reflecting the extent of joint investments, roughly defined by the length of the marriage. Jana Singer, for example, suggests that divorcing couples equally share their combined income after divorce for a period equal to one-half the length of the marriage.[40] Joan Williams suggests equalization of post-divorce household standards of living during the dependency of minor children, followed by a second period of income sharing equal to half the length of the marriage.[41] Stephen Sugarman suggests that each spouse take "a percentage interest in the other's human capital/future earnings based upon the duration of the marriage."[42] By way of example, he suggests 1.5 percent to 2 percent per year, after perhaps a minimum vesting period of three to five years, and with a cap of 40 percent.[43] Robert Kirkman Collins proposes a series of postmarital income adjustments, each with a presumptive calculation formula. During the first period (immediately following separation), the couple would share equally all disposable income; thereafter, they would share a decreasing percentage of the disparity in disposable income, declining by 10 percent in each period.[44] The "length of each period—and hence the angle of the decline in transfers—is set as a function of the length of the marriage."[45] At the end of the "economic phase-out period," the parties would be "financially independent."

Gain theorists have much in common. Their focus is on the collaboration, teamwork, and partnership between spouses who join together to produce mutual benefits the couple expects to share—income and a home with children. If the parties divorce, the couple continues to share children, but without a divorce court's intervention, the primary wage-earner will take all the human capital benefits of the marital division of labor. As an equal stakeholder in the marriage, the primary caregiver is entitled to an equal share of the financial fruits of marriage. This right to share in the returns on joint investments and in the pool of collective human capital is gain theorists' rationale for alimony.

Gain theory is generally not interested in relative spousal contributions. The assumption is that spouses are equals—a default rule drawn from visions of contemporary marriage. Equality of status does not depend on the type or size of each spouses' contribution. As equals, spouses are entitled to share equally in the returns on joint investments, and in what has become a collective pool of human capital—no matter who brought home the bigger paycheck, no matter who cooked dinner more often or better. In the next chapter, we will explore a compelling extension of gain theory based on these principles.

C. LOSS THEORY

Loss theorists focus on the reliance costs of participating in a "failed" marriage. Compensation thus aims to put an injured party "in as good a position as he would have been in had the contract not been made."[46] In the family setting, Margaret Brinig and June Carbone describe two types of reliance: (1) "a lost opportunity to marry someone else," and (2) "sacrifices in career development."[47]

In 1989, Ira Mark Ellman offered a theory of alimony that closely tracks the classic reliance interest. Ellman reasons that "[t]he main residual financial consequence of a failed marriage is a reduction in one spouse's earning capacity (usually the wife's) compared to the earning capacity she would have had if she had not married."[48] Ellman's model aims to compensate a spouse for lost earning capacity arising from "economically rational marital sharing behavior," since without such compensation a "rational spouse will pause before making a marital investment." The purpose of alimony, concludes Ellman, is "to reallocate the post-divorce financial consequences of marriage in order to prevent distorting incentives."

Whatever its conceptual appeal, Ellman's theory poses difficult practical challenges. As he acknowledges, quantification of a spouse's loss requires comparison of "the claimant's economic situation at the end of marriage with the situation she would have been in if she had not married. . . . The difference equals [the] general measure of the alimony claim."[49] But how are we to know what a spouse might have become but for her marriage? To his credit, Ellman concedes that answering this question is "in some sense . . . impossible even in theory, as is any 'might have been.'" "In the end," says Ellman, "precision is not obtainable," and so alimony under his loss theory depends on "the rough justice of trial court discretion."[50]

Other scholars have offered variations on loss theory. Richard Posner, for example, analogizes alimony to severance pay or unemployment benefits for the wife who has specialized in household production;[51] Elizabeth Scott and Robert Scott analogize alimony to insurance payments;[52] and Twila Perry turns to tort principles, casting alimony as compensation for disproportionate economic loss caused by the "accident" of divorce.[53]

The most detailed version of loss theory comes from the American Law Institute. In a "principal conceptual innovation," the *ALI Principles* cast alimony as "compensation for loss rather than relief of need."[54] Spousal need, reasons the ALI, "results from the unfair allocation of the financial losses arising from the marital failure" and should thus be shared according to "equitable principles."[55] The ALI gives alimony a new name—compensatory spousal payments—and claims that its recharacterization transforms an alimony petition from a "plea for help" to a "claim of entitlement."

The ALI implements its loss-allocation model by identifying three primary types of compensable loss: (1) loss of the marital standard of living (section 5.04); (2) loss of earning capacity by a primary caregiver (section 5.05); and (3) loss of earning capacity by the caregiver of certain third parties in fulfillment of a moral obligation (section 5.11). These awards all appear in Topic 2 of the *Principles*, and each section sets out presumptive eligibility requirements and quantification formulae, which are intended as templates for statewide reform. These Topic 2 awards may be combined, but the combined award may not exceed a cap set by state rule makers.[56] In Topic 3, the *ALI Principles* offer two alternative awards, based on restitution and rescission, which will be available only to a small number of claimants after short marriages.[57]

Of the Topic 2 awards, section 5.04 most closely reflects current alimony practice. Under this section, a spouse may partially recover for loss of the marital living standard if her spouse's earning capacity is "significantly greater" than her own, and the marriage is of "sufficient" duration.[58] "The basis for the award," explains the ALI, "is disproportionate vulnerability to the financial consequences of divorce."[59] As an example of such vulnerability, the ALI cites the case of the traditional wife whose "economic dependence . . . grows as the marriage ages."[60] Compensation for this wife is appropriate, it reasons, since "[t]o leave the financially dependent spouse in a long marriage without a remedy would facilitate the exploitation of the trusting spouse and discourage domestic investment by the nervous one."[61]

Section 5.05 of the *ALI Principles* is more radical. Alimony under this section is available to a primary caregiver whose earning capacity at divorce is "substantially less" than that of her spouse. Caregiving responsibilities, says the ALI, often limit market labor and "typically result . . . in a residual loss in earning capacity that continues after the children no longer require close parental supervision."[62] Primary caregivers, which the ALI observes are usually women, "sacrifice earnings opportunities to care for their children, in reliance upon continued market labor by their husbands."[63] The ALI concludes that lost opportunities resulting from caregiving should be compensated. Also radical, but likely to apply to far fewer cases, is section 5.11, which recognizes compensable loss in the case of a spouse who cares for a third party in fulfillment of a moral obligation owed by both spouses. The provisions of section 5.11 are similar to those of 5.05.

To presumptively value awards under its two primary alimony sections, 5.04 and 5.05, the ALI proposes a two-step process: (1) calculate the disparity in the spouses' incomes at divorce, and (2) multiply that figure by a percentage based on the length of the marriage (section 5.04) or the length of the past child care period (section 5.05). To presumptively calculate the duration of a fixed-term award, the ALI suggests multiplying the length of the marriage (section 5.04) or past child care period (section 5.05) by a percentage set out in a rule of statewide application. By way of example, the ALI suggests the duration of an award under section 5.04 might equal half the length of the marriage.[64]

While the ALI quantification formulae add a much-needed certainty to alimony law, it is not clear that these formulae are actually measuring the loss they aim to compensate. Indeed, by comparing the parties' (expected) incomes and requiring the parties to share any disparity, the formulae are actually measuring *expected gain* rather than loss. The ALI formulae essentially identify the party who takes more of the family wage and then require that party to share part of that wage with the other spouse. This is basic gain theory. Conceding as much, the ALI reasons that since loss is just the flip side of gain, loss of the marital living standard in section 5.04 can be measured by calculating the disparity in the spouse's post-divorce expected earnings. Evidently, the reasoning is that the disparity in income at divorce roughly reflects the disparity in post-divorce standards of living, which roughly reflects the disparity in lost marital standard of living.

The inability to actually quantify loss is more difficult to finesse in the case of section 5.05. The ALI admits "intractable practical problems in implementing the principle that both spouses should share in the earning-capacity loss" of a primary caregiver.[65] Most fundamentally, it is usually impossible to measure loss caused by primary caregiving. Such a calculation would require comparison of "an individual's actual earning capacity with the hypothetical earning capacity of the same person" who was not a primary caregiver. Yet it is virtually impossible to know "what the claimant's earning capacity would have been if he or she had not, and had never intended to, provide the major portion of parental care for the marital children." As the ALI concedes, "[a]ccurate measurements based on that hypothetical possibility are not ordinarily available."[66] As a result, "the basic principle—that the residual loss in earning capacity arising from child-care responsibilities should be shared—cannot be perfectly expressed in an administrable rule."[67] Quantification of loss, concludes the ALI, thus requires "pragmatic accommodation"—evidently, a willingness to co-opt gain theory formulae.

The ALI offers three justifications for resorting to measures of expected gain in order to calculate loss under section 5.05. First, it claims that basing compensation on the disparity in spousal earnings is actually a good proxy for earning capacity loss, since statistics suggest that spouses are more "similar in socioeconomic status" than "randomly chosen pairs of people."[68] Thus, reasons the ALI, a mate's earnings approximate what a primary caregiver's earnings would have been but for caregiving. Second, an expectation formula compensates a primary caregiver's lost opportunity "to have had children with someone with whom she would enjoy an enduring relationship," evidently again on the theory that a hypothetical, more-enduring mate would have earning capacity much like her husband's, which, but for caregiving, would have been her own earnings.

Finally, and most curiously, the ALI reasons that its proxy measure compensates loss by "providing a more balanced allocation at dissolution of the benefits created by both spouses' contributions to the marriage."[69] That is, the ALI's proxy measure of loss is more attractive because it apportions expected marital benefits . . . like gain theory. The ALI then offers a one-paragraph classic expectation rationale, emphasizing parents' joint responsibility for children and the contributions of primary caregivers, and suggesting that the primary caregiver has a claim to a wage-earner's post-divorce earnings. Of course, this rationale has little to do with measuring loss and much to do with measuring gain. The ALI acknowledges that benefits-based proposals reach "very similar conclusions," at least in cases of long-term marriages.[70]

Something is amiss. After insisting that loss theory is superior to gain theory, the ALI concedes the impossibility of quantifying loss, resorts to a gain formula, and then notes that its loss model approximates an expectation outcome. One is left to wonder why the ALI insisted on a loss rationale in the first place, if a gains-based rationale would avoid the intractable problems of quantification of loss and support the same mathematical model.

The ALI's insistence on loss theory is even more problematic because of the negative message it sends. Good intentions notwithstanding, the ALI's rationale and vocabulary signal a dispiriting view of caregivers as losers who are economically incapacitated by their unpaid family labor. The ALI seriously underestimates the significance of its extensive rhetoric of economic vulnerability, loss, and exploitation, rather casually suggesting that the "choice of language is of course less important than the underlying rule it describes."[71] Not so. Language can have a powerful effect on the way caregivers view themselves and are viewed by others. Cast as casualties of marriage, caregivers may deserve pity and even compensation, but they are denied the status of equal partners and full stakeholders in marriage entitled to dignity and a share of marital gain. The ALI's loss-based rationale is objectionable both for the intractable quantification problems it poses and for the dispiriting message it sends. Fortunately, there is a far better alimony rationale and reform alternative, and it to this alternative that we now turn.

PART IV

Alimony Reform

[T]here would seem to be no reason why [a satisfactory alimony outcome] could not come to be more nearly the rule if alimony could be treated as a business matter dealing with the sharing of mutual resources between the spouses involved, rather than as tribute to be levied on the guilty party by the innocent one, or, even worse, as charity to be exacted from the man for the benefit of the woman merely because he is a man and she a woman.
—Catherine Groves Peele, "Social and Psychological Effects of the Availability and the Granting of Alimony on the Spouses," *Law and Contemporary Problems* 6 (1939): 292

If alimony is to serve as an exit price when a marriage ends, it must do so in a way that is consistent with no-fault principles. The challenge is to identify an exit price that does not depend on who files for divorce, or who commits adultery or some other act of traditional marital fault; and one that does not punish a spouse who wants out or compel specific performance of the marriage promise. In chapter 8 I take on this challenge, offering a fresh perspective on the partnership metaphor that inspired the no-fault reforms almost forty years ago and advancing an enriched partnership model that analogizes alimony to a buyout. Two variations of this buyout model are described: the first based on enhanced earnings and the second based on pooled earnings. Chapter 9 addresses a second distinct partnership—a co-parenting partnership between committed couples who share children. Disentangled from the marriage partnership, the co-parenting partnership provides a conceptual basis for income sharing between divorced parents of minor children and a solution to the vexing problem of the disparate costs of *post-divorce* caregiving.

8

A Marital Partnership Model

Alimony as Buyout

They had trusted each other to the point that no one had ever raised the prospect of a written partnership agreement let alone dissolution. But sitting at the end of the conference table was one of the partners having just announced that he wanted to dissolve the partnership and take his considerable collection of contingency fee cases with him. The other partners were stunned. Could he really expect to keep these cases and not share the income realized from them?
—Mark I. Weinstein, "The Revised Uniform Partnership Act: An Analysis of Its Impact on the Relationship of Law Firm Dissolution, Contingent Fee Cases and the No Compensation Rule," *Duquesne Law Review* 33 (1995): 857

A. The Partnership Metaphor: Concept, Fact, and Law

Partnership is an intuitive metaphor for marriage. The "ideal to which marriage aspires [is] that of equal partnerships between spouses who share resources, responsibilities, and risks," and thus perhaps some limited duty to sacrifice individually for the good of the partnership.[1] This norm encourages commitments between spouses, promotes gender equality, and supports the privatized care of children and elderly dependents. Indeed, much of the contemporary writing on divorce reform espouses such an ideal relationship, even when the writer declines to endorse a partnership metaphor. The most powerful support for a partnership model thus lies in its egalitarian principles of mutual contribution, reciprocal responsibility, and shared fate—principles that infuse family norms if not all family realities.

Partnership also offers a fresh, gender-neutral vocabulary for the family, an alternative reform discourse free of the stubborn remnants

This chapter draws on two of my previous articles: "Mothers as Suckers: Pity, Partnership, and Divorce Discourse," *Iowa Law Review* 90 (2005): 1513; and "Divorce and the Displaced Homemaker: A Discourse on Playing with Dolls, Partnership Buyouts and Dissociation under No-Fault," *University of Chicago Law Review* 60 (1993): 67.

of old ideologies that sabotage reform efforts long after those ideologies have ceased to be openly expressed. As we saw in the last chapter, reform discourse has the power to assign status; the loss theory favored by some reformers casts primary caregivers as victims of marriage, damaged by their family labor, and deserving of reparations. A partnership metaphor assigns caregivers a very different status, casting them as full stakeholders in marriage, equal in status to primary wage-earners, no matter who brings home the bigger paycheck. Under a partnership metaphor, the equality of spouses—in contribution, in responsibility, in right—becomes an analytical starting point against which all departures must be justified.

In addition to its conceptual appeal, support for a partnership model can be found in the many de facto similarities between a marriage and a handshake partnership. Both are consensual relationships that typically commence with the exchange of promises and without written agreements or advice of counsel.[2] Like many business partners, spouses may begin their relationship as starry-eyed optimists, full of hope and trust, eschewing the need for a written partnership or prenuptial agreement. Both relationships often involve specialization, with one party primarily contributing money, and the other primarily services, a practice that describes both the traditional marriage and many contemporary ones between primary wage-earners and primary caregivers.

Expectations of gain, broadly understood, generally motivate both business partners and spouses to enter the relationship. In marriage, anticipated gain may be emotional, social, spiritual, and sexual as well as financial, but in some way, couples ordinarily expect that marriage will make life better, a hope evident in the celebration that commonly accompanies marriage. As Elizabeth Scott observes, marrying couples are often motivated by self-interest, each believing that "individual self-fulfillment will be promoted by a substantial investment in a stable, interdependent, long-term relationship with a marital partner."[3] Couples may also believe that "having and raising children together in a loving home is important to self-realization."[4] While the nature of expected gain in marriage is surely more personal, more intimate, and more complex than in a commercial partnership, an expectation of gain broadly describes both relationships.

Additional support for a partnership metaphor lies in the law governing partnerships. The Uniform Partnership Act (UPA) codifies the law of partnership in most states. Promulgated in 1914, the UPA has undergone numerous revisions, most recently in 1997. The UPA contains both mandatory rules and an array of default rules triggered by the frequent failure of commercial partners, like spouses, to negotiate the terms of their relationship. Many key UPA provisions identify principles and rules that are as essential to a marriage as to a purely commercial relationship. Under the UPA, for example, partners undertake a duty of loyalty,[5] and of good faith and fair dealing toward each other,[6] obligations consistent with social norms of mutual trust and responsibility between spouses. In a passage often quoted in partnership cases, Justice Cardozo describes the duty of loyalty between joint venturers in terms that suggest normative visions of the spousal relationship:

> Joint adventurers, like copartners, owe to one another, while the enterprise continues, the duty of the finest loyalty. Many forms of conduct permissible in a workaday world for those acting at arm's length, are forbidden to those bound by fiduciary ties. A trustee is held to something stricter than the morals of the market place. Not honesty alone, but the punctilio of an honor the most sensitive, is then the standard of behavior.[7]

Absent an agreement otherwise, the UPA also recognizes that "[e]ach partner has equal rights in the management and conduct of the partnership business,"[8] a rule consistent with modern equality rhetoric and with statutes that make spouses co-managers of community property.[9] Not unlike spouses, partners have "the right to know what is going on in the partnership, the right to be involved in conducting the business . . . , the right to participate in collective decision making [and] the right to veto certain other types of decisions."[10] Distinctions between status as a partner and status as a mere participant such as a wage-earner are significant: a partner participates in important decisions, while a wage-earner obeys instructions; a partner invests in the enterprise, while a wage-earner works for the enterprise; a partner may agree to share losses while a wage-earner expects a paycheck even when the enterprise is losing money.[11] To be sure, not every business partner or every spouse will fully exercise partnership rights. One spouse, for example, may be terrible with money and may be perfectly content to delegate control of the marital purse to the other spouse. The important point, however, is that such deference represents a delegation of rights rather than the absence of rights.

The UPA also makes partners co-owners rather than individual owners of partnership property,[12] a rule that mirrors many state statutes that presume property acquired during marriage is marital (or community) property.[13] UPA default provisions also provide that partners share equally all profits and losses,[14] a rule that encourages partners "to view their economic fate as linked with the fate of the enterprise as a whole."[15] A similar sense of shared fate is inherent in normative concepts of egalitarian marriage. As one court observed,

> When couples enter marriage, they ordinarily commit themselves to an indefinite shared future of which shared finances are a part. Acquisitions are made, foregone or replaced for the good of the family unit rather than for the financial interests of either spouse. Property is bought, sold, enhanced, diminished, intermixed and used without regard to ease of division upon termination of the marriage. All this may be modified by agreement, of course, but, by the nature of the marital relationship, couples ordinarily pledge their troth for better or worse until death parts them and their financial affairs are conducted accordingly.[16]

Partnership, of course, does not perfectly describe marriage. The question, however, is not whether partnership is a perfect metaphor but rather whether it is a useful one. Such an analogy need not be an all-or-nothing proposition, for partnership can inform discourse without dominating it. Much can indeed be gained from an analogy to partnership, as the drafters of no-fault divorce laws understood.

B. The Birth of Partnership Marriage: The UMDA Clean-Break Model

Especially attractive to the drafters of the harbinger of no-fault divorce, the Uniform Marriage and Divorce Act (UMDA),[17] was the historical partnership principle of at-will dissolution, the unalterable power of a partner to dissolve the partnership at any time.[18] As we saw in chapter 2, this dissolution right is the linchpin of no-fault divorce, which authorizes divorce at the will of either party upon a finding that the marriage is "irretriev-ably broken." Indeed, the UMDA drafters went so far as to substitute the partnership term "dissolution" for the more traditional term "divorce."[19] UMDA drafters also expressly adopted a partnership model for the divi-sion of marital property,[20] recognizing that the power to dissolve the mar-riage does not entitle a spouse to walk away without financial consequence, an outcome that traditionally describes cohabitation rather than marriage.

While its reasoning is not fully articulated, the UMDA suggests a view of marriage as a consensual relationship the dissolution of which, in the absence of an agreement otherwise, should be governed by leg-islatively supplied rules similar to those of partnership law. Key among these rules is the borrowed partnership rule that dissolution of the part-nership triggers a winding up of partnership business and termination of the partnership. Winding up includes the completion of unfinished partnership business, liquidation of assets, payment of debts, and dis-tribution of any remaining proceeds to the partners,[21] a process analo-gous to the final settlement of property rights on divorce. As part of this process, any capital furnished (but not contributed) to the partnership by a partner is returned.[22] This rule resembles many property distribu-tion statutes that require return of a spouse's separate property prior to the distribution of marital property.[23] Winding up terminates the part-ners' mutual rights and obligations.[24] This consequence underscores the clean-break aspiration of no-fault divorce statutes; the distribution of marital property marks an end to the parties' financial entanglement, thus affording each spouse a fresh start.

As we saw in chapter 2, adherence to this clean-break partnership model made divorce a financial catastrophe for caregivers in the early years of no-fault. Especially hard-hit were full-time, long-term caregiv-ers in marriages with few assets. As critics searched for an explanation and solution to the problem of the displaced homemaker, the partner-ship model for marriage became a convenient scapegoat. Theorists attacked the partnership metaphor for its failure to provide a concep-tual basis for alimony,[25] its mischaracterization of marriage as "profit-seeking,"[26] its hidden bias against women,[27] and its failure to recognize the different ways a business partnership and a marital relationship commence.[28] Theorists who rejected the partnership model, together with those who tacitly dismissed it, launched a search for a framework that would provide a conceptual foundation for alimony. In the forty years since promulgation of the UMDA, the belief that a partnership model provides no satisfactory basis for alimony has spawned numerous reform proposals, many of which we reviewed in the last chapter.

The problem with divorce law lies not in partnership, however, but in the simplistic use of partnership principles. No-fault divorce laws fail to recognize both the common case in which partnership business continues after the dissociation of a partner and the critical distinction between dissolution, windup, and termination. The remedy is not to scrap partnership, but to expand it; not to abandon the powerful, egalitarian, gender-neutral principles that drew no-fault reformers in the first place, but to enrich our understanding of those principles.

C. The Maturing of Partnership Marriage: Alimony as Buyout

The clean-break partnership model of divorce misses the critical point that a partner's dissociation does not immediately or invariably trigger a winding up and termination of partnership business. In practice, partnership business typically is not wound up, but continues after a partner's departure, sometimes by a new partnership that rises from the ashes of the first.[29] In a fixed-term partnership, remaining partners may elect to continue rather than wind up the partnership business.[30] In such cases, the partners who continue the business must buy out the interest of the dissociated partner.[31] This buyout right of the departing partner is usually more valuable than the right to a windup, because it can be realized more quickly and avoids judicial reluctance to extinguish the remaining partners' means of livelihood.

The 1997 revision of the UPA preserves the rule that a partner may leave the partnership at any time,[32] but expands and details the right of a departing partner to force a buyout rather than a winding up.[33] Such a buyout commonly occurs when a partner dissociates before the expiration of a fixed term, in which case partnership business may continue.[34] If the business does continue, the UPA requires a buyout of the dissociated partner's interest.[35]

The UPA buyout rules provide a useful analogy for family law. Contemporary marriage is a partnership for a term (the life of one partner), although spouses, like commercial partners, have the power to leave the relationship at any time. A spouse's decision to leave the partnership does not necessarily trigger a winding up of any shared marital enterprise. If this enterprise continues, a dissociated spouse should receive a buyout of his or her interest.

This reasoning raises some immediate conceptual concerns. First, is marriage analogous to a fixed-term partnership even in an age of easy divorce? The answer is that the ability to escape a commitment does not alter the terms of the commitment. From both a traditional and a normative perspective, marriage is a commitment for life. Marriage licenses do not designate a term other than life, although everyone understands that spouses are free to change their minds, to break their promises of lifetime commitment at any time and for virtually any reason. Marriage, however, need not be an inescapable commitment in order to be a lifetime one. No-fault divorce laws recognize spouses' freedom to end their relationship, but no-fault does not change the terms of the marital commitment any more than the ability to terminate a business contract alters its terms. In neither case are parties compelled to specifically perform their promises, nor are their broken promises ordinarily penalized through punitive damage awards.[36] The point is that breaking a promise is not the same as never having made one.

But if promises can be broken, what is the point of insisting they were made? The answer is that freedom to terminate a relationship does not necessarily mean freedom to terminate it without consequence. To say that a spouse may dissolve the marriage upon request and without penalty is *not* to say that she may walk away with all the marital assets or earnings. Unlike cohabitation, which parties traditionally may end without legal involvement or economic consequence, marriage is a lifetime legal status that may end prematurely only with state involvement. Absent an agreement otherwise, the state determines the economic price of exit, or, in partnership terms, the buyout price. And it is important that the state fix this price, for if the marriage promise matters, it must have consequences.

The buyout metaphor raises another conceptual concern: In the case of marriage, who should buy out whom—that is, which spouse is the dissociated spouse? Even more fundamentally, is there a shared enterprise that continues after divorce, thus requiring the spouse who continues it to buy out the interest of the dissociated spouse? The answer to these questions draws heavily on human capital theory.[37]

1. An Enhanced-Earnings Buyout Model

An enhanced-earnings model begins with a view of marriage as, among other things, a mutual commitment to pool labor, time, and talent in the expectation that these contributions will generate shared value in the form of income and a family home. When the couple adds children to the family, pragmatism often leads one spouse to assume primary responsibility for family care, a role that frees the other spouse to invest more fully in the job market. These disparate marital roles often generate a higher income stream and enhanced human capital for the spouse who invests more extensively in paid employment. Although divorce terminates the parties' relationship, it usually does not terminate this enhanced income stream, which continues to reflect value produced through joint marital effort. In such a case, the higher-income spouse should buy out the other spouse's interest in the financial arm of the marital partnership.

Consider, for example, the story of Stacy and Tracy, whom we first met in part 1. At marriage, Stacy and Tracy exchange lifetime promises to care for each other, to live together as a family, to share income, to nurture any mutual children. In a common pattern, Stacy and Tracy are similarly positioned at marriage, but once they add children to the family, expediency leads Tracy to assume primary responsibility for home and children. This role prompts gaps in Tracy's employment, part-time or part-year employment, and employment choices that offer flexibility, limited travel, a short commute, and other incidentals that facilitate family care. Meanwhile, Tracy's primary assumption of family labor has freed Stacy to enjoy a family while investing more fully in the job market, pursuing employment options that offer little flexibility, require long hours and extensive travel, and permit limited time off.

From a partnership perspective, Stacy and Tracy are equals, each contributing capital and labor to the marital partnership in the expectation that their mutual contributions will generate shared value in the form of enhanced income and an adequately (or comfortably) tended home with children. Over time, however, the spouses' marital roles disparately impact their individual human capital—Stacy's human capital increases while Tracy's declines. During marriage this disparate impact is masked, as the marital partnership enjoys the benefits of the partners' specialized labor. Divorce, however, unmasks the reality that family roles have left Stacy and Tracy with markedly different earning capacity.

Although divorce terminates the parties' marriage, it usually does not terminate Stacy's income stream, which continues to reflect the enhanced value produced through the spouses' joint efforts. In such a case, Stacy should buy out Tracy's interest in the financial arm of the marital partnership. To implement this buyout model and guard against its gender-biased application, I propose bright-line legislation that presumptively establishes (1) a simple mathematical formula for determining alimony eligibility and (2) a quantification formula patterned after the spousal elective share provisions of the Uniform Probate Code.

This buyout model, which I first proposed in 1993,[38] works best in a robust economy where investments in paid labor pay off with increased earnings over time. In a stagnant or declining economy, however, an enhanced-earnings model will sometimes provide no basis for alimony in cases where most folks would think it is appropriate. Consider, for example, the case of a full-time family caregiver married for many years to a spouse whose earnings (measured in constant dollars) are high at divorce but no higher than at the beginning of marriage. The intuition that such a caregiver deserves alimony can best be explained by a variation of my enhanced-earnings buyout model that draws on the work of Stephen Sugarman.

2. A Pooled-Earnings Buyout Model

As we saw in the previous chapter, Sugarman argues that over time spouses' human capital merges. The longer the marriage, says Sugarman, the more the spouses' human capital is

> intertwined rather than affixed to the individual spouse in whose body it resides. This idea is consistent with the notion that human capital needs constant renewal—a regular tune-up, repair, and parts replacement model, if you like. After a while, one can less and less distinguish between what was brought into the marriage and what was produced by the marriage.[39]

Sugarman notes that his merger-over-time model is analogous to marital property patterns. Spouses typically begin marriage with only separate property, but over time, as marital earnings produce new property and as separate property is commingled with marital property, property holdings become predominantly marital.

Another application of merger principles comes from the American Law Institute (ALI). In its 2002 *Principles of the Law of Family Dissolution (ALI Principles)*, the ALI offers a rule that gradually recharacterizes separate property into marital property.[40] This recharacterization occurs at a specified rate per year, beginning once the marriage lasts for a threshold period. The ALI leaves the question of the appropriate rate of recharacterization and the duration of the threshold period to state rule makers. By way of example, they suggest that after the fifth year of marriage, separate property owned by either spouse prior to marriage might be recharacterized as marital property at the rate of 4 percent per year. Under this formula, after thirty years of marriage, all separate property owned prior to marriage would become shared property. A different formula applies to separate property acquired during marriage (e.g., through gift or inheritance). The ALI labels its recharacterization rule "modest" since it is subject to several exceptions. Separate property is not recharacterized where such sharing would be inconsistent with the parties' intent (expressed, for example, in a premarital agreement) or with the intent of a donor or testator who gives or bequeaths property to an individual spouse during marriage; or where application of the rule would work a "substantial injustice."[41]

Whether or not its proposal is modest, the ALI offers a compelling rationale for recharacterization:

> After many years of marriage, spouses typically do not think of their separate-property assets as separate, even if they would be so classified under the technical property rules. Both spouses are likely to believe, for example, that such assets will be available to provide for their joint retirement, for a medical crisis of either spouse, or for other personal emergencies. The longer the marriage the more likely it is that the spouses will have made decisions about their employment or the use of their marital assets that are premised in part on such expectations about the separate property of both spouses.[42]

As the ALI explains, the effect of its recharacterization rule is to establish that spouses who live together for many years commit at least some of their resources to one another, in a proportion that increases with the duration of their relationship, unless there is good reason to think that they did not intend that result. This is surely more reasonable than assuming that spouses who live together for many years do not intend to commit any of their resources to one another.[43]

The ALI reasoning is compelling partly because of its recognition that the parties' intent should matter. And, while the recharacterization rule applies only to property, the ALI's reasoning seems equally applicable to earnings. If a couple increasingly expects to share assets as their marriage endures, don't they also increasingly expect to share earnings? If a couple plans for retirement, for medical crises, and for personal emergencies on the assumption that they will share assets, isn't it at least as likely that they base these plans on an assumption that they will also share earnings? If a couple makes decisions about employment and marital property in the expectation that they will share separate property, won't they also base these decisions on an expectation that they will share earnings?

Yes, say the co-directors of the Canadian alimony guideline project. As we saw in chapter 5, the Canadian guidelines quantify the duration and value of alimony awards in a series of detailed, nonmandatory formulae that have profoundly affected alimony decision making in that country. As a rationale for alimony in cases without children, Carol Rogerson and Rollie Thompson draw on merger principles. "As a marriage or relationship lengthens," they explain,

> spouses merge their economic and noneconomic lives more deeply, in both direct and indirect ways, with each spouse making countless decisions to mould his or her skills, behavior and finances around those of the other spouse. The longer the marriage or relationship, the greater is the claim by the recipient spouse to maintain the marital standard of living and for a longer period after separation.[44]

While the ALI itself rejects an expectation-based model of alimony, its rationale for alimony also draws on merger principles.[45] In a variation of Sugarman's model, the ALI reasons that as a marriage endures, a spouse's economic vulnerability to divorce increasingly becomes a shared responsibility; that is, over time, losses are increasingly shared. If loss, why not gain? Indeed, marriage is a signal that two individuals have committed themselves to share the costs *and the benefits* of life together. As we have seen, marriage is, among other things, a mutual commitment to pool labor, time, and talent in the expectation that this pooling will generate value that the couple will share.

To return to the partnership metaphor, as a marriage endures, increasing portions of each spouse's human capital become a collective resource, generating benefits that belong to the marital partnership rather than to either spouse alone. In this variation on Sugarman's model, the spouses' individual human capital is not intertwined so much as it is pooled, increasingly creating a collective resource that generates *marital* rather than individual benefits. Each spouse's individual human capital remains identifiable, but over time the right to enjoy the benefits that human capital produces increasingly belongs to the marital unit rather than to an individual spouse. Portions of each spouse's human capital and the earnings generated by that human capital are thus pooled and so belong to the marital partnership rather than to either spouse alone.

The basis for a buyout is now clear. If divorce ends the parties' marriage, it does not usually end the earnings-generating potential of this collective marital resource, which continues to function in the marketplace in the hands of one or both spouses. If one divorcing spouse reaps disproportionate post-divorce benefits from what is a collective resource, that spouse must buy out the interest of the other spouse. The obligation to buy out a spouse thus depends not on which spouse initiates divorce proceedings, but rather on which spouse walks away at divorce with a larger share of wage-earning human capital that has become part of the marital pool. This buyout obligation is the partnership analogue of alimony.

A default rule based on this pooled-earnings buyout model is consistent with normative visions of contemporary marriage. If, as we have seen, the "ideal to which marriage aspires [is] that of equal partnerships between spouses who share resources, responsibilities, and risks,"[46] then default rules should be chosen to reflect and reinforce this ideal rather than to contravene and discourage it. As Thaler and Sunstein explain, default rules are sticky, affecting what people do, what they want to do, and what they feel entitled to do.[47] If the law is to pick a default rule, it should be one that nudges intimate partners toward an expectation that resources will be increasingly shared as their commitment endures, rather than toward an expectation that no matter how long the relationship, in the end it is "every man for himself." Couples who intend this latter-type relationship can *opt into* it.

A default rule that assumes increased sharing over time will not only encourage normative expectations, but will also protect primary caregivers by recognizing that as time passes, increasing portions of each spouse's human capital become a collective resource. As Thaler and Sunstein note, "the stickiness of default rules can easily be enlisted to insulate the most vulnerable people from the worst outcomes."[48] A default rule based on the pooling of human capital over time will reinforce a normative, egalitarian, communal vision of marriage, encourage expectations consistent with that vision, and protect primary caregivers. Not a bad day's work for a single default rule. The next question is how to calculate the buyout price.

D. Quantifying a Buyout: The Pooling and Disentanglement Principles

Buyout quantification requires answers to three important questions: How much? How long? When modification?

1. How Much?

As previously noted, a buyout is appropriate when marital human capital continues to generate earnings after divorce, primarily to the benefit of one spouse. Determining a spouse's eligibility for a buyout thus begins with identification of each spouse's earnings at divorce and then calculating the portion of those earnings attributable to marital human capital. To avoid creating distorting incentives, each spouse's earnings at divorce might be presumptively measured by averaging earnings over the three- to five-year period immediately preceding divorce. Determining what portion of each spouse's earnings is attributable to marital human capital then requires two policy choices: the pooling rate and the threshold period, if any, that precedes the onset of pooling. Whatever these policy choices may be, it is important that quantification of marital human capital be a presumptive figure only. Both spouses should have an opportunity to show that quantification under the presumptive formula would work a substantial injustice because of special circumstances not present in most cases, in particular, because the parties agreed to a different arrangement.[49]

Sugarman suggests that the threshold period be set at three or five years, after which each spouse would acquire a 1.5 percent to 2 percent interest in the human capital of the other spouse. If, for example, state rule makers chose a five-year threshold period and a 2 percent pooling rate, then after a twenty-year marriage each spouse would have an interest in 30 percent (fifteen years times 2 percent per year) of the other's wage-earning human capital. If spouse A's annual earnings at divorce were $100,000 and spouse B's earnings were $40,000, then $30,000 of A's earnings and $12,000 of B's earnings would be presumptively attributable to marital human capital. Total earnings produced by marital human capital would thus be $42,000 ($30,000 plus $12,000). If each spouse is entitled to an equal share of marital human capital, as equality principles suggest, then B would be presumptively entitled to an annual buyout of $9,000. A's payment of this sum would leave each party with $21,000 of post-divorce earnings produced by marital human capital. Couples who intend a different arrangement could opt out via an agreement.

Clearly, the pooling rate and threshold period are key policy choices that will significantly affect the calculation of marital human capital. In addition to their monetary impact, these choices will send important signals about the meaning of marriage promises. In the case of the threshold period, the message is a negative one, suggesting that marriage promises don't mean much unless the couple survives a probationary period. Only after probation do couples begin to develop a pool of shared property and earnings. This scheme devalues the couple's commitment to each other, casting marriage in its early years as a trial relationship that is little more than cohabitation. Moreover, it is not clear on what principled basis a state could choose a threshold period. Is five years better than three? Better than seven? No matter where the threshold period is set, it will create a distorting incentive for the higher wage-earner to terminate the relationship prior to that threshold. A five-year threshold, for example, would give a higher wage-earner an incentive to terminate the marriage at 4.9 years—prior to any pooling—a result inconsistent with marriage norms. On balance, states would be well advised to reject the notion of a threshold period and begin pooling at the time the marriage begins.

A more generous pooling rate without a threshold period might be patterned after the marital-property rule of the Uniform Probate Code (UPC). The UPC recognizes the right of a surviving spouse to 50 percent of the marital-property portion of a deceased's estate. The portion of an estate characterized as marital increases with the length of the marriage under a sliding scale set out in the UPC.[50] Interestingly, UPC Comments, which appear under the heading "The Partnership Theory of Marriage," explain that "the economic rights of each spouse are seen as deriving from an unspoken marital bargain under which the partners agree that each is to enjoy a half interest in the fruits of marriage."[51] Using the UPC as a model, the pooling rate, for example, would be 6 percent for a marriage that lasted more than one year but less than two years, 30 percent for a marriage that lasted five years but less than six years, 42 percent for a marriage that lasted seven years but less than eight years, 60 percent for a marriage that lasted ten years but less than eleven years, and 100 percent for a marriage of fifteen years or more. To return to our previous example, if after a twenty-year marriage A's earnings at divorce are $100,000 and B's earnings are $40,000, then both parties' earnings would presumptively be fully attributable to marital human capital. Total earnings produced by marital human capital would thus be $140,000 ($100,000 plus $40,000). If each spouse is entitled to an equal share of marital human capital, then B would be presumptively entitled to an annual buyout of $30,000. A's payment of this sum would leave each party with $70,000 of post-divorce earnings produced by marital human capital.

If the parties' marriage lasted seven (rather than twenty) years, then under the UPC model, 42 percent of each party's earnings would be presumptively attributable to marital human capital. Total earnings produced by marital human capital would thus be $58,800 ($42,000 plus $16,800). If each spouse is entitled to an equal share of marital human capital, then B would be presumptively entitled to an annual buyout of $12,600. A's payment of this sum would leave each party with $29,400 of post-divorce earnings produced by marital human capital.

2. How Long? The Disentanglement Principle

Once marital human capital is measured and an annual buyout price set, the next step is to determine the duration of a buyout. Because a buyout reflects the right to a share of earnings attributable to marital human capital, it should continue for as long as this marital resource generates earnings. So far, the quantification of a buyout reflects only a snapshot vision of marital human capital as measured at the time of divorce. But life goes on. While divorce does not extinguish marital human capital, neither does divorce freeze it. Over time, the pooling process reverses, gradually converting what was once marital human capital into separate human capital. This *disentanglement principle* is the pooling principle in reverse and is based on similar reasoning. To flip Sugarman's merger principle (something he does not do),

> the longer the [period since divorce], the more [marital] human capital [becomes disentangled and] affixe[s] to the individual spouse in whose body it resides. This idea is consistent with the notion that human capital needs constant renewal—a regular tune-up, repair, and parts replacement model, if you like. After a while, one can less and less distinguish between what was [taken from the marriage] and what was produced by the [individual former spouse].[52]

Over time, a former spouse's individual effort (or non-effort) thus converts what was once marital human capital into human capital that is predominantly, and then totally, a separate resource. Ultimately, the earnings-generating capacity of marital human capital ceases to function in the marketplace. In partnership terms, the marital enterprise has wound down and the basis for a buyout disappears.

To return to our previous example based on a UPC pooling model, suppose that after a twenty-year marriage A's earnings at divorce are $100,000 and B's earnings are $40,000. As we saw, both parties' earnings would presumptively be fully attributable to marital human capital. Total earnings produced by marital human capital would thus be $140,000. If each spouse is entitled to an equal share of marital human capital, then B would be presumptively entitled to an annual buyout of $30,000. A's payment of this sum would leave each party with $70,000 of post-divorce earnings produced by marital human capital. How would the disentanglement principle affect this picture five and fifteen years after the parties' divorce?

Assume for simplicity's sake that the earnings of A and B remain constant. Five years after their divorce, 30 percent of A's earnings would be newly attributed to A's separate human capital ($100,000 times 30 percent equals $30,000), reducing the portion of A's earnings attributable to marital human capital from $100,000 to $70,000. Similarly, 30 percent of B's earnings would be newly attributed to B's separate human capital ($40,000 times 30 percent equals $12,000), reducing the portion of B's earnings attributable to marital human capital from $40,000 to $28,000. Marital human capital five years after divorce would thus total $98,000, down from $140,000 at the time of divorce. B's buyout would thus be reduced from $30,000 to $21,000. A's payment of this sum would leave each party with $49,000 of post-divorce earnings presumptively produced by marital human capital. As with the initial buyout calculation, this figure should operate as a presumptive amount only, subject to either party's showing that this buyout amount would result in a substantial injustice.

Under a UPC-based model, fifteen years after divorce the pool of collective human capital would fully convert to separate human capital and the buyout obligation would terminate. There is nothing sacrosanct about fifteen years, and state rule makers might prefer a longer disentanglement period. Moreover, while symmetry has intuitive appeal, there is no reason why the pooling rate and disentanglement rate must be identical. A state might determine that fairness to primary caregivers warrants a slower disentanglement rate, justified perhaps by the ceiling on earnings primary caregivers are likely to experience because of the years in which they sacrificed development of wage-earning human capital. The mom, for example, who begins a career as a welder at age fifty will start at the bottom of the organizational hierarchy and because she is older will not likely attain the earnings level she would have enjoyed had she started her work at age twenty-five or thirty.[53] Even under a UPC-style disentanglement model that presumptively terminates a buyout at fifteen years, the buyout would continue beyond this point if termination would work a substantial injustice. The presence of minor children will not likely establish such an injustice, but will rather establish grounds for a monetary award distinct from a buyout, which is discussed in the next chapter.

Examples of the disentanglement principle have so far been limited to cases in which the former spouses' earnings remain constant, which is an unlikely scenario. Should a buyout also be subject to modification based on changes in the earnings of one or both former spouses?

3. Modifying a Buyout

Investing in another human being is risky business. A life partner may die, become ill or incapacitated; give up a good salary to join the seminary, the carnival, or Doctors Without Borders; or simply decide that life is better sitting on the sofa eating bonbons. This is not to say that investing in a life partner is a bad idea, but only that, financially speaking, it is a risky one. Former life partners, unlike stocks or houses or cars, are human beings who may exercise free will. A buyout does not change this fact. A buyout obligation should not enslave a former spouse to a particular job; nor should a buyout right entitle a former spouse to a lifetime paycheck. The key is to return to the foundation on which a buyout is based—the right of each spouse to a share of post-divorce earnings generated by marital human capital, whatever those earnings may be. If earnings attributable to marital human capital decline, so should the buyout amount. And the converse is also true—if earnings attributable to marital human capital increase, so should the buyout amount.

Since changes in earnings will ordinarily be linked to a former spouse's human capital, which is partly a marital resource, a presumption should arise that a modification is appropriate when earnings change. As with the initial buyout calculation, an objecting spouse could rebut this presumption by showing that modification would work a substantial injustice because of circumstances not present in most cases. The costs of obtaining a modification might be reduced under a scheme that automatically adjusts the buyout amount each year based on income tax returns and the disentanglement rate.

The principle that a buyout should reflect current earnings attributable to marital resources is an important one, for it renders unnecessary many of the troubling questions that complicate current modification actions. Most significantly, the reason for a drop in earnings becomes irrelevant. Former spouses have no obligation to continue on any particular earnings course, but rather retain the freedom to vary that course or to forgo earnings altogether. A buyout is not a shackle. There is thus no need to question the voluntariness of a reduction in earnings; no need to ask whether a retirement was taken prematurely; no need to inquire into a payor's good faith; no need to determine a payor's potential earnings; no need to impute income; no need to ask whether a payor gave up a paycheck in order to avoid paying a buyout. Indeed, these inquiries become inappropriate. Suffice it to say that the earnings of a person with free will have dropped. The same reasoning applies to cases in which the earnings of one or both spouses increase. Any harsh effects of an increase in the buyout amount is ameliorated by the disentanglement principle, which gradually reduces the percentage of earnings attributable to marital human capital so that even if the buyout price increases, it will represent a smaller and smaller portion of the payor's total earnings. Any harsh effects of this simple modification principle could be avoided by allowing an adversely affected party to show that operation of the general rule would work a substantial injustice because of facts not present in most cases.

The principle that a buyout amount depends on the stream of post-divorce earnings attributable to marital human capital also makes clear that the remarriage or cohabitation of a former spouse is irrelevant to modification. A buyout is not based on old notions of a husband's duty to support a wife, a duty that can be passed on to another man. On the contrary, a buyout reflects an entitlement to share the post-divorce benefits flowing from marital resources—calculated according to the applicable pooling rate, disentanglement rate, and earnings of former spouses. There is no conceptual justification for terminating or even modifying a buyout based on a former spouse's decision to begin a new intimate relationship. If a buyout recipient marries a brain surgeon and quits her job, or marries a starving artist and doubles her work hours and earnings, her change in earnings will affect the buyout amount, but the reason for those changes—her remarriage—is irrelevant. Nor is the remarriage or cohabitation of a buyout payor relevant. The payor who marries a high earner may experience an improved standard of living, and the payor who marries an unemployed person with a gambling addiction may experience a decreased standard of living, but neither of these scenarios is relevant to buyout quantification. A buyout is based on the earnings of former spouses flowing from marital human capital, not on the former spouses' standards of living. In the end, a buyout metaphor for alimony makes modification decision making more predictable, more affordable, and more conceptually sound than under current law.

No one of course would mistake a marriage for a commercial partnership. But an analogy to partnership buyouts achieves much, offering a conceptual rationale for alimony lacking in current law, and an explanation for the common intuition that alimony should depend on marriage duration and spousal earning disparities. The buyout analogy does all this in an egalitarian, gender-neutral framework that casts caregivers as equal stakeholders in marriage rather than victims of marriage. While this buyout model addresses cases in which the spouses' shared efforts end with divorce, it does not address cases in which the presence of minor children requires the continuing, combined efforts of former spouses. For these latter cases I propose an additional, complementary partnership model set out in the next chapter.

9

Beyond Alimony

Lovers, Parents, and Partners

"What's for dinner?" she asks, adding "Dad," as if to remind him who he is.

Nate finds this question suddenly so mournful that for a moment he can't answer. It's a question from former times, the olden days. His eyes blur. He wants to drop the casserole on the floor and pick her up, hug her, but instead he closes the oven door gently.

"Macaroni and cheese," he says.

—Margaret Atwood, *Life before Man* (New York: Simon and Schuster, 1979), 10

Divorce is not a tool for spinning off children. While divorce may deeply affect children, divorce is not about them. Divorcing parents understand this point well enough; at least it's what they tell their children: "We will still love you, still be there for you, still be your parents after divorce." Custody norms reinforce such parental assurances, increasingly reflecting the premise that shared custody is best for children and that divorce ordinarily should not end the spouses' role as co-parents. This shared-parenting norm has its most recent incarnation in the ALI's approximation model, which assigns custodial responsibility after divorce in a way that quantitatively approximates each parent's share of child care prior to divorce.[1] Rejecting the traditional sole-custodian, winner-take-all custody model, the ALI advances a vision of continued, shared parenting that survives divorce. The ALI model, like contemporary custody norms in general, nudges parents toward an expectation

This chapter incorporates portions of an earlier work published as "Lovers, Parents, and Partners; Disentangling Spousal and Co-Parenting Commitments," *Arizona Law Review* 54 (2012): 197.

that while divorce ends their status as spouses, it will not end their status as co-parents.[2]

Laws governing the economics of divorce send parents a very different message, nudging them to expect that divorce will end all inter-spousal ties. As we saw in chapter 2, no-fault's clean-break philosophy preaches spousal disentanglement—a fresh start for former spouses who are told they should each be free to begin new lives unshackled by a dead relationship. The clash between the clean-break norm in divorce economics and the sharing norm in custody arrangements is more than a conceptual curiosity.[3] As we saw in chapter 1, primary caregiving often constrains labor force participation, resulting in lost opportunities and ultimately in reduced human capital. This constraint applies both to caregiving that occurs during marriage and to caregiving that occurs after divorce. While the shared-parenting norm ensures that custodial rights are shared, the clean-break norm ensures that the post-divorce costs of primary physical responsibility for children will fall disproportionately on the parent who provides the majority of children's daily physical care.[4] These residential parents, most often mothers,[5] are left alone to bear the immediate and long-term opportunity costs associated with post-divorce parenting.

Consider, for example, the common case of the couple who after eight years and two children decide to divorce.[6] The mother earns far less than the father, partly because her role as primary family caregiver compromised her investment in the workplace, leading to gaps in employment; part-time employment; or family-friendly, full-time employment that is more flexible but less remunerative than available alternatives—all market disinvestment strategies that as we saw in chapter 1 are often associated with primary caregiving. In a common storyline, the divorce court will strive to give these spouses an economic clean break, dividing scant marital property and awarding the mother little or no alimony. While the custody order speaks of shared parenting, the practicalities of everyday life soon lead the mother to undertake primary responsibility for the children's daily physical care. The father will pay child support in an amount designed to approximate spending on the children during marriage, but this sum will leave the standard of living of the mother and children far below that of the father.[7] If this mother's post-divorce parenting responsibilities generate new opportunity costs and new reductions in earning capacity, these costs are hers alone to bear. There is something troubling about this state of things. If parents continue to share parenting *rights* after divorce, why shouldn't they also share parenting *costs*, including the human capital costs of post-divorce parenting?

Family law's failure to acknowledge parents' shared responsibility for the costs of parenting stems from a more systemic tendency to conflate marital and parental promises and to assume that divorce terminates all commitments between spouses whether or not they share children. The solution to the problem of post-divorce parenting begins with recognition that marital commitments and co-parenting commitments are two distinct undertakings.

A. Disentangling Marital and Co-Parenting Commitments
1. The Marital Partnership

As we have seen, marriage signals a lifetime commitment between intimate partners who typically exchange promises, comply with state formalities, and so acquire the legal status of spouses. Less often, couples forgo formalities, entering common-law marriages, which generally require a present agreement to be husband and wife and a holding out to the community.[8] Couples who choose marriage through either method are joined in a marital partnership, as diagrammed in figure 9.1.

If spouses happen to be parents, current law connects each parent to the child in a relationship line distinct from the marital partnership, as shown in figure 9.2.

Figures 9.1 and 9.2 depict two free-standing, unconnected relationship lines, one for spouses and another for parents. Responsibility for a child's financial support and physical care is thus viewed as the

Figure 9.1. The Marital Partnership

(spousal commitment)

Spouse 1   Spouse 2

(spousal commitment)

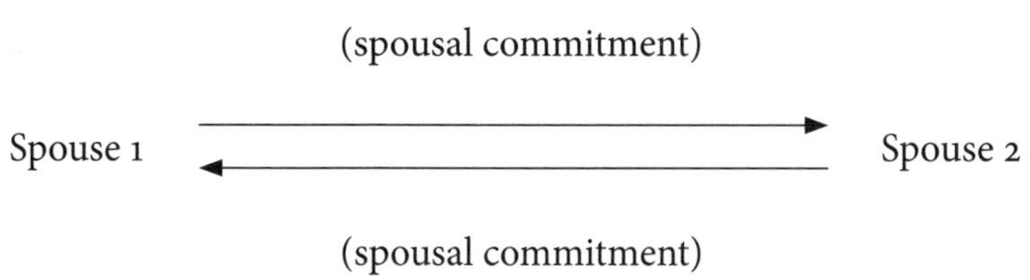

Figure 9.2. The Parent-Child Relationship

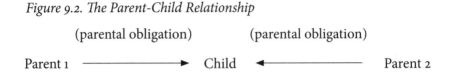

individual obligation of each parent. As a practical matter, married parents may combine and share their responsibilities, as for example where one parent serves as primary caregiver and the other as primary wage-earner. But such private arrangements are largely irrelevant to the state, which continues to view each parent as individually responsible for the child's welfare. So long as the child is not subject to abuse or neglect, the state assumes that each parent has met his or her individual responsibility to the child.

In a simple world, the marital partnership enjoys a natural life span, enduring until the death of one spouse. In the real world, however, affection may fade, and if it does, no-fault divorce laws allow parents to end their marital partnership freely and often unilaterally. As we have seen, under no-fault's partnership model, divorce triggers a winding up of partnership affairs, during which property, alimony, custody, and child support decisions are made. At this point, a final divorce decree is entered, and each spouse emerges with an individual obligation to his or her child but, at least as clean-break principles teach, otherwise set free to enjoy a fresh start, disentangled from a dead marriage. In its analogy to partnership, current divorce law stops here, erroneously assuming that marriages with children are no more complex than those without children and that termination of the marital partnership ends all commitments between former spouses whether or not they share children. Not so.

2. The Co-Parenting Partnership

Simple visions of spousehood on the one hand and parenthood on the other fail to capture the complexity of marriages with children. A married parent is not simply a participant in two independent relationships—one with a spouse and another with a child. From both a normative and a practical perspective, children add another dimension to marriage, as adults who are legally committed to each other as spouses

undertake a new mutual commitment as parents. This parental commitment runs not only to the child, to whom each parent owes an independent, state-imposed obligation, but also to the other parent, both
spouses understanding that they will share the physical and financial
costs of parenting. The result is a second layer of commitment between
intimate partners—a co-parenting partnership—that supplements the
marital partnership. The co-parenting partnership builds on each parent's individual obligation to the child, as shown in figure 9.3.

The co-parenting promises may be express, but more often they are
implied, both spouses understanding that the addition of children to
their family means a shared commitment to raise those children. The
child benefits from the stability of the co-parenting partnership and
from the mutuality of the parents' commitment, which, at least as a
normative matter, makes child care more dependable, more bountiful,
more efficient, and more manageable for parents.

While the state-imposed parental obligation requires only a minimal standard of care enforced by actions for abuse or neglect, the co-
parenting commitment may incorporate the parents' desire to provide
more. The state, for example, requires parents to feed their children. If
macaroni and cheese is on the menu, some parents believe it should

Figure 9.3. The Co-Parenting Partnership

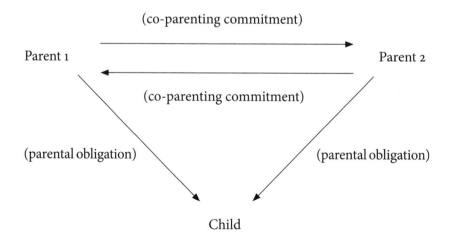

be homemade with fontina and aged cheddar, while others are content with the boxed variety. Neither type of macaroni and cheese is legally compelled, but for some parents, only one type will do, and that type, metaphorically speaking, becomes part of their co-parenting commitment. The point, of course, is not to disparage boxed dinners, but rather to suggest the pluralism that describes parental decisions about what is adequate and appropriate for their children.

The co-parenting partnership does not displace the marital partnership. While children may enrich and stretch and test a marriage, they do not, at least normatively speaking, end a marriage. Children are often an important part of marriage, but marriage is a relationship between adults that exists apart from children. Marriages with children thus involve two simultaneous, complementary partnerships—a marital partnership between two adults who make a commitment to live as lifetime intimate partners, and a co-parenting partnership between two parents who make a commitment to share the rights and responsibilities of parenting. During marriage, the marital partnership and the co-parenting partnership work together to form a multilayered family partnership. If the parents divorce, their marital partnership ends, but what of their co-parenting partnership?

B. Divorce and the Co-Parenting Commitment

I smiled at him.
> "And my ex-husband has money."
> "Alimony?"
> "Oh God, no," I said. "I'd never ask Richie for alimony."
> Farrell nodded.
> "Of course not," he said.
> "Alimony destroys a relationship."
> "I figured the divorce usually did that."
> "It doesn't have to."
—Robert B. Parker, *Perish Twice* (New York: Putnam's, 2000), 253

When parents divorce during their child's minority, the marital partnership terminates, but divorce does not so swiftly terminate the co-parenting partnership, which endures at least until its work is complete—that is, until the couple's children reach majority. Divorcing parents may not love or even like each other, but while the loss of intimate affection is a basis for ending a marriage, it is not a basis for ending a commitment to share parenting. Indeed, custody norms are premised on an assumption that the end of intimacy should *not* trigger the end of co-parenting. Continuation of the co-parenting partnership thus does not depend on love, intimacy, or friendship between former spouses, but rather on the parents' mutual commitment to take on the economic support and physical labor required to raise shared children. In a best-case scenario, of course, parents will retain some modicum of good will toward each other, or at least not become enemies, and there is some evidence that this outcome is more likely than generally assumed. As Tali Schaefer observes, "judges get a distorted picture of how acrimonious divorce is and how unreasonable and self-involved parents are because the worst cases are the ones that they get to hear."[9] In any event, as friends or enemies, former spouses with shared children continue to be bound by their mutual promises to share the responsibilities of parenting. Although the relationship has lost its intimate connection, the couple's shared children continue to link them.

Continuation of the co-parenting partnership does not depend on the parents' desire or ability to cooperate with each other. Divorced parents may coordinate their care for the children or they may refuse to speak to each other. Whatever their inclination toward cooperation, as a de facto matter, each divorced parent benefits from the other's physical labor on behalf of a child, since what one parent does for a child the other parent need not do. As the ALI observes, while parents "can allocate responsibility [for children] they cannot avoid it and the spouse who assumes it discharges a legal obligation of both parents."[10] Simply put, if one parent provides a child with breakfast, the other parent need not; if one parent shops for a winter coat or shoes or crayons, the other need not; if one parent tutors a child, washes her pajamas, transports her to school and soccer practice, or prepares her macaroni and cheese, the other need not. The point is that labor expended on behalf of a child by one parent frees the other parent from the legal and moral obligation to perform it. While parenting may be pleasant work, it is work nonetheless—a point babysitters for pay understand well enough.

As divorced co-parents continue to raise their children, the co-parenting commitment thus endures and their promise to share the costs of raising their children continues. Current tools governing divorce economics—property distribution, alimony, and child support—ignore co-parenting promises and so also ignore divorced parents' shared responsibility for the post-divorce costs of parenting.

1. Clean-Break Tools: Property Distribution,
Alimony, and Child Support

As we saw in chapter 2, the distribution of marital property is designed to be a onetime, nonmodifiable event that allocates marital (or community) property rights at the time of divorce. The no-fault aspiration is that the property distribution will address any economic inequities between spouses so that they can swiftly be set free to begin new lives. As we also saw, this aspiration has proved to be wishful thinking, as most marriages end without enough property to give courts much to work with. Even when property abounds, the property distribution is an awkward tool for dealing with divorced parents' shared responsibility for the post-divorce costs of parenting. Although a sizable, disparately large share of marital property could theoretically offset these costs, they are difficult to estimate. Because property awards are not modifiable, an award intended to address co-parenting responsibilities might lock parents into obligations that are inappropriately large or inappropriately small. Moreover, there is no satisfactory theoretical basis for conscripting the property distribution to address the costs of post-divorce parenting. Property rules were designed to bring an equitable conclusion to the marital partnership, which exists quite apart from any continuing co-parenting obligations, and the partnership analogy strongly supports an equal-division rule for marital property.

Like property distribution, alimony does not, and should not, address co-parenting commitments. Alimony is a tool for addressing the consequences of broken marriage promises. Its role does not depend on the presence or absence of shared children. To be sure, if primary caregiving during marriage has *already* reduced a caregiver's earning potential at the time of divorce, she may qualify for alimony under current law on the ground that she is needy, although as we have seen, neediness is no guarantee of an alimony award. Alimony is rare,

partly because of its awful reputation, and partly because it is inconsistent with the clean-break imperative. Moreover, alimony tends to
punish rather than compensate residential parents whose caregiving
responsibilities reduce their earnings. Unless a residential parent is caring for a disabled child or perhaps for a very young child, she may be
the target of income imputation. Income imputation serves to reduce
the size of an alimony award, and may even disqualify a claimant from
receiving alimony, effectively punishing a caregiver for family labor that
a court or legislature deems "excessive."[11] On balance, alimony is doing
a poor enough job addressing termination of the marital partnership;
it would be a mistake to conscript it for a new assignment. Even if alimony were analogized to a partnership buyout, as described in the last
chapter, its function is to impose an exit price upon premature termination of the marital partnership, a relationship that imposes rights and
responsibilities distinct from those associated with shared parenting.

Nor does child support address the opportunity costs of post-divorce
primary parenting. Child support awards essentially aim to disentangle
divorcing parents by identifying, separating, and assigning each parent's liability for the child. The premise is that each parent is individually responsible for the child's support, but that the parents owe nothing
to each other. Even under income-shares models, which combine the
parents' incomes to determine support levels,[12] the goal of child support
is fundamentally to convert what was once shared family responsibility
for children into the individual responsibilities of two "single" parents.
Calculation of child support thus recognizes no continuing obligations
between parents, but only between each individual parent and the child.

The clean-break goal of child support and the sense of individual
entitlement it fosters is evident in the frequent complaint of nonresidential parents that their child support payments are benefitting the
residential parent, an event that is assumed to be inappropriate.[13] As the
American Law Institute (ALI) explains, "the payor parent has an interest
in limiting the *measure* of his child support obligation to his relationship
to the child, rather than to the residential household."[14] Of course, it is
not possible to fully protect this interest, legitimate or not, since as the
ALI observes, "any transfer of income to the child's residential household may also be enjoyed by other members of the household, including
the residential parent. This is an inevitable and unavoidable effect of any

child-support transfer, and is not itself an adequate reason for limiting or disapproving child support."[15] Sharing with a co-parent is thus cast as an unfortunate but unavoidable price of supporting one's child.

But why shouldn't a nonresidential parent share income with a co-parent who is caring for shared children on a daily basis? If a residential parent experiences opportunity costs as a result of post-divorce parenting, why should these costs be hers alone to bear? If responsibility for children's daily physical care is the responsibility of *both* co-parents, why should a residential parent bear the lion's share of these costs? If a nanny were caring for their children, parents would likely share the cost of her salary, but if a divorced co-parent performs this same daily labor, she is entitled to no compensation and no reimbursement for her lost market opportunities. At worst, divorce converts a mother into an unpaid employee of the father. Evidently, when it comes to financial responsibility for children's daily physical care, the status of a residential parent is worse than that of a third-party stranger. In the end, child support laws, like laws governing property distribution and alimony, encourage parents to assume that divorce should end all commitments between them. This sense of entitlement, justified by the clean-break principle, lies at the core of laws governing the economics of divorce. If the law is to nudge divorcing parents to expect to keep their co-parenting commitment to share the responsibilities of nurturing shared children, it must look beyond current tools governing the economics of divorce.

2. Co-Parenting Orders and the Next Conversation

Continuation of the co-parenting commitment provides a conceptual basis for income sharing between divorced co-parents. This commitment lays the groundwork for new default rules that recognize, for the first time, a nonresidential parent's affirmative responsibility to share income not only with his or her child, but also with the residential parent who is undertaking the lion's share of the daily labor required to raise shared children. Disentangled from the marital commitment, the co-parenting commitment stands as a distinct undertaking, one the law should encourage parents to honor. As we have seen, however, current law does just the opposite, ignoring the co-parenting commitment and encouraging divorcing partners to assume that divorce signals the end of *all* commitments between them whether or not they share children. The default rules[16] that produce this result are sticky, nudging spouses to believe that this is an appropriate divorce outcome.[17] It is not. Divorce law must be reconceptualized to reinforce people's general inclination to keep their commitments, or at least to take them seriously,[18] and to reflect policy goals more consistent with the best interests of children, their caregivers, and society at large.[19]

Income sharing between divorced co-parents will raise many questions—some new, some old, and many tough. And so there must be a next conversation, one that builds on the conceptual foundation for income sharing offered here. A threshold question is the appropriate form of income sharing. The most radical but most conceptually sound approach would be to craft a new financial remedy for enforcing the co-parenting commitment. This new tool would supplement the marital-termination tools of property, alimony, and child support, and might be termed a *co-parenting order*. Karen Czapanskiy has proposed something similar, if more limited, in the form of "chalimony," which would be paid by nonresidential parents to primary caregivers of children with disabilities or chronic illnesses when caregiving impairs the caregiver's labor force participation.[20]

Less radically, the co-parenting commitment provides the basis for an expansion of child support. In this new version of child support, parents would share not only the costs of their children's food, clothing, and shelter, but also the human capital costs of parenting. This approach might begin with a redefinition of "parental expenditures on the child" to include the residential parent's forgone wages and declining human capital. As others have pointed out, the definition of "parental expenditures on the child" is a policy choice, "not something one looks up in a technical manual on economic statistics."[21]

Another approach would be to include an allowance for the costs of post-divorce parenting in an alimony award. This appears to be the approach of the Canadian alimony guidelines. As we saw in chapter 5, the Canadian guidelines offer two basic formulae for calculating the duration and value of an alimony award. As the guideline project co-directors explain, the formula that applies in cases with minor children (where child support is also being paid) is based on the principle of "parental partnership," reflecting compensation for the indirect costs of primary caregiving both during and after marriage.[22]

Another important issue for the next conversation is the appropriate level of income sharing. Since measuring the costs of parenting for a particular primary caregiver is impractical, these costs might be presumptively identified as the difference between the divorced parents' incomes, a method employed by the ALI to measure the costs of *past* caretaking.[23] The level of income sharing must be carefully calibrated to ensure that the residential parent does not bear an unfair share of the costs of parenting, and also to ensure that neither parent is inappropriately discouraged from job investments. The nonresidential parent should thus not give up too much; the residential parent should not gain too much. How much is "too much" is of course no easy question. The ALI suggests in its new alimony formulation that the value of an alimony award should not exceed 40 percent of the spouses' income differential.[24] An alternative approach would focus on the parents' household standards of living, equalizing or at least minimizing any disparities. Whatever level of income sharing is chosen, it should be clear, predictable, and widely known, published perhaps in the form of guidelines. As Thaler and Sunstein observe, "Families facing divorce will gain if the law provides an anchor or range, helping people know what constitutes a fair or likely outcome."[25]

The next conversation should also identify intimate relationships other than marriage that evidence commitment. Parents, of course, may expressly contract into a co-parenting commitment. Without such an express agreement, some intimate relationships clearly evidence commitment, so that the addition of children to these families signals an implicit co-parenting commitment. Easy examples of such relationships include registered domestic partnerships and civil unions. Just as easily, couples engaged in a one-night stand are clearly not committed and so do not enter a co-parenting partnership. Nor do marriage-eligible cohabiting intimates qualify as committed couples, unless perhaps the circumstances of their relationship trigger a state-imposed status, as the ALI has proposed.[26] A related question involves couples who commit to each other as intimate partners *after* they bear or adopt a child. In such cases, the co-parenting commitment should date from the time of the couple's commitment rather than to the date of their child's birth or adoption.

One complicating issue in inferring a co-parenting partnership between committed intimates is the possibility that the parents are divided on their desire to add a child to their family. The couple, for example, may agree never to have children, but later the wife decides unilaterally to discontinue birth control. Another couple may become "accidentally" pregnant, with one party advocating abortion and the other resisting. One possible response to these cases is to say that the addition of a child to the family signals the couple's understanding that they will share responsibility for their child, whether or not they are joyful about the prospect. Under this reasoning, the couple who breaks up because of their disagreement about a new child does not enter a co-parenting commitment relating to that child. A pragmatic approach to these cases and others like them might be to create a rebuttable presumption that spouses (and other committed intimates) who add children to their family *presumptively* enter a co-parenting partnership; outside these relationships, no such presumption arises.[27] These default rules won't get all cases right, but they will get most cases right.

Yet another issue goes to the parents' ability to terminate the co-parenting partnership. Because their commitment is voluntarily undertaken, it should be capable of voluntary termination. But, like the marital partnership, termination of the co-parenting partnership would require payment of an exit price. This exit price, paid by the nonresidential parent, would be designed to compensate the primary caregiver for the lost earnings and earning capacity she is likely to experience as a result of post-divorce caregiving. The size of the exit price will reflect a policy choice about how difficult it should be to abandon a promise to share the costs of parenting shared children.[28] Termination of the co-parenting partnership, of course, would not affect the obligation of each individual parent to support the child, but only the obligation to share the lost earnings and lost earning capacity of the parent who assumes the responsibilities of primary caregiving.

Merle Weiner has recently argued that caregiver payments should be based on status without regard to any commitment between co-parents.[29] While this approach finesses the challenge of identifying co-parenting commitments, it raises tough new questions about the rationale for forced income sharing beyond child support, especially in cases where parents are little more than strangers. Her argument, however, should enrich the next conversation about the nature and role of commitments between parents. Other issues that should drive the next conversation include many with which family law is currently grappling: how to deal with new families,[30] multiple parents,[31] and unemployed or underemployed parents.[32]

3. The Psychic Joy Objection

Some may object to income sharing between co-parents on the ground that such sharing would overcompensate residential parents, who already reap a huge reward in the form of psychic joy stemming from their extensive time with children. This argument is unpersuasive. Most fundamentally, psychic joy is simply not measureable and so cannot be quantified and then offset against a monetary award. Measurement is made more challenging by the fact that time spent with children is a poor indicator of the extent of psychic joy. A primary caregiver may spend much time tending to daily chores that produce little joy—cooking, cleaning, shopping, laundering, wiping macaroni and cheese off the floor. The parent who spends less time with children may actually experience more psychic joy than the other parent, especially if that time is devoted more exclusively to child-intensive endeavors—time perhaps at the zoo, the soccer field, the ice cream shop, or the library. Time is a poor proxy for psychic joy. Moreover, the suggestion that psychic joy is time-dependent raises uncomfortable questions about the children themselves and their tendency to inspire joy rather than sorrow or worry or frustration or any of the other psychic costs of parenting that are likely to fall disproportionately on the parent with primary residential responsibility.

The partnership metaphor provides an interesting perspective on the argument that income sharing would overcompensate a primary caregiver. Imagine the following exchange between equal partners:

> "Did you enjoy your day—working at the office [or the shop, the restaurant, the car wash]?"
>
> "Yes, very much."
>
> "Well then, you have reaped your reward and we will reduce your share of partnership income accordingly."

Psychic joy is a dubious basis for keeping primary caregivers and their children at a lower standard of living than the other parent.

In the end, this chapter advances the "radical" proposition that the law should listen when parents say that divorce is not about children. The clean-break philosophy of no-fault, and the default rules it inspires, however, encourage parents to believe that divorce ends all ties between them, including their commitment to share the costs of raising children. The result is a sense of individual entitlement that nudges parents to break their co-parenting promises and to assume that the parent who provides the lion's share of children's daily care after divorce should alone bear the financial costs of that work. The law is sending the wrong message. Family law must expand its understanding of commitment to include both intimate and co-parenting partnerships, and refine its vision of divorce as a tool for ending some but not all commitments between married parents. Disentangled from the marital commitment, the co-parenting commitment provides a compelling basis for new default rules that recognize divorced parents' joint liability for the full costs of parenting shared children. Implementing co-parenting orders should be the focus of new reform efforts.

Conclusion

Many of the primary caregivers at work in today's homes are going about their business unaware that if their marriages end they are likely to become the law's suckers, set free to alone bear the long-term costs of the role they thought was part of marital teamwork. Archaic alimony laws are to blame. Alimony is often the only available tool for ensuring that divorce does not impose all the long-term costs of marital roles on caregivers while freeing the other spouse to enjoy all the long-term benefits. Yet in its current incarnation, alimony is not up to the task before it. Beset by myths, disdain, and neglect, the law of alimony inspires orders that are unpredictable, inconsistent, short-lived, and uncommon. Alimony's problems are exacerbated by the absence of any contemporary rationale to justify its existence in an age of no-fault divorce and supposed gender equality. Concerned commentators have offered an array of alimony theories and reform proposals, but none has carried the day. Meanwhile, grassroots alimony reform groups in numerous states are working hard to publicize alimony horror stories and promote legislative reform to limit alimony, most recently succeeding in Massachusetts.

Alimony may be a broken tool, but it is an essential tool for avoiding injustice when marriage ends. Drawing on a loose analogy to partnership, I have proposed that alimony be reconceptualized as a marriage buyout. Buyouts may be based on either an enhanced-earnings or a pooled-human-capital model and, in either case, can be quantified under presumptive formulae designed to make these new awards more certain and predictable than their current alimony counterparts. In addition to their practical importance, buyouts support new default rules that reinforce egalitarian, gender-neutral, communal visions of marriage, encourage expectations consistent with that vision, and in all but very low-income cases, protect primary caregivers who rely on marriage promises. Looking beyond alimony, I also propose a new co-parenting partnership model, which provides the conceptual basis for income sharing between divorced parents of minor children and an answer to the vexing problem of how to deal with the opportunity costs associated with post-divorce caregiving.

Alimony's future is uncertain, and much is at stake—for today's primary caregivers, for those who care about them and benefit from their labor, and for everyone concerned about the integrity of family law. My hope is that this book will inform reform discourse and ensure that Casey's story is a part of it.

NOTES

NOTES TO THE INTRODUCTION

1. *Alimony Madness* (Mayfair Pictures Corporation, 1933).
2. *Alimony—Preying on Innocent Dupes* (Orbit Productions, 1949).
3. *Guilty Conscience* (CBS Entertainment, 1985).
4. Bethany True, *Remember the Alimony* (New York: Dorchester, 2007).
5. *See* http://www.alimonynightmares.com/.
6. *See* http://www.njalimonyreform.org/stories.php.
7. *See* http://alimonyslaves.blogspot.com/.

NOTES TO CHAPTER 1

1. Joan Williams, *Unbending Gender: Why Family and Work Conflict and What to Do about It* (New York: Oxford University Press, 2000), 5 ("the ideal worker's wage is the product of two adults: the ideal worker's market work and the marginalized caregiver's family work.").
2. *See, e.g., In re Marriage of Harris*, 244 P.3d 801, 805–6 (Or. 2010), in which a caregiver sought alimony despite a pool of marital property approximating $1.5 million. A lower court rejected the caregiver's alimony claim, but the Oregon Supreme Court reversed, stating that a large property award should not preclude alimony.

3. The title of this section translates literally as "children, kitchen, church." This German phrase suggests that women should be confined to their biological role.

4. *See Orr v. Orr*, 440 U.S. 268 (1979).

5. Anita Raghaven, "Men Receiving Alimony Want a Little Respect," *Wall Street Journal*, April 1, 2008, A1.

6. Hilary Stout, "The Controversial Rise in Manimony," *Marie-Claire*, April 19, 2011.

7. *Bradwell v. Illinois*, 83 U.S. (16 Wall) 130, 141–42 (1872) (concurring opinion).

8. *See* Nancy Dowd, *The Man Question: Male Subordination and Privilege* (New York: New York University Press, 2010), 119–20 ("Men are blocked from embracing nurture by the command of masculinity that they not be like girls or women and that identifies care as feminine. . . . As characteristic and as action, nurture is unmanly. Just as significantly, men embrace the role of breadwinner as the defining characteristic of partnership with women and of being a parent.").

9. Max Lerner, *America as a Civilization* (New York: Simon and Schuster, 1957), 611.

10. William H. Chafe, *Women and Equality* (New York: Oxford University Press, 1977), 15.

11. Betty Friedan, *The Feminine Mystique* (New York: Dell, 1984), 59 (quoting *Look* magazine, October 16, 1956).

12. *Id.* at 95 (quoting *Life* magazine, Christmas 1956).

13. Chafe, *supra* note 10 at 32.

14. Friedan, *supra* note 11 at 59 (quoting *Look* magazine, October 16, 1956).

15. Chafe, *supra* note 10 at 95.

16. Alice Kessler-Harris, *Out to Work* (New York: Oxford University Press, 1982), 381n26.

17. Stephanie Coontz, *The Way We Never Were: American Families and the Nostalgia Trap* (New York: Basic Books, 1992), 37.

18. Friedan, *supra* note 11 at 16.

19. *Id.* at 25 (quoting *Redbook* magazine).

20. *Id.* at 24, 25 (quoting *New York Times*).

21. Anne Slaughter, "Why Women Still Can't Have It All," *Atlantic*, July/August 2012, 92.

22. Lisa Belkin, "The Opt-Out Revolution," *New York Times*, October 23, 2003.

23. Katy McLaughlin, "New Dreams, When the Old Ones Don't Fit," *Wall Street Journal*, October 7, 2012.

24. Arlie Hochschild, *The Second Shift* (New York: Viking, 1989).

25. U.S. Bureau of Labor Statistics, *American Time-Use Survey—2012 Results* (Washington, D.C.: U.S. Government Printing Office, 2012) (hereinafter BLS 2012a), http://www.bls.gov/news.release/pdf/atus.pdf.

26. Suzanne M. Bianchi, John P. Robinson, and Melissa A. Milkie, *Changing Rhythms of American Family Life* (New York: Russell Sage Foundation, 2006), 93.

27. Diane Swanbrow, "Exactly How Much Housework Does a Husband Create?" *Michigan Today—Research News* (2008), http://ns.umich.edu/new/releases/6452.

28. Bianchi et al., *supra* note 26 at 66.

29. *Id.*

30. *Id.* at 64, table 4.1.

31. *Id.* at 85.

32. American Law Institute, *Principles of the Law of Family Dissolution: Analysis and Recommendations* (St. Paul, MN: American Law Institute, 2002), § 5.05, reporter's notes, cmt. d.

33. Swanbrow, *supra* note 27.

34. *Id.*

35. Bianchi et al., *supra* note 26 at 93, table 5.1.

36. *Id.* at 115.

37. *Id.* at 55.

38. Christopher Carrington, "Domesticity and Political Economy of Lesbigay Families," in *Families at Work: Expanding the Bounds*, ed. Naomi Gerstel et al. (Nashville: Vanderbilt University Press, 2002), 91.

39. U.S. Bureau of Labor Statistics, *Employment Characteristics of Families—2011* (2012), tables 4, 6, http://www.bls.gov/news.release/famee.htm.

40. *Id.* at Technical Notes.

41. *Id.* at tables 4, 6.

42. *Id.* at table 5.

43. Christy Spivey, "Time Off at What Price? The Effects of Career Interruptions on Earnings," *Industrial and Labor Relations Review* 59 (2005): 119.

44. Sylvia Ann Hewlett, *Off-Ramps and On-Ramps: Keeping Talented Women on the Road to Success* (Boston: Harvard Business School Press, 2007), 1, 29–36.

45. *Id.* at 29.

46. *Id.* at 32.

47. *Id.* at 33.

48. *Id.* at 36.

49. *Id.* at 35.

50. Joan Williams, *Reshaping the Work-Family Debate: Why Men and Class Matter* (Cambridge: Harvard University Press, 2010).

51. *Id.* at 48.

52. *Id.* at 31.

53. Belkin, *supra* note 22.

54. Pew Research Center, *The Harried Life of the Working Mother* (2009), http://www.pewsocialtrends.org/2009/10/01/the-harried-life-of-the-working-mother.

55. Joan Williams and Heather Boushey, *The Three Faces of Work-Family Conflict: The Poor, the Professionals and the Missing Middle*, Report of the Center for American Progress and the Center for Worklife Law, University of California Hastings College of the Law (2010), table 2, http://www.worklifelaw.org/pubs/ThreeFacesofWork-FamilyConflict.pdf.

56. Pew Research Center, *supra* note 54.

57. Williams, *supra* note 50 at 147–48.

58. Riche Jeneen Daniel Barnes, "Black Women Have Always Worked: Is There a Work-Family Conflict among the Black Middle Class?" in *The Changing Landscape of Work and Family in the American Middle Class: Reports from the Field*, ed. E. Rudd and L. Descartes (Lanham, MD: Lexington Books, 2008), 190–92.

59. *See* A. Michele Dickerson, "Race Matters in Bankruptcy," *Washington and Lee Law Review* 61 (2004): 1725, 1749.

60. Gina Bellafonte, "Two Fathers, One Happy to Stay at Home," *New York Times*, November 12, 2004.

61. U.S. Department of Labor, *Women's Employment during the Recovery* (2011), 1, http://www.dol.gov/_sec/media/reports/FemaleLaborForce/FemaleLaborForce. pdf.

62. H. Luke Shaefer, "Part-Time Workers: Some Key Differences between Primary and Secondary Earners," *Monthly Labor Review*, October 2009, 4.

63. *Id.*

64. U.S. Bureau of Labor Statistics, "Part-Time Workers: Who They Are and How Much They Earn," November 4, 2004, http://www.bls.gov/opub/ted/2004/nov/wk1/art04.htm.

65. Hewlett, *supra* note 44.

66. Pew Research Center, *supra* note 54.

67. BLS 2012a, *supra* note 25.

68. Bianchi et al., *supra* note 26 at 46, 58.

69. Ann Crittenden, *The Price of Motherhood: Why the Most Important Job in the World Is Still the Least Valued* (New York: Metropolitan Books, 2001), 18.

70. Janet C. Gornick and Marcia K. Meyers, *Families That Work: Policies for Reconciling Parenthood and Employment* (New York: Russell Sage Foundation, 2003), table 2.3 at 47.

71. Bianchi et al., *supra* note 26 at 51.

72. *Id.* at 124.

73. Bellafonte, *supra* note 60.

74. Victor Fuchs, *Women's Quest for Economic Equality* (Cambridge: Harvard University Press, 1988), 147.

75. Crittenden, *supra* note 69 at 88.

76. *Id.*

77. Jane Waldfogel, "Understanding the 'Family Gap' in Pay for Women with Children," *Journal of Economic Perspectives* 12 (1998): 137.

78. Deborah Anderson et al., "The Motherhood Wage Penalty Revisited: Experience, Heterogeneity, Work Effort, and Work-Schedule Flexibility," *Industrial and Labor Relations Review* 56 (2003): 273–94.

79. Michelle J. Budig and Melissa J. Hodges, "Differences in Disadvantage: Variation in the Motherhood Penalty across White Women's Earnings Distribution," *American Sociological Review* 75 (2010): 705, 717, 725.

80. Shaefer, *supra* note 62 at 5.

81. Spivey, *supra* note 43.

82. Wendy Sigle-Rushton and Jane Waldfogel, *Motherhood and Women's Earnings in Anglo-American, Continental European, and Nordic Countries*, Luxembourg Income Study Working Paper Series No. 454 (2006), http://www.lisproject.org/publications/liswps/454.pdf.

83. Hewlett, *supra* note 44 at 43–46.

84. *Id.* at 43.

85. Williams, *supra* note 1.

86. Terry Hekker, "The Satisfactions of Housewifery and Motherhood in 'an Age of Do-Your-Own-Thing,'" *New York Times*, December 20, 1977.

87. Terry Hekker, "Paradise Lost (Domestic Division)," *New York Times*, January 1, 2006.

88. Herma Hill Kay, "Equality and Difference: A Perspective on No-Fault Divorce and Its Aftermath," *University of Cincinnati Law Review* 56 (1989): 80. *See also* June Carbone, "Economics, Feminism, and the Reinvention of Alimony," *Vanderbilt Law Review* 43 (1990): 1463.

89. Kay, *supra* note 88 at 85.

90. Williams, *supra* note 1 at 122.

91. Twila L. Perry, "Alimony: Race, Privilege and Dependency in the Search for Theory," *Georgetown Law Journal* 82 (1994): 2481, 2493, 2504. *See also* Keith L. Shoji, "Review: Alimony: Race, Privilege, and Dependency in the Search for Theory," *Journal of Contemporary Legal Issues* 11 (2000): 309.

92. Regina Austin, "Nest Eggs and Stormy Weather: Law, Culture, and Black Women's Lack of Wealth," in *Feminism Confronts Homo Economicus: Gender, Law, and Society*, ed. Martha Albertson Fineman and Terence Dougherty (Ithaca: Cornell University Press, 2005), 131, 139.

93. Laura T. Kessler, "Getting Class," *Buffalo Law Review* 56 (2008): 915, 923–24.

94. Martha Albertson Fineman, "The Nature of Dependencies and Welfare 'Reform,'" *Santa Clara Law Review* 36 (1996): 287, 299–304.

95. Vicki Schultz, "Life's Work," *Columbia Law Review* 100 (2000): 1881, 1912.

96. *Id.* at 1908.

97. Martha Albertson Fineman, *The Neutered Mother, the Sexual Family and Other Twentieth Century Tragedies* (New York: Routledge, 1995), 161–64, 231–33.

98. Martha Albertson Fineman, "Contract and Care," *Chicago-Kent Law Review* 76 (2001): 1403, 1410–11.

NOTES TO CHAPTER 2

1. *In re Marriage of Brantner*, 136 Cal. Rptr. 635, 637 (1977).

2. Sally Herigstad, "Q and A with Terry Hekker, author of 'Disregard First Book,'" CreditCards.com, November 23, 2011, http://finance.yahoo.com/news/q-terry-hekker-author-disregard-130000485.html.

3. William Blackstone, *Commentaries on the Laws of England*, book 1(Oxford: Clarendon, 1765-69), 430.

4. *Id.* at 433.

5. Reva Siegel, "Modernization of Marital Status Law: Adjudicating Wives' Rights to Earnings, 1860–1930," *Georgetown Law Journal* 82 (1994): 2128.

6. N.C. Gen. Stat. § 50.16.3A (2011). *See* American Law Institute, *Principles of the Law of Family Dissolution: Analysis and Recommendations* (St. Paul, MN: American Law Institute, 2002) (hereinafter *ALI Principles*), 82–83.

7. S.C. Code Ann. § 20-3-130(A) (2008).

8. Uniform Marriage and Divorce Act § 302(a) (1973) (hereinafter UMDA).

9. Doris Jonas Freed and Timothy B. Walker, "Family Law in the Fifty States: An Overview," *Family Law Quarterly* 18 (1985): 379–82.

10. Diana Pearce, "The More Things Change . . . A Status Report on Displaced Caregivers and Single Parents in the 1980s" (Washington, D.C.: Displaced Homemakers Network, 1990), 60 (on file with the University of Chicago Law Review).

11. Lenore J. Weitzman, *The Divorce Revolution: The Unexpected Social and Economic Social Consequences for Women and Children in America* (New York: Free Press, 1985), 323.

12. *See, e.g.,* J. Herbie Difonzo and Ruth C. Stern, "The Winding Road from Form to Function: A Brief History of Contemporary Marriage," *Journal of the American Academy of Matrimonial Lawyers* 21 (2008): 1.

13. *See* Greg J. Duncan and Saul D. Hoffman, "Economic Consequences of Marital Instability," in *Horizontal Equity, Uncertainty, and Economic Well-Being*, ed. Martin David and Timothy Smeeding (Chicago: University of Chicago Press, 1985), 427, 437 (reporting that five years after divorce, single women averaged a standard of living that was about 94 percent of the standard they enjoyed in the year prior to divorce, while remarried women averaged a standard of living that was about 25 percent higher than in the year prior to divorce).

14. *See* Lenore Weitzman, "The Economic Consequences of Divorce Are Still Unequal: Comment on Peterson," *American Sociological Review* 61 (1996): 537 (conceding that her figures were exaggerated).

15. U.S. Bureau of the Census, *Current Population Survey—1989. See also* Displaced Homemakers Self-Sufficiency Assistance Act, 29 U.S.C.A. § 2301(a)(3) (1990) (repealed 1998) (hereinafter DHSSAA) (stating the Congressional finding that "there are approximately 15,600,000 displaced homemakers in the United States, the majority of whom are women not in the labor force, who live in poverty and who require educational, vocational, training and other services to obtain financial independence and economic security").

16. Pearce, *supra* note 10 at 20–21.

17. National Displaced Caregivers Network, *A Handbook on State Displaced Caregiver Legislation: 1990–1991*; Update 7 (1991) (on file with the University of Chicago Law Review).

18. DHSSAA, *supra* note 15.

19. *Id.* at § 2301(b).

20. UMDA , *supra* note 8 at § 308, Official Comment.

21. Weitzman, *supra* note 11 at 30–31.

22. Cal. Civ. Code § 4700.10(a)(2) (West Supp. 1991), repealed by Stats. 1992, c. 162 (A.B.2650), § 3, operative Jan. 1, 1994.

23. *O'Brien v. O'Brien*, 489 N.E.2d 712 (1985).

24. Weitzman, *supra* note 11 at 396–97.

25. For surveys of early gender bias studies, see Lynn Hecht Schafran, "Documenting Gender Bias in the Courts: The Task Force Approach," *Judicature* 70 (1987): 280; and Lynn Hecht Schafran, "Gender and Justice: Florida and the Nation," *Florida Law Review* 42 (1990): 181.

26. Schafran, "Documenting Gender Bias," *supra* note 25 at 285.

27. Michigan Supreme Court Task Force on Gender Issues in the Courts, "Conclusions and Recommendations" (1990), 1 (on file with the University of Chicago Law Review).

28. Schafran, "Documenting Gender Bias," *supra* note 25 at 285.

29. Pub. L. No. 297, 1973 Ind. Acts 1585, formerly codified at Ind. Code Ann. § 31-1-11.5-11.

30. *Luedke v. Luedke*, 487 N.E.2d 133 (Ind. 1985)

31. *Luedke v. Luedke*, 476 N.E.2d 853, 855, 860 (Ind. App. 1985), rev'd 487 N.E.2d 133 (Ind. 1985).

32. *Luedke*, 476 N.E.2d at 859–60.

33. *Id.* at 860.

34. *Baker v. Baker*, 488 N.E.2d 361, 366–67 (Ind. App. 1986) (Young, J., concurring).

35. Ind. Code Ann. § 31-15-7-5 (Lexis 2012).

36. Herma Hill Kay, "Equality and Difference: A Perspective on No-Fault Divorce and Its Aftermath," *University of Cincinnati Law Review* 56 (1989): 80.

37. *Id.* at 85.

38. UMDA, *supra* note 8 at § 308, Official Comment.

39. *Id.* at § 308(a).

40. Jana B. Singer, "Alimony and Efficiency: The Gendered Costs and Benefits of the Economic Justification for Alimony," *Georgetown Law Journal* 82 (1994): 2423, 2424n5.

41. Paul H. Jacobson, *American Marriage and Divorce* (New York: Rinehart, 1959), 127–28.

42. U.S. Bureau of the Census, *Child Support and Alimony*, Current Population Report, Series P-60, No. 173 (Washington, D.C.: U.S. Government Printing Office, 1989).

43. Marsha Garrison, "The Economics of Divorce: Changing Rules, Changing Results," in *Divorce Reform at the Crossroads*, ed. Stephen D. Sugarman and Herma Hill Kay (New Haven: Yale University Press, 1990), 91, table 3.11.

44. Weitzman, *supra* note 11 at 169.

45. U.S. Bureau of the Census, *supra* note 42. *See also* Heather Ruth Wishik, "Economics of Divorce: An Exploratory Study," *Family Law Quarterly* 20 (1986–1987): 79, 81, 85–86 (reporting that in Vermont, of divorces closed from October

1982 through February 1983, fewer than 7 percent of spouses received alimony awards, and fewer than 2 percent received awards of unlimited duration).

46. Marsha Garrison, "Good Intentions Gone Awry: The Impact of New York's Equitable Distribution Law on Divorce Outcomes," *Brooklyn Law Review* 57 (1991): 700.

47. David H. Kelsey and Patrick P. Fry, "The Relationship between Permanent and Rehabilitative Alimony," *Journal of the American Academy of Matrimonial Lawyers* 4 (1988): 6.

48. *The Displaced Caregivers Network: The Woman It Serves, the Problems It Addresses, Its Accomplishments and Current Activities*, 2 (pamphlet on file with the University of Chicago Law Review), quoting Laurie Shields.

49. Jill Miller, "Working Paper on Displaced Caregivers in the Employment and Training System" (1988), 11 (on file with the University of Chicago Law Review).

50. Jacob Mincer and Solomon Polachek, "Family Investments in Human Capital: Earnings of Women," in *Economics of the Family: Marriage, Children, and Human Capital*, ed. Theodore W. Schultz (Chicago: University of Chicago Press, 1974), 397, 415.

51. Betty Friedan, *It Changed My Life: Writings on the Women's Movement* (New York: Random House, 1976), 325–26.

52. Ind. Code Ann. § 31-15-7-2 (Lexis 2012), formerly codified at Ind. Code Ann. § 31-1-11.5-11, provides as follows:

> Sec. 2. A court may make the following findings concerning maintenance:
>
> (1) If the court finds a spouse to be physically or mentally incapacitated to the extent that the ability of the incapacitated spouse to support himself or herself is materially affected, the court may find that maintenance for that spouse is necessary during the period of incapacity, subject to further order of the court.
>
> (2) If the court finds that:
>
> (a) a spouse lacks sufficient property, including marital property apportioned to that spouse, to provide for that spouse's needs; *and*
>
> (b) the spouse is the custodian of a child whose physical or mental incapacity requires the custodian to forgo employment;
>
> the court may find that maintenance is necessary for that spouse in an amount and for a period of time that the court deems appropriate. (emphasis added)

Curiously, this section closely parallels § 308 of the UMDA, except that the word "and" (italicized in section (2) above) reads "or" in the UMDA. UMDA § 308(a)(2) (1973). This singular change from the text of the uniform act drastically alters the thrust of the statute.

53. *Liszkai v. Liszkai*, 168 Ind. App 532, 343 N.E.2d 799, 806 (1976) (Sullivan, J., concurring).

54. Pub. L. No. 150 § 2, 1984 Ind. Acts, formerly codified at Ind. Code Ann. § 31-1-11.5-11(e)(3):

After considering [the statutory factors]; a court may find that rehabilitative maintenance for the spouse seeking maintenance is necessary in an amount and for a period of time that the court considers appropriate but not to exceed two (2) years from the date of the final decree.

55. Ind. Code Ann. § 31-1-11.5-11(e) (West Supp. 1992), as added by 1987 Ind. Acts 283 § 4. Repealed by P.L. 1-1 157.

56. *See In re Marriage of Battles*, 564 N.E.2d 565, 567 (Ind. App. 1991) (affirming denial of rehabilitative maintenance to military wife who had "substantial opportunity to complete her college degree through university extension courses at various military bases"). *See also Dahnke v. Dahnke*, 535 N.E.2d 172, 174–75 (Ind. App. 1989) (reversing trial court denial of rehabilitative maintenance to mother of three children who began college after fourteen-year marriage).

57. UMDA, *supra* note 8 at § 308(b).

58. Minn. Stat. Ann. § 518.06 et seq. (2012).

59. *Otis v. Otis*, 299 N.W.2d 114, 116-17 (Minn. 1980).

60. *Id.* at 117-18 (Otis, J., dissenting).

61. *Id.* at 118.

62. *In re Marriage of Napier*, 374 N.W.2d 512 (Minn. App. 1985).

63. *Id.* at 514, 516.

64. *In re Marriage of Rohling*, 379 N.W.2d 519, 524 (Minn. 1986).

65. *Id.* at 522 (citing *Bollenbach v. Bollenbach*, 175 N.W.2d 148, 154 (Minn. 1970)).

66. Minn. Stat. Ann. § 518.522 (2012) (Act of May 31, 1985, ch. 266 § 52, 1985 Minn. Laws 1186, 1186-87 (amending Minn. Stat. Ann. § 518.552 (1984))).

67. *Nardini v. Nardini*, 414 N.W.2d 184, 197-98 (Minn. 1987).

68. *See, e.g., Lovato v. Lovato*, 98 N.M. 11, 644 P.2d 525, 527 (1982) (reducing alimony to wife who had never worked in order to encourage her to support herself); *In re Marriage of Schlenker*, 300 N.W.2d 164, 166 (Iowa 1981) (after twenty-three-year marriage, wife with no employment skills and kidney disorder awarded alimony for only two years).

69. Wis. Stat. Ann. § 767.26 (West 1981) (Renumbered 767.56, 767.531 and amended by 2005 Act 443 §§ 112, 113, eff. Jan. 1, 2007).

70. *Bahr v. Bahr*, 318 N.W.2d 391 (1982).

71. *Hubert v. Hubert*, 465 N.W.2d 252, 259-60 (Wis. App. 1990).

NOTES TO CHAPTER 3

1. Ann Crittenden, *The Price of Motherhood: Why the Most Important Job in the World Is Still the Least Valued* (New York: Metropolitan Books, 2001), 72.

2. *Burchard v. Garay*, 724 P.2d 486 (Cal. 1986) (Byrd, C.J., concurring).

3. Crittenden, *supra* note 1 at 53 (citing Jeanne Boydston, *Home and Work: Housework, Wages, and the Ideology of Labor in the Early Republic* (New York: Oxford University Press, 1990), 284).

4. This reference appeared beside a 1961 photo in a 1993–1994 exhibit on mechanical brides at New York's Cooper-Hewitt Museum. For a discussion of this

rhetoric, *see* Cynthia Starnes, "Reflections on Betty Crocker, Soccer Mom and Divorce: A Message from Detergent Manufacturers," *Wisconsin Law Review* 1997, 285.

5. A 2000 *New York Times* article, for example, touted the fact that the two-working-parent family has become a 51 percent majority of all two-parent families. *See* Tamar Lewin, "Now a Majority: Families with 2 Parents Who Work," *New York Times*, October 24, 2000. What is surprising is actually the flip side of this figure: in 49 percent of two-parent families, one or both parents do *not* work outside the home.

6. American Law Institute, *Principles of the Law of Family Dissolution: Analysis and Recommendations* (St. Paul, MN: American Law Institute, 2002) (hereinafter *ALI Principles*), § 3.03, cmt. d.

7. U.S. Bureau of Labor Statistics, *Employment Characteristics of Families—2011* (2012), tables 4 and 6, http://www.bls.gov/news.release/famee.htm.

8. U.S. Bureau of Labor Statistics, *American Time-Use Survey—2012 Results* (Washington, D.C.: U.S. Government Printing Office, 2012), http://www.bls.gov/news.release/pdf/atus.pdf.

9. Suzanne M. Bianchi, John P. Robinson, and Melissa A. Milkie, *Changing Rhythms of American Family Life* (New York: Russell Sage Foundation, 2006), 93.

10. "Betty Crocker" is used here to refer to a full-time caregiver.

11. "Soccer mom" is used here to refer to a primary caregiver who also works in the paid economy, either part-time or full-time. The term "soccer mom" was coined by Susan Casey in her 1995 campaign for Denver City Council. *See* Christopher Cox, "Original Soccer Mom Spurs Kick," *Boston Herald*, October 24, 1996, 1. In Casey's words, "We arrange our lives around our kids and support them. . . . I wanted people to understand that. I've been a teacher, I have a Ph.D., I've managed national presidential campaigns, but when I wake up in the morning and when I go to bed at night, my heart and soul are in my family." *Id.*

12. Lynn Hecht Schafran, "Documenting Gender Bias in the Courts: The Task Force Approach," *Judicature* 70 (1987): 280, 285 (quoting a New York legislator's description of judicial attitudes).

13. *Hartung v. Hartung*, 306 N.W.2d 16, 19 (1981). This case is discussed in Ann Laquer Estin, "Maintenance, Alimony, and the Rehabilitation of Family Care," *North Carolina Law Review* 70 (1993): 732.

14. In close to 90 percent of divorces, mothers obtain primary physical custody of children. Ira Mark Ellman et al., *Family Law: Cases, Text, Problems*, 4th ed. (Newark: LexisNexis, 2004), 571.

15. E. Allan Farnsworth, *Contracts*, 4th ed. (New York: Aspen, 2004), § 12.1.

16. Diana Pearce, "The More Things Change . . . A Status Report on Displaced Caregivers and Single Parents in the 1980s" (Washington D.C.: Displaced Homemakers Network, 1990) 60 (on file with the University of Chicago Law Review).

17. *ALI Principles, supra* note 6 at § 5.05, cmt. d. "[W]ives continue in the great majority of cases," adds the ALI, "to sacrifice earnings opportunities *to care for their children." Id.* at § 5.05, reporter's notes, cmt. c (emphasis added).

18. *Grimms' Fairy Tales by the Brothers Grimm*, trans. Mrs. E. V. Lucas, Lucy Crane, and Marian Edwardes (New York: Grosset and Dunlap, 1945), 337.

19. Idaho Child Support Guidelines, § 6(c)(1), in Idaho Rules of Civil Procedure 6(c)(6) ("Ordinarily, a parent shall not be deemed underemployed if the parent is caring for a child not more than 6 months of age.").

20. Alaska Civ. R. 90.3(a)(4)(2012) ("A determination of potential income may not be made for a parent who is physically or mentally incapacitated, or who is caring for a child under two years of age to whom the parents owe a joint legal responsibility.").

21. Md. Code Ann., Fam. Law § 12-204(b)(2) (2012) ("A determination of potential income may not be made for a parent who . . . is caring for a child under the age of 2 years for whom the parents are jointly and severally responsible.").

22. Colo. Rev. Stat. § 14-10-115(7)(b)(I) (2012) ("If a parent is voluntarily unemployed or underemployed, child support shall be calculated based on a determination of potential income; except that a determination of potential income shall not be made for a parent who is physically or mentally incapacitated or is caring for a child under the age of thirty months for whom the parents owe a joint legal responsibility.").

23. Ky. Rev. Stat. Ann. § 403.212(2)(d) (2012) ("a determination of potential income shall not be made for a parent who is physically or mentally incapacitated or is caring for a very young child, age three (3) or younger, for whom the parents owe a joint legal responsibility.").

24. Me. Rev. Stat. Ann. tit. 19-A, § 2001(5)(D) (2012) ("In the absence of evidence in the record to the contrary, a party that is personally providing primary care for a child under the age of 3 years is deemed not available for employment.").

25. Administrative Office of the Courts, AOC-A-162, North Carolina Child Support Guidelines 3 (2011), http://www.nccourts.org/forms/documents/1226.pdf.

26. La. Rev. Stat. Ann. § 9:315.9 (2012) ("If a party is voluntarily unemployed or underemployed, child support shall be calculated based on a determination of his or her income earning potential, unless the party is physically or mentally incapacitated, or is caring for a child of the parties under the age of five years.").

27. N.M. Stat. Ann. § 40-4-11.1(C)(1) (2012) ("'income' means actual gross income of a parent if employed to full capacity or potential income if unemployed or underemployed. Income need not be imputed to the primary custodial parent actively caring for a child of the parties who is under the age of six or disabled.").

28. *ALI Principles, supra* note 6 at § 3.04, cmt. e (emphasis added).

29. Jane Lazarre, "Fictions of Home," in *Representations of Motherhood*, ed. Donna Bassin et al. (New Haven: Yale University Press, 1994), 47, 50.

NOTES TO CHAPTER 4

1. U.S. Census Bureau, *Current Population Survey* (2007), table PINC-02, part 49, http://www.census.gov/hhes/www/income/incomestats.html.

2. *Id.* at table PINC-08, pt. 190.

3. American Law Institute, *Principles of the Law of Family Dissolution: Analysis and Recommendations* (St. Paul, MN: American Law Institute, 2002) (hereinafter *ALI Principles*), 21–23.

4. The Uniform Marriage and Divorce Act, for example, directs courts to consider

   [t]he duration of the marriage, the age, health, station, occupation, amount and source of income, vocational skills, employability, estate, liabilities, and needs of each of the parties, custodial provisions, whether the appointment is in lieu of or in addition to maintenance, and the opportunity of each for future acquisition of capital assets and income.

   Uniform Marriage and Divorce Act § 307 (Alternative A) (1998). The court must also consider "the contribution or dissipation of each party in the acquisition, preservation, depreciation, or appreciation in value of the respective estates, and the contribution of a spouse as a homemaker or to the family unit." *Id.*

5. *See, e.g.,* 23 Pa. Cons. Stat. § 3502(a)(7) (West 2010) (authorizing court to consider the "contribution or dissipation of each party in the acquisition, preservation, depreciation or appreciation of the marital property, including the contribution of a party as homemaker.").

6. *See ALI Principles, supra* note 3 at § 4.09, cmt. a.

7. *See, e.g.,* Ark. Code Ann. § 9-12-315(a)(1)(A) (2012) ("All marital property shall be distributed one-half (½) to each party unless the court finds such a division to be inequitable."); and N.C. Gen. Stat. Ann. § 50-20(c) (2012) ("There shall be an equal division . . . unless the court determines that an equal division is not equitable.").

8. Ira Mark Ellman et al., *Family Law: Cases, Text, Problems,* 5th ed. (New Providence, NJ: LexisNexis, 2010), 336.

9. Alfred O. Gottschalk, *Net Worth and Asset Ownership of Households: 2002,* U.S. Census Bureau Publication No. P70-115, U.S. Census Current Population Reports (2008), 15.

10. Emily Brandon, "Retiree Net Worth Declines," *U.S. News and World Report,* July 23, 2012.

11. E. S. Browning, "Retiring Boomers Find 401(k) Plans Fall Short," *Wall Street Journal,* February 19, 2011.

12. *See, e.g.,* Illinois Marriage and Dissolution of Marriage Act, 750 Ill. Comp. Stat. 5/510(a-5) (West 2012) (alimony modifiable upon a substantial change in circumstance).

13. Mass. Gen. Laws ch. 208 § 48 (2005).

14. Linda D. Elrod and Robert G. Spector, "A Review in the Year of Family Law: Working toward More Uniformity in Laws Relating to Families," *Family Law Quarterly* 44 (Winter 2011): 510.

15. Illinois Marriage and Dissolution of Marriage Act, *supra* note 12 at 5/504 (emphasis added).
16. *ALI Principles, supra* note 3 at § 5.02 comment a.
17. *Id.* at 25.
18. Tenn. Code Ann. § 36-5-121 (2012).
19. Elrod and Spector, *supra* note 14 at 510.
20. N.C. Gen. Stat. Ann. § 50-16.3A (2012)
21. Va. Code Ann. § 20-107.1(B), (-E) (2012).
22. Illinois Marriage and Dissolution of Marriage Act, 750 Ill. Comp. Stat. 5/504(a) (West 2012).
23. *Id.*
24. *ALI Principles, supra* note 3 at 51–52.
25. *Sparks v. Sparks*, 485 N.W.2d 893, 905 (Mich. 1992) (Levin, J., dissenting).
26. For an argument criticizing the ALI's position that marital fault, including murder, should not be relevant to the economics of divorce, see David Westfall, "Unprincipled Family Dissolution: The American Law Institute's Recommendations for Spousal Support and Division of Property," *Harvard Journal of Law and Public Policy* 27 (2003–2004): 917. Westfall suggests as an alternative that the duration of an alimony award be shortened by a period equal to the duration of a claimant's adultery. *Id.* at 936.
27. N.J. Stat. Ann. § 2A-34-23i (West 2012) (citations omitted).
28. *Id.* (emphasis added).
29. For helpful reviews of state guidelines, see Twila B. Larkin, "Guidelines for Alimony: The New Mexico Experiment," *Family Law Quarterly* 38 (Spring 2004): 29; and Mary Kay Kisthardt, "Re-Thinking Alimony: The AAML's Considerations for Calculating Alimony, Spousal Support or Maintenance," *Journal of the American Academy of Matrimonial Lawyers* 21 (2008): 61.
30. Cal. Santa Clara Co. L.R. 3.1, § 3; Cal. Super. Ct., Alameda Co. L. R. § 11.2, Cal. Marin Co. L.R. 6.21(B)(1) and (2).
31. Fairfax Bar Association, *Child and Spousal Support Guidelines,* Item No. 0206 (Fairfax, Va., November 2002).
32. Kansas, Johnson Co. Bar Assoc., *Family Law Guidelines, Maintenance,* pt. V (rev. February 2001).
33. Ariz. Super. Ct., Maricopa Co., Fam. Ct. Dep't, *Spousal Maintenance Guidelines* (approved April 2000, rev. October 2002).
34. Support 2013: Providing Software Solutions for the Active Family Law Attorney, http://www.marginsoft.net/.
35. Me. Rev. Stat. tit. 19-A, 951-A(2)(A)(1) (2012).
36. *Id.*
37. Tex. Fam. Code § 8.051(2) (2012).
38. Me. Rev. Stat. tit. 19-A § 951-A(2)(A)(1) (2012).
39. Del. Code Ann. tit. 13 § 1512(d) (2009).
40. Utah Code Ann. § 30-3-5(8)(a) (2012).

41. Tex. Fam. Code § 8.054(a)(1)(A)-(C) (2012).

42. *Id.* at § 8.055(a) (2012).

43. 23 Pa. Cons. Stat. § 4322(a) (West 2010).

44. Pa. R. Civ. P. 1910.16-4 (2012).

45. *Id.* at 1910.16-1(d) (2012).

46. Colo. Rev. Stat. 14-10-114 (2012).

47. N.Y. Dom. Rel. Law § 236(B) (West 2010).

48. Alexandra Harwin, "Ending the Alimony Guessing Game," *New York Times,* July 3, 2011.

49. *J.H. v. W.H.,* 2011 N.Y. Slip Op. 50478(U) (N.Y. Sup. Ct. 2011).

50. Victoria M. Ho and Jennifer J. Cohen, "An Update on Florida Alimony Case Law," *Florida Bar Journal* 77 (2003): 85.

51. *Tarkow v. Tarkow,* 805 So.2d 854 (Fla. Dist. Ct. App. 2001).

52. *Merkin v. Merkin,* 804 So.2d 595 (Fla. Dist. Ct. App. 2002).

53. *Thomas v. Thomas,* 776 So.2d 1092 (Fla. Dist. Ct. App. 2001).

54. Kisthardt, *supra* note 29 at 61, 62, 65–73.

55. Jess Bidgood, "Alimony in Massachusetts Gets Overhaul, with Limits," *New York Times,* September 26, 2011.

56. Mass. Gen. Laws. Ann. ch. 208, §§ 48-54 (West 2011).

57. *Id.* at ch. 208, § 53(c).

58. Bidgood, *supra* note 55.

59. Wendy Murphy, "New Alimony Law Is Bad for Women," CNN, March 9, 2012, http://www.cnn.com/2012/03/09/opinion/murphy-alimony-overhaul-con/index.html.

60. *Id.*

61. Martine Powers, "Legislation Overhauls Bay State Alimony Law," *Boston Globe,* September 26, 2011.

62. Murphy, *supra* note 59.

63. Yamiche Alcindor, "Should Alimony Laws Be Changed?" USAToday.com, January 18, 2012, http://usatoday30.usatoday.com/money/perfi/basics/story/2012-01-05/alimony-law-reform/52642100/1.

64. Samuel H. Hofstadter and Shirley R. Levittan, "Alimony—A Reformulation," *Journal of Family Law* 7 (1967): 51, 55.

65. Lynn Hecht Schafran, "Documenting Gender Bias in the Courts: The Task Force Approach," *Judicature* 70 (1987): 285.

66. *In re Marriage of Brantner,* 136 Cal. Rptr. 635, 637 (1977).

NOTES TO CHAPTER 5

1. For a review of alimony law in Ireland, see Geoffrey Shannon, "Grounds for Divorce and Maintenance between Former Spouses: Republic of Ireland," August 2002, http://www.ceflonline.net/index.php/country-reports-by-subject/. This article was one of a series of reports on alimony (dubbed "maintenance") in various countries prepared for the Commission on European Family Law. *See*

also Frank Martin, "From Prohibition to Approval: The Limitations of the 'No Clean Break' Divorce Regime in the Republic of Ireland," *International Journal of Law, Policy and the Family* 16 (2002): 223, 248.

2. *See, e.g.*, Martin, *supra* note 1 at 248.

3. *G. v. G.* [2011] 1ESC 40. A summary of the case is available at http://www.independent.ie/national-news/courts/rich-businessman-wins-appeal-in-key-divorce.

4. This description of alimony in Malaysia is based on Anis Shuhaiza Bt Md Salleh and Noor'Aza Bt Ahmad, "Cross Boundary Marriage under Malaysian Family Law: Between a Dream of Life and Reality of Legal Requirements," *Journal of Politics and Law* 3, no. 2 (September 2010): 148, 149, 152–53.

5. Masha Antokolskaia, "Grounds for Divorce and Maintenance between Former Spouses: Russia," September 2002, http://www.ceflonline.net/index.php/country-reports-by-subject/. This article was one of a series of reports on alimony in various countries prepared for the Commission on European Family Law.

6. *Id.* at 26.

7. *Id.* at 30.

8. *Id.* at 26.

9. This summary of Samoan alimony law is based on an article by Lalotoa Mulitalo and Jennifer Corrin, "Reform of Maintenance and Divorce Laws in Samoa: Appropriate for the 'AIGA'?" in *The International Survey of Family Law*, ed. Bill Atkin (Bristol, UK: Jordan Publishing, 2012), 283–98, 291.

10. *Id.* at 291.

11. For a summary of the CEFL's project, see Katharina Boele-Woelki, "The Principles of European Family Law: Its Aims and Prospects," *Utrecht Law Review* 1, no. 2 (December 2005): 160, http://www.utrechtlawreview.org.

12. See http://www.ceflonline.net/index.php/country-reports-by-subject/.

13. These principles are available on the CEFL website and also at Esin Orucu and Jane Mair, eds., *Juxtaposing Legal Systems and the Principles of European Family Law on Divorce and Maintenance* (Cambridge, UK: Intersentia, 2007), 265–68.

14. For a comprehensive and in-depth review of alimony in Canada and the guideline project, see Carol Rogerson and Rollie Thompson, "The Canadian Experiment with Spousal Support Guidelines," *Family Law Quarterly* 45 (2011): 241; and Carol Rogerson, "The Canadian Law of Spousal Support," *Family Law Quarterly* 38 (2004–2005): 69. This section relies heavily on these articles.

15. Julien D. Payne and Marilyn A. Payne, *Canadian Family Law*, 2d ed. (Toronto: Irwin Law Publishers, 2006), 8-20.

16. *Id.* at 17.

17. *Pelech v. Pelech* [1987] 1 S.C.R. 801.

18. The two other cases on spousal support decided at the same time as *Pelech* were *Richardson v. Richardson* [1987] 1 S.C.R. 857; and *Caron v. Caron* [1987] 1 S.C.R. 892.

19. *Moge v. Moge* [1992] 3 S.C.R. 813.

20. *Id.* at 864.

21. Rogerson, *supra* note 14 at 86.

22. *Id.* at 87.
23. *Bracklow v. Bracklow* [1999] 1 S.C.R. 420.
24. Rogerson, *supra* note 14 at 91–93.
25. This section draws heavily on the firsthand description of the guidelines by the co-directors, Carol Rogerson and Rollie Thompson. *See* Rogerson and Thompson, *supra* note 14.
26. *Id.* at 249-50.
27. *Id* at 257-58.
28. *Id.* at 258-59.
29. *Yemchuk v. Yemchuk*, 2005 B.C.C.A 406 (2005).
30. Rogerson and Thompson, *supra* note 14 at 258-59.
31. *Id.* at 259.
32. *See S.C. v. J.C.*, 2006 N.B.C.A. 46; and *Fisher v. Fisher*, 2008 O.N.C.A. 11.
33. Rogerson and Thompson, *supra* note 14 at 259.
34. *G.V. v. C.G.*, 2006 Q. C.C.A. 763.
35. Rogerson and Thompson, *supra* note 14 at 261–63.
36. *Id.* at 264–66.

NOTES TO CHAPTER 6

1. U.S. Department of Health and Human Services, *Cohabitation, Marriage, Divorce, and Remarriage in the United States: Vital and Health Statistics* (July 2002), 1, 22, http://purl.access.gpo.gov/GPO/LPS22381.
2. Based on 1996 data, the Census Bureau reports that women who entered second marriages in 1975 through 1984 were less likely to reach their tenth anniversary than were women entering first marriages during the same period. U.S. Bureau of the Census, *Number, Timing, and Duration of Marriages and Divorces: 1996*, Current Population Reports (2002), 3, http://purl.access.gpo.gov/GPO/LPS18539. The average duration of a first marriage that ends in divorce is about eight years; for second marriages the duration is about seven years. *Id.* at 9.
3. Although alimony is available to both men and women, *see Orr v. Orr*, 440 U.S. 268 (1979), this chapter will refer to an alimony recipient as "she" and an alimony payor as "he" for convenience and because the vast majority of alimony recipients are women.
4. American Law Institute, *Principles of the Law of Family Dissolution: Analysis and Recommendations* (St. Paul, MN: American Law Institute, 2002) (hereinafter *ALI Principles*), § 5.07, cmt. a.
5. The facts in this paragraph are taken from *Keller v. O'Brien*, 652 N.E.2d 589 (Mass. 1995) (*Keller I*), *appeal after remand*, 683 N.E.2d 1026 (Mass. 1997) (*Keller II*).
6. Uniform Marriage and Divorce Act § 316(a) (1973) (hereinafter UMDA). Many states require a less significant showing of changed circumstances.
7. *See, e.g.*, La. Civ. Code Ann. art. 115 (2012); N.J. Stat. Ann. § 2A:34-25 (West 2010); N.C. Gen. Stat. Ann. § 50-16.9(b) (Lexis 2011); 23 Pa. Cons. Stat. § 3701(e)

(West 2012); R.I. Gen. Laws § 15-5-16(c)(2) (2012); S.C. Code Ann. § 20-3-150 (2012); Tenn. Code Ann. § 36-5-101(a)(2)(B) (West 2012).

8. *See, e.g.,* N.Y. Dom. Rel. Law § 248 (2010); Wis. Stat. Ann. § 767.32(3) (West 2009).

9. *See, e.g.,* Ark. Code Ann. § 9-12-312(a)(1) (2012); Cal. Fam. Code § 4337 (West 2012); Colo. Rev. Stat. Ann. § 14-10-122(2) (2012); Del. Code Ann. 13, § 1519(b) (West 2009); Ga. Code Ann. § 19-6-5(b) (West 2012); Haw. Rev. Stat. Ann. § 580-51(a) (2012); 750 Ill. Comp. Stat. Ann. 5/510(c) (West 2012); Ky. Rev. Stat. Ann. § 403.250(2) (2012); Md. Code Ann. Fam. Law § 11-108 (2012); Mo. Ann. Stat. § 452.370(3) (2012); Mont. Code Ann. § 40-4-208(4) (2012); Neb. Rev. Stat. § 42-365 (2012); Nev. Rev. Stat. § 125.150(5) (2012); Utah Code Ann. § 30-3-5(8) (2012); Va. Code Ann. § 20-109 (2012); Wash. Rev. Code § 26.09.170(2) (West 2005).

10. This language appears in both the UMDA § 316(b) and Ariz. Rev Stat. Ann. § 25-327(B) (2012).

11. *In re Marriage of Glasser,* 226 Cal. Rptr. 229, 230 (1986).

12. Okla. Stat. Ann. tit. 43 § 134 (B) (2012).

13. *Mathis v. Mathis,* 91 P.3d 662, 666 (Okla. Civ. App. 2004).

14. *Voyles v. Voyles,* 644 P.2d 847, 849 (Alaska 1982). *See also McHan v. McHan,* 84 P.2d 984 (Idaho 1938); *Hubbard v. Hubbard,* 656 So.2d 124 (Miss. 1995); and *Kelley v. State Dept. of Revenue,* 796 So.2d 1114 (Ala. Civ. App. 2000), *cert. denied* (Apr. 27, 2001).

15. *Voyles,* 644 P.2d at 848.

16. *Keller I,* 652 N.E.2d at 593.

17. *See, e.g., Sleicher v. Sleicher,* 167 N.E. 501 (N.Y. 1929); and *Peters v. Peters,* 214 N.W.2d 151 (Iowa 1974).

18. *See, e.g., Sefton v. Sefton,* 291 P.2d 439 (Cal. 1955) (*en banc*) (annulment of second marriage does not revive alimony rights). Annulment might alternatively be viewed not as an extraordinary circumstance justifying an exception to the remarriage-termination rule, but rather as a definitional failure to trigger the rule at all, on the theory that if the remarriage did not legally occur, the remarriage-termination rule is inapplicable. The modern view, however, is that, at least for purposes of the economics of divorce, an annulment should be viewed as a divorce.

19. The ALI remarriage-termination rule provides as follows:

> An obligation to make periodic payments imposed under § 5.04 [alimony based on duration of marriage and disparity in spousal earnings] or § 5.05 [alimony based on duration of caretaking and disparity in spousal earnings] ends automatically at the remarriage of the obligee or at the death of either party, without regard to the award's term as fixed in the decree, unless either
> (1) the original decree provides otherwise, or
> (2) the court makes written findings . . . establishing that termination of the award would work a substantial injustice because of facts not present in most cases to which this section applies.

ALI Principles, supra note 4 at § 5.07.

20. *Id.*

21. *Id.* at § 5.07, illustration 4.

22. *Id.* at §§ 5.07, cmt. a, 5.12(5), 5.13(5).

23. *See id.* at §§ 5.12, cmt. a (one spouse finances the other's education or training within a specified number of years of divorce and that education or training substantially enhances the other spouse's earning capacity), and 5.13, cmt. a (short, childless marriage in which one spouse is disparately and unfairly unable to regain a premarital living standard).

24. William Blackstone, *Commentaries on the Laws of England*, book 1, 442.

25. *ALI Principles, supra* note 4 at intro. n44 (quoting Chester G. Vernier and John B. Hurlbut, "The Historical Background of Alimony Law and Its Present Statutory Structure," *Law and Contemporary Problems* 6 (1939): 197, 199).

26. E. Allan Farnsworth, *Contracts*, 4th ed. (New York: Aspen, 2004), § 12.12. The purpose of the rule is clearly to encourage an injured party to minimize the costs of breach.

27. *ALI Principles, supra* note 4 at § 5.07, cmt. a.

28. *Id.*

29. *Id.*

30. *Id.*

31. *Id.*

32. *Id.*

33. *Cary v. Cary*, 152 A. 302, 303 (Conn. 1930) (emphasis added).

34. *Wolter v. Wolter*, 158 N.W.2d 616, 619 (Neb. 1968) (quoting *Bowman v. Bowman*, 79 N.W.2d 554 (Neb. 1956)). "The essential keystone," said the court in *Wolter*, "that supports a decree for true alimony payable in the future for support and maintenance of a divorced wife is the continued unmarried status of the wife." *Id.* at 619.

35. *Herzmark v. Herzmark*, 427 P.2d 465, 470 (Kan. 1967) (emphasis added). Curiously, the court thought "it would be even *more repugnant* for a man to receive support from both wife and former wife." *Id.* (emphasis added).

36. *Voyles*, 644 P.2d at 849.

37. *Keller I*, 652 N.E.2d at 594 (quoting *Marquardt v. Marquardt*, 396 N.W.2d 753, 754 (S.D. 1986)).

38. *In the Matter of Quint*, 907 P.2d 818, 821 (Kan. 1995) (emphasis added).

39. *Tillis v. Tillis*, 405 So.2d 938, 940 (Ala. Civ. App. 1981).

40. *Wolter*, 158 N.W.2d at 619 (quoting *Bowman*, 79 N.W.2d 554) (emphasis added). *See also In re Marriage of Shima*, 360 N.W.2d 827, 828 (Iowa 1985) (quoting *Wolter's* "election" rationale); *Keller I*, 652 N.E.2d at 594 ("remarriage should serve as an election between the support provided by the alimony award and the legal obligation of support embodied in the new marital relationship").

41. *Voyles*, 644 P.2d at 849 (emphasis added). The court in *Voyles* added that "[f]or support to continue to a dependent spouse when he or she has *chosen* to form a new marital relationship is, in our judgment, unsound as a matter of public policy." *Id.* (emphasis added).

42. *Dunaway v. Dunaway*, 560 N.E.2d 171, 175 (Ohio 1990) (emphasis added). An Ohio statute now limits judicial authority to terminate alimony to cases in which a divorce decree contains an express reservation of jurisdiction. *See* Ohio Rev. Code Ann. § 3105.18(E) (LexisNexis 2003). Applying this statute, the Ohio Supreme Court reversed a trial court's termination of alimony upon the recipient's remarriage on the ground that the trial court failed to reserve jurisdiction over alimony issues. *See Kimble v. Kimble*, 780 N.E.2d 273 (Ohio 2002).
43. *Id.* at 176.
44. *Id.*
45. *Bowman*, 79 N.W.2d at 560. *See* Neb. Rev. Stat. § 42-365 (2012). *See also Voyles*, 644 P.2d at 849 ("Because there is a legal obligation of support embodied in the new marital relationship, the obligation of support from the past marital relationship should end.").
46. *Keller I*, 652 N.E.2d at 594. In 2004, the Supreme Judicial Court of Massachusetts, Middlesex, expressly adopted the automatic remarriage-termination rule of *ALI Principles* § 5.07, although the facts of that case presented only the issue of whether alimony survives the payor's death. *See Cohan v. Feuer*, 810 N.E.2d 1222, 1228 (Mass. 2004).
47. *Marquardt*, 396 N.W.2d at 755 (concurring specially and supporting an automatic termination rule).
48. *Greene v. Greene*, 643 P.2d 1061, 1067 (Idaho 1982) (denying wife's claim to unpaid alimony that accrued after her remarriage but before husband's modification motion).

NOTES TO CHAPTER 7
1. Elisabeth M. Landes, "Economics of Alimony," *Journal of Legal Studies* 7 (1978): 35, 41.
2. Elizabeth S. Beninger and Jeanne Wielage Smith, "Career Opportunity Cost: A Factor in Spousal Support Determination," *Family Law Quarterly* 16 (1982): 201 (emphasis added).
3. *Id.* at 210.
4. *Id.* at 207-8.
5. *Id.* at 208.
6. Margaret F. Brinig and June Carbone, "The Reliance Interest in Marriage and Divorce," *Tulane Law Review* 62 (1988): 855, 869.
7. *Id.* at 877-78.
8. Jana Singer, "Divorce Reform and Gender Justice," *North Carolina Law Review* 67 (1988-1989): 1103, 1114–15 (emphasis added).
9. Ira Mark Ellman, "The Theory of Alimony," *California Law Review* 77 (1989): 1, 48 (emphasis added).
10. *Id.* at 48.
11. *Id.*

12. *Id.* at 49.

13. Joan Williams, "Is Coverture Dead? Beyond a New Theory of Alimony," *Georgetown Law Journal* 82 (1993–1994): 2227, 2229.

14. Joan Williams, *Unbending Gender: Why Family and Work Conflict and What to Do about It* (New York: Oxford University Press, 2000), 3–5.

15. American Law Institute, *Principles of the Law of Family Dissolution: Analysis and Recommendations* (St. Paul, MN: American Law Institute, 2002) (hereinafter *ALI Principles*), § 5.05, comments a through e (emphasis added).

16. Carolyn J. Frantz and Hanoch Dagan, "Properties of Marriage," *Columbia Law Review* 104 (January 2004): 75, 108 (emphasis added).

17. Alicia Brokars Kelly, "The Marital Partnership Pretense and Career Assets: The Ascendency of Self over the Marital Community," *Boston University Law Review* 81 (2001): 59, 61–63.

18. Nancy E. Cott, *Public Vows: A History of Marriage and the Nation* (Cambridge: Harvard University Press, 2000), 1.

19. Georg Wilhelm Friedrich Hegel, *The Philosophy of Right* (Chicago: Encyclopedia Britannica, 1952), 32.

20. *Maynard v. Hill*, 125 U.S. 190, 205, 210-11 (1888).

21. Uniform Marriage and Divorce Act § 201 (1973) (hereinafter UMDA).

22. *Id.* at Refs. and Annos. Prefatory Note.

23. E. Allan Farnsworth, *Contracts*, 4th ed. (New York: Aspen, 2004), § 1.1.

24. *In re Marriage Cases*, 183 P.3d 384, 433 (Cal. 2008) (emphasis added).

25. *Goodridge v. Dep't of Public Health*, 798 N.E.2d 941, 948 (Mass. 2003) (holding Massachusetts's ban on same-sex marriage unconstitutional).

26. *Id.* at § 344(c).

27. Joan M. Krauskopf, "Recompense for Financing Spouse's Education: Legal Protection for the Marital Investor in Human Capital," *University of Kansas Law Review* 28 (Spring 1980): 379, 391.

28. *ALI Principles, supra* note 15 at § 5.12. For examples of cases recognizing "reimbursement alimony," *see Mahoney v. Mahoney*, 453 A.2d 527 (N.J. 1982); and *Marriage of Francis*, 442 N.W.2d 59 (Iowa 1989).

29. June Carbone, "Economics, Feminism, and the Reinvention of Alimony: A Reply to Ira Ellman," *Vanderbilt Law Review* 43 (1990): 1463n87.

30. Krauskopf, *supra* note 27 at 417.

31. Landes, *supra* note 1 at 40.

32. *Id.* at 45.

33. Williams, *supra* note 13 at 2236-48.

34. Singer, *supra* note 8 at 1114.

35. *Id.*

36. Stephen D. Sugarman, "Dividing Financial Interests on Divorce," in *Divorce Reform at the Crossroads*, ed. Stephen D. Sugarman and Herma Hill Kay (New Haven: Yale University Press, 1990), 130, 159-60.

37. Robert Kirkman Collins, "The Theory of Marital Residuals: Applying an Income Adjustment Calculus to the Enigma of Alimony," *Harvard Women's Law Journal* 24 (Spring 2001): 23, 49-50.

38. *Id.* at 50.

39. Jane Rutherford, "Duty in Divorce: Shared Income as a Path to Equality," *Fordham Law Review* 58 (1990): 539.

40. Singer, *supra* note 8 at 1117.

41. Williams, *supra* note 13 at 2258-61.

42. Sugarman, *supra* note 36 at 160.

43. *Id.*

44. Collins, *supra* note 37 at 51.

45. *Id.*

46. *Restatement (Second) Contracts* § 344(b) (St. Paul: American Law Institute, 1981).

47. Brinig and Carbone, *supra* note 6 at 881–82.

48. Ellman, *supra* note 9 at 49-51.

49. *Id.* at 53–54.

50. *Id.* at 80.

51. Richard Posner, *Economic Analysis of Law* (New York: Aspen, 2011), 194.

52. Elizabeth Scott and Robert Scott, "Marriage as Relational Contract," *Virginia Law Review* 84 (1998): 1225, 1309-11.

53. Twila L. Perry, "No-Fault Divorce and Liability without Fault: Can Family Law Learn from Torts?," *Ohio State Law Journal* 52 (1991): 55, 66-67.

54. *ALI Principles, supra* note 15 at § 5.02 and cmt. a.

55. *Id.* at § 5.02 and cmt. a.

56. *Id.* at § 5.10(2)(d).

57. *Id.* at §§ 5.12 to 5.14 ("compensation for contributions to the other spouse's education or training," and "restoration of premarital living standards after a short marriage").

58. *Id.* at § 5.04.

59. *Id.* at § 5.04, cmt. e.

60. *Id.* at § 5.04, cmt. c.

61. *Id.*

62. *Id.* at § 5.05, cmt. a and reporter's notes, cmt. c.

63. *Id.* at § 5.05, cmt. c.

64. *Id.* at § 5.06, cmt. b.

65. *Id.* at § 5.05, cmt. d.

66. *Id.* at § 5.05, cmt. e.

67. *Id.* at § 5.05, cmt. d.

68. *Id.* at § 5.05, cmt. e.

69. *Id.*

70. *Id.* at § 5.04, reporter's notes, cmt. c.

71. *Id.* at § 5.02, cmt. a.

NOTES TO CHAPTER 8

1. Deborah L. Rhode and Martha Minow, "Reforming the Questions, Questioning the Reforms," in *Divorce Reform at the Crossroads*, ed. Stephen D. Sugarman and Herma Hill Kay (New Haven: Yale University Press, 1990), 198.

2. *See* Alfred F. Conard et al., *Enterprise Organization: Cases, Statutes, and Analysis*, 4th ed. (Mineola, NY: Foundation Press, 1987), 18 ("The great mass of ordinary partnerships are probably in that form because the parties never gave their organizational structure much attention. Their agreements are informal, and often unwritten."); Daniel S. Kleinberger, *Agency, Partnerships and LLCs*, 4th ed. (New York: Wolters Kluwer Law and Business, 2002), § 7.2.1 (stating that some partnerships "arise from a handshake").

3. Elizabeth Scott, "Rational Decisionmaking about Marriage and Divorce," *Virginia Law Review* 76 (1990): 9, 12. Scott contrasts this view of marriage with the "conventional 'story' of modern marriage [as] one of limited investment and individual pursuit of self-gratification, followed by disappointment and the breakdown of the relationship." *Id.* at 11.

4. *Id.* at 12.

5. Uniform Partnership Act, § 404(a), (b) (1997) (hereinafter UPA).

6. *Id.* at § 404 (d). This section provides, "A partner shall discharge the duties to the partnership and the other partners under this [Act] or under the partnership agreement and exercise any rights consistently with the obligation of good faith and fair dealing."

7. *Meinhard v. Salmon*, 164 N.E. 545, 546 (N.Y. 1928).

8. UPA, *supra* note 5 at § 401(f).

9. *See, e.g.*, Cal Fam. Code § 1100 (West 2012).

10. Kleinberger, *supra* note 2 at § 9.1.

11. *Id.* at § 7.4.4.

12. *See* UPA, *supra* note 5 at § 25(1)-(2).

13. *See, e.g.*, N.M. Stat. Ann. § 40-3-8 (2012), Tex. Fam. Code Ann. § 3.003 (West 2012), Wash. Rev. Code § 26.16.030 (West 2012).

14. UPA, *supra* note 5 at § 401(b) ("Each partner is entitled to an equal share of the partnership profits and is chargeable with a share of the partnership losses in proportion to the partner's share of the profits.").

15. Kleinberger, *supra* note 2 at § 7.2.3. Sharing profits (gross income less expenses) tends to produce a different attitude than having a share of revenues (gross income). *Id.* "A person with a revenue share naturally focuses on the business generating as much revenue as possible. Such a person may have little direct concern for the costs of providing goods or services. In contrast, for someone who shares profits, sales (and revenues) are only part of the equation; a profit will exist only if the whole business is functioning well." *Id.* Like business partners, spouses may view themselves as sharing not just paychecks, but ultimate gains and losses.

16. *Matter of Stice*, 779 P.2d 1020, 1026-27 (Or. 1989) (*en banc*) (quoting *In re Marriage of Jenks*, 656 P.2d 286, 290 (Or. 1982)).
17. Uniform Marriage and Divorce Act (amended 1973) (hereinafter UMDA).
18. UPA, *supra* note 5 at §§ 29, 31.
19. *See id.* at §§ 302, 305.
20. In a prefatory note, the drafters state, "The distribution of property upon the termination of a marriage should be treated, as nearly as possible, like the distribution of assets incident to the dissolution of a partnership." *Id.* at Prefatory Note.
21. As Professor Gregory explains,
    Under the UPA, dissolution designates the point in time when the partners cease to carry on the business together; in contrast, termination is the point in time when all the partnership affairs have been wound up. Winding up is the period of time subsequent to dissolution and prior to termination during which the process of settling partnership affairs takes place.
    William A. Gregory, *The Law of Agency and Partnership*, 3d ed. (St. Paul, MN: West, 2001), § 227.
22. Section 40 of the UPA details the rules for distribution of partnership property. Essentially, that section requires distributions to (1) creditors; (2) partners for loans to the partnership; (3) partners in respect of capital; and (4) partners in respect of profits. *See* Alan R. Bromberg and Larry E. Ribstein, *Bromberg and Ribstein on Partnership* (New York: Aspen, 2005), § 7.10.
23. *See, e.g.*, UMDA, *supra* note 17 at § 307 (Alternative B), which authorizes the return of "each spouse's separate property" before community property is divided.
24. *See* Bromberg and Ribstein, *supra* note 22 at § 7.08. The parties' mutual rights and obligations are thus not terminated by the dissolution but continue until the winding up is completed, which occurs when every obligation has been discharged by performance.
25. Professor Ira Mark Ellman, for example, maintains that partnership law authorizes post-dissolution compensation only where the dissolution is "wrongful" or where a partner has provided either extraordinary or inadequate service. Ira Mark Ellman, "The Theory of Alimony," *California Law Review* 77 (1989): 35–40. He concludes that "[p]artnership makes no provision for alimony." *Id.* at 35. *See also* Stephen D. Sugarman, "Dividing Financial Interests on Divorce," in *Divorce Reform at the Crossroads*, ed. Stephen D. Sugarman and Herma Hill Kay (New Haven: Yale University Press, 1990), 140 ("under the partnership analogy there would be no spousal support").
26. Ellman, *supra* note 25 at 33.
27. *See* Mary E. O'Connell, "Alimony after No-Fault: A Practice in Search of a Theory," *New England Law Review* 23 (1988): 497-98. Professor O'Connell reasons that if each partner walks away from a business partnership with 50 percent of the assets, theoretically each has an equal opportunity for future success. In contrast, a woman usually does not leave a marriage with an equal opportunity for future success. Data suggest that she is economically damaged

by participation in a failed marriage. *Id.* at 497n342. *See also* Martha Albertson Fineman, *The Illusion of Equality: The Rhetoric and Reality of Divorce Reform* (Chicago: University of Chicago Press, 1991), 176 ("As it currently stands, the partnership concept of sharing responsibility and contribution is typically translated into assuming equal economic responsibility after divorce, a result that is unrealistic, even cruel, given the material situation of many women.").

28. Professor Mary Ann Glendon, for example, observes that while business partners typically negotiate a general agreement governing the terms of the partnership, including dissolution, marriage partners relegate the crucial terms of partnership to tacit assumption. Mary Ann Glendon, *The New Family and the New Property* (Toronto: Butterworths, 1981), 65.

29. *See* Donald J. Weidner, "The Revised Uniform Partnership Act Midstream: Major Policy Decisions," *University of Toledo Law Review* 21 (1990): 825, 837.

30. UPA, *supra* note 17 at § 801(2)(i).

31. *Id.* at § 701(a).

32. *See id.* at § 601(1) and comment.

33. UPA § 801 states that a partnership dissolves and its business must be wound up only upon the occurrence of listed events, suggesting a starting point of continuation rather than dissolution. The UPA distinguishes between a "dissociation" (the departure of a partner) and a "dissolution" (the winding up of its business and termination of a partnership). In Article 7, the UPA details the effects of dissociation; in Article 8, it details the effects of dissolution. *See also id.* at § 801, comment.

34. *Id.* at § 801(2)(i).

35. *Id.* at § 701(a).

36. As Allan Farnsworth explains,

    Somewhat surprisingly, our system of contract remedies rejects, for the most part, compulsion of the promisor as a goal. It does not impose criminal penalties on one who refuses to perform one's promise, nor does it generally require one to pay punitive damages. Our system of contract remedies is not directed at *compulsion of promisors to prevent breach*; it is aimed, instead at *relief to promisees to redress breach.*

    E. Allan Farnsworth, *Contracts*, 4th ed. (New York: Aspen, 2004), § 12.1 (emphasis in original).

37. Human capital concepts, which date to the time of Plato, have enjoyed great popularity among economists since the early 1960s. Joan M. Krauskopf, "Recompense for Financing Spouse's Education: Legal Protection for the Marital Investor in Human Capital," *University of Kansas Law Review* 28 (Spring 1980): 379. Other theorists who advocate the application of human capital concepts to marriage include Deborah A. Batts, "Remedy Refocus: In Search of Equity in 'Enhanced Spouse/Other Spouse' Divorce," *New York University Law Review* 63 (1988): 751; Elizabeth S. Beninger and Jeanne Wielage Smith, "Career Opportunity Cost: A Factor in Spousal Support Determination," *Family Law Quarterly*

16 (1982): 201; E. Raedene Combs, "The Human Capital Concept as a Basis for Property Settlement at Divorce," *Journal of Divorce* 2, vol. 4 (1979): 329; Elisabeth M. Landes, "Economics of Alimony," *Journal of Legal Studies* 7 (1978): 35; and Allen M. Parkman, "The Recognition of Human Capital as Property in Divorce Settlements," *Arkansas Law Review* 40 (1987): 439. Not all of these theorists advocate human capital theory as a basis for maintenance. For example, Professors Parkman and Combs urge that human capital is property that should be valued and divided like other marital property on divorce. *See* Parkman, *supra* at 440-41 (income stream expected for future services is an asset, like a house); Combs, *supra* at 333 (earning ability is an asset to be divided).

38. *See* Cynthia Starnes, "Divorce and the Displaced Homemaker: A Discourse on Playing with Dolls, Partnership Buyouts and Dissociation under No-Fault," *University of Chicago Law Review* 60 (1993): 67.

39. Sugarman, *supra* note 25 at 130, 140.

40. American Law Institute, *Principles of the Law of Family Dissolution: Analysis and Recommendations* (St. Paul, MN: American Law Institute, 2002) (hereinafter *ALI Principles*), § 4.12.

41. *Id.* at § 4.12(6).

42. *Id.* at § 4.12, cmt. a.

43. *Id.*

44. Carol Rogerson and Rollie Thompson, "The Canadian Experiment with Spousal Support Guidelines," *Family Law Quarterly* 45 (2011): 241, 254–55.

45. *See ALI Principles, supra* note 40 at §§ 5.05, cmt. a, 5.04, reporter's notes, cmt. c. The basic scheme of § 5.04(1) is to authorize alimony when a marriage is "of sufficient duration" that equity requires that loss of the marital standard of living be shared. *Id.* at § 5.05(1).

46. Rhode and Minow, *supra* note 1 at 198.

47. Richard H. Thaler and Cass R. Sunstein, *Nudge: Improving Decisions about Health, Wealth, and Happiness* (New York: Penguin, 2008), 227.

48. *Id.*

49. The "substantial injustice" standard is borrowed from the ALI recharacterization rule. *See ALI Principles, supra* note 40 at § 4.12.

50. *See* Uniform Probate Code § 2-203(b), which establishes the following sliding scale:

> The value of the marital property portion of the augmented estate consists of . . . the augmented estate . . . multiplied by the following percentage:
>
> *If the decedent and the spouse were married to each other: The percentage is:*

Less than 1 year	3%
1 year but less than 2 years	6%
2 years but less than 3 years	12%
3 years but less than 4 years	18%

4 years but less than 5 years	24%
5 years but less than 6 years	30%
6 years but less than 7 years	36%
7 years but less than 8 years	42%
8 years but less than 9 years	48%
9 years but less than 10 years	54%
10 years but less than 11 years	60%
11 years but less than 12 years	68%
12 years but less than 13 years	76%
13 years but less than 14 years	84%
14 years but less than 15 years	92%
15 years or more	100%

51. *Id.* at 89 (comment).
52. Sugarman, *supra* note 25 at 159-60.
53. For this point and example, I am indebted to Matt Piszczek.

NOTES TO CHAPTER 9

1. American Law Institute, *Principles of the Law of Family Dissolution: Analysis and Recommendations* (St. Paul, MN: American Law Institute, 2002) (hereinafter *ALI Principles*), § 2.08(1) ("Unless otherwise resolved by agreement of the parents . . . the court should allocate custodial responsibility so that the proportion of custodial time the child spends with each parent approximates the proportion of time each parent spent performing caretaking functions for the child prior to the parents' separation."). The ALI recommends a rebuttable presumption in favor of joint legal custody. *Id.* at § 2.09.

2. *See* Richard H. Thaler and Cass R. Sunstein, *Nudge: Improving Decisions about Health, Wealth, and Happiness* (New York: Penguin, 2008), 225–26 (suggesting that default rules can be used to nudge people in committed relationships toward an outcome that helps the most vulnerable, usually women and children).

3. For an insightful look at the clash between clean-break and co-parenting models in the context of parental relocation disputes, *see* Theresa Glennon, "Still Partners? Examining the Consequences of Post-Dissolution Parenting," *Family Law Quarterly* 41, no. 1 (2007-2008): 105. Professor Glennon argues that parents should share the costs of a custodian's denied petition to relocate. *Id.* at 138-43.

4. As the ALI observes, "Bearing primary responsibility for a child additionally constrains the residential parent's labor-force opportunities after dissolution." *ALI Principles, supra* note 1 at § 3.04, cmt. i.

5. Despite the supposed abandonment of gender-biased custody decision making, mothers are far more likely than fathers to be residential parents.

"Many studies show that around 90 percent of custodial parents are mothers," although this figure may be dropping somewhat. Ira Mark Ellman et al., "Intuitive Lawmaking: The Example of Child Support," *Journal of Empirical Legal Studies* 6 (2009): 69n1. *See also* Ira Mark Ellman et al., *Family Law: Cases, Text, Problems*, 5th ed. (New Providence, NJ: LexisNexis, 2010), 637 ("most divorces still conclude with the mother as the primary custodial parent"); and Ann Crittenden, *The Price of Motherhood: Why the Most Important Job in the World Is Still the Least Valued* (New York: Metropolitan Books, 2001), 26 ("Despite the media's fondness for Mr. Mom, he remains an aberration. Of the 20.5 million American children under the age of five, only about 320,000 have fathers as their primary guardian—a minuscule 1.5 percent."). In one widely cited study, researchers found that in 70 percent of the cases, children of divorced parents resided primarily with their mothers. *See* Robert Mnookin and Eleanor Maccoby, "Facing the Dilemmas of Child Custody," *Virginia Journal of Social Policy and Law* 10, no. 1 (2002): 54, 57. The Census Bureau reports that children who live with only one parent are four times more likely to live with their mother than with their father. Jason Fields, *Children's Living Arrangements and Characteristics: March 2002*, U.S. Census Bureau Publication No. P20-547, Current Population Reports (2003), 2, http://www.census.gov/prod/2003pubs/p20-547.pdf.

6. First marriages that end in divorce last a median of eight years. Rose M. Kreider, *Number, Timing, and Duration of Marriages and Divorces: 2001*, U.S. Census Bureau Publication No. P79-97, Current Population Reports (2005), 9, http://www.census.gov/prod/2005pubs/p70-97.pdf.

7. For a critique of current child support laws on the ground that the amounts are too low, *see* Nancy E. Dowd, *Redefining Fatherhood* (New York: New York University Press, 2000), 222 ("Strong evidence demonstrates that even if . . . all support were paid, the support would be inadequate to meet the needs of children.").

8. Ellman et al., "Intuitive Lawmaking," *supra* note 5 at 134. Ten states as well as Washington, D.C., recognize common-law marriages contracted within their borders. *Id.* at 133. While most marriages begin with the legal formalities of licensing and solemnization, not all do. *See, e.g., State v. Denton*, 983 P.2d 693, 695 (Wash. Ct. App. 1999) (upholding the validity of a marriage contracted without a license and noting "the common law principle that a marriage without a license is universally held to be valid in the absence of an express declaration by the Legislature that such a marriage is void.").

9. Tali Schaefer, "Saving Children or Blaming Parents? Lessons from Mandated Parenting Classes," *Columbia Journal of Gender and Law* 19, no. 2 (2010): 491, 513. *See also* Eleanor E. Maccoby and Robert H. Mnookin et al., *Dividing the Child: Social and Legal Dilemmas of Custody* (Cambridge: Harvard University Press, 1992), 159 (75 percent of families studied had low-conflict divorces).

10. *ALI Principles, supra* note 1 at § 5.05, reporter's notes, cmt. a.

11. For a review and critique of state laws governing imputation of income to caretakers, *see* Cynthia Lee Starnes, "Mothers, Myths, and the Law of Divorce: One More Feminist Case for Partnership," *William and Mary Journal of Women and the Law* 13 (2006): 203, 227-30. For a list of alimony statutes that include references to custodial responsibility, *see* Linda Elrod and Robert Spector, "A Review of the Year in Family Law 2007-2008: Federalization and Nationalization Continue," *Family Law Quarterly* 42 (2008-2009): 757, chart 1.

12. Child support is generally based on the principle of continuity of expenditure, under which the amount of child support is measured according to average spending on children. Income-shares models take the total amount of support and divide it between the parents on a pro rata basis—that is, in proportion to their income.

13. The payor's complaint sometimes takes the form of a charge that his child support payments are actually "disguised additional maintenance." *See, e.g., Smith v. Stewart*, 684 A.2d 265, 269 (Ver. 1996) (noting that while "increased child support necessarily has an incidental benefit for the custodial parent, the real beneficiaries are the children."). In order to guard against a custodian's inappropriate use of child support on herself, many states authorize courts to order the custodian to provide an accounting of her spending. *See, e.g.,* Mo. Rev. Stat. § 452.342 (2008).

14. *ALI Principles, supra* note 1 at § 3.04, cmt. f (emphasis in original).

15. *Id.*

16. Default rules are those that govern in the absence of an agreement otherwise. Default rules thus apply if the parties do not enter an agreement or if their agreement contains gaps or ambiguities. On default rules in general, see Randy Barnett, "The Sound of Silence: Default Rules and Contractual Content," *Virginia Law Review* 78 (1992): 821. In the case of marriage, divorce laws governing property distribution and alimony are largely default rules, since they generally apply only when spouses fail to agree on these economic exit terms.

17. *See* Thaler and Sunstein, *supra* note 2 at 227. As Thaler and Sunstein explain, "what people wish to do is likely to be affected by the law's default rules. If the law establishes a standard practice, many people will follow it." *Id.* As Adrienne Davis notes, marital default rules are "notoriously sticky" and "crucial" since "[e]ven when parties are predisposed to bargain around them, their best efforts to do so may come under heightened legal scrutiny and not be enforced." Adrienne D. Davis, "Regulating Polygamy: Intimacy, Default Rules, and Bargaining for Equality," *Columbia Law Review* 110 (2010): 1955, 2000-2001.

18. *See* Thaler and Sunstein, *supra* note 2 at 224 ("even without a government licensing scheme or legal sanction, people take their private commitments seriously.").

19. Some commentators have argued that the nuclear family should not be expected to alone absorb the costs of children's care, either during or after marriage, since the costs of dependency are more properly borne by society at large. These scholars point to the parent-child relationship rather than the spousal

relationship as the core source of legal obligation and the appropriate focus of family law regulation. Some call for abrogation of marriage altogether. While my model of co-parenting commitments furthers a private-law response to the costs of post-divorce caretaking, it also endorses calls for public responsibility as a backup to private obligation. As Martha Fineman has so compellingly charged, in the end dependency is everyone's responsibility. *See* Martha Fineman, "Dominant Discourse, Professional Language, and Legal Change in Child Custody Decisionmaking," *Harvard Law Review* 101, no. 4 (1998): 727.

20. Karen Syma Czapanskiy, "Chalimony: Seeking Equity between Parents of Children with Disabilities and Chronic Illnesses," *New York University Review of Law and Social Change* 34 (2010): 253. For a call for a new legal framework to allocate the costs of child rearing between parents, see Ayelet Blecher-Prigat, "The Costs of Raising Children: Toward a Theory of Financial Obligations between Co-Parents," *Theoretical Inquiries in Law* 13 (2012): 179.

21. Ira Mark Ellman and Tara O'Toole Ellman, "The Theory of Child Support," *Harvard Journal on Legislation* 45 (2008): 107, 116.

22. Carol Rogerson and Rollie Thompson, "The Canadian Experiment with Spousal Support Guidelines," *Family Law Quarterly* 45 (2011): 241, 255–56.

23. To presumptively measure earning capacity loss resulting from primary caregiving during marriage, the ALI calculates the spouses' income disparity and multiplies that figure by a "child care durational factor" based on the length of the child care period. *See ALI Principles, supra* note 1 at § 5.05(4). This approach rests on the proposition that "spouses are, on average, more similar in socioeconomic status, at the time of their marriage, than are randomly chosen pairs of people, [and so] a more accurate estimate of the forgone earning capacity is obtained by comparing the obligee's income to the obligor's than to an average obtained from the general population." *Id.* at § 5.05, cmt. e.

24. *Id.* at §§ 5.04(3), cmt. a (illustration), 5.05(5).

25. Thaler and Sunstein, *supra* note 2 at 227.

26. *See ALI Principles, supra* note 1 at Chap. 6 (proposing that the status of "domestic partners" be imposed on couples who fall within an identified fact pattern). Washington state currently recognizes such a status. *See Olver v. Fowler,* 168 P.3d 348 (Wash. 2007) (recognizing the status of "committed intimate relationship"). For a critique of this status-based approach to cohabitants, *see* Marsha Garrison, "Is Consent Necessary? An Evaluation of the Emerging Law of Cohabitant Obligation," *University of California Los Angeles Law Review* 52 (2005): 815, 846 ("Cohabitation usually functions, in the eyes of cohabitants themselves, as a substitute for being single, not for being married. Cohabitation thus does not imply marital commitment.").

27. For this point I am indebted to my colleague Brian Kalt.

28. As Professors Thaler and Sunstein have noted, setting an exit price is an important function of divorce law: "a primary reason for the official institution of marriage has been not to limit entry but to police exit—to make it difficult for

people to abandon their commitments to one another." Thaler and Sunstein, *supra* note 2 at 221.

29. Merle H. Weiner, "Caregiver Payments and the Obligation to Give Care or Share," *Villanova Law Review* 59 (2014): 000-00.

30. The perplexing question is whether new children, born subsequent to a child support order, provide a basis for a reduction in child support. Courts are split on the answer—some taking a "first in time, first in right" position that denies a reduction, others allowing a reduction on the ground that all children deserve to share on a pro rata basis in their parents' income. *See* Ellman et al., *Family Law, supra* note 5 at 567-68. If there is no good answer to this question, one possibility is a compromise: new children provide a basis for resisting an action to increase child support, but not a basis for an action to reduce child support. *See* Laura W. Morgan, *Child Support Guidelines: Interpretation and Application* (New York: Aspen Law and Business, 1996), 3–51.

31. As Stephanie Coontz has noted,

> The reproductive revolution has shaken up all the relationships once taken for granted. . . . People who could not become parents before can now do so in such bewildering combinations that a child can potentially have five different parents: a sperm donor, an egg donor, a birth mother, and the social father and mother who raise the child.

Stephanie Coontz, *Marriage, a History: From Obedience to Intimacy, or How Love Conquered Marriage* (New York: Viking, 2005), 250.

This possibility, however, should not pose much of a problem for co-parenting partnerships, which are based on commitments to raise children rather than biology.

32. The question is whether it is appropriate to impute income to a parent who earns less than he or she could earn. Imputing income to a parent will generally increase that parent's proportional share of the child support obligation. For a parent paying child support, this means a higher payment; for the parent receiving child support, this means a decrease in household income.

ABOUT THE AUTHOR

Cynthia Lee Starnes is the John F. Schaefer Chair in Matrimonial Law at Michigan State University College of Law. She is known for her work on the law and theory of divorce economics, work-family balance, and the interplay between private commitments and social justice. Starnes is a leading proponent of the partnership metaphor for marriage, and her pioneering reform proposals have provoked widespread commentary.